D1580790

At War with Metaphor

Media, Propaganda, and Racism in the War on Terror

Erin Steuter and Deborah Wills

LIS - LIBRARY

Date	Fund
18.7.2011	070 pt STE

Order No.

02212468

University of Chester

36133020

LEXINGTON BOOKS

A division of
ROWMAN & LITTLEFIELD PUBLISHERS, INC.
Lanham • Boulder • New York • Toronto • Plymouth, UK

LEXINGTON BOOKS

A division of Rowman & Littlefield Publishers, Inc.
A wholly owned subsidiary of The Rowman & Littlefield Publishing Group, Inc.
4501 Forbes Boulevard, Suite 200
Lanham, MD 20706

Estover Road
Plymouth PL6 7PY
United Kingdom

Copyright © 2008 by Lexington Books
First paperback edition 2009

All rights reserved. No part of this publication may be reproduced,
stored in a retrieval system, or transmitted in any form or by any
means, electronic, mechanical, photocopying, recording, or otherwise,
without the prior permission of the publisher.

British Library Cataloguing in Publication Information Available

Library of Congress Cataloging-in-Publication Data

Steuter, Erin, 1963–
   At war with metaphor: media, propaganda, and racism in the war on terror / Erin
Steuter and Deborah Wills.
      p. cm.
 1. Mass media—Social aspects. 2. Mass media and public opinion. 3. Terrorism in
mass media. 4. Fear. 5. Propaganda. 6. Social control. I. Wills, Deborah, 1962– II.
Title.
   HM1206.S74143 2008
   070.4'49909831—dc22   2008016776

   ISBN: 978-0-7391-2198-6 (cloth : alk. paper)
   ISBN: 978-0-7391-2199-5 (pbk. : alk. paper)
   ISBN: 978-0-7391-3031-5 (electronic)

Printed in the United States of America

♾™ The paper used in this publication meets the minimum requirements of
American National Standard for Information Sciences—Permanence of Paper
for Printed Library Materials, ANSI/NISO Z39.48-1992.

Accession no.
36133020

At War with Metaphor

Contents

             Fomenting Backlash   189

Chapter 9   Talking our Way to Peace: New Metaphors
             for Change   201

             Bibliography   213

             Index   237

             About the Authors   245

Acknowledgments

In this book we argue that the mainstream media can act as a stenographer to power, "spin" even horrific acts of brutality, and characterize opposition as disloyalty. Thus to research and write a book that challenges the official story and provides documentation of events and issues not normally explored by the media involves accessing the work of a phenomenal network of investigative independent journalists and social justice activists. This book could not have been written without all the intellectuals, reporters, and citizen journalists who dedicated themselves to doing the hard work of investigative reporting and sharing their findings even when it was not always popular to do so. While the mainstream news media bears the blame for boiling the blood and narrowing the mind of so many readers, the alternative news media deserves considerable credit for speaking the truth to power. Progressive magazines and radical newsletters such as Z, *The Nation*, *CounterPunch*, *The New Statesman*, *Dissident Voice*, *In these Times*, and *Left Turn Magazine* have led the way in providing a forum for the insights of progressive intellectuals and journalists. Alternative news centers such as *AlterNet*, *Common Dreams*, and *Democracy Now* generate news and provide a venue for alternative voices and independent media sources that often fall below the public's radar. Tremendous care and careful documentation is evident in web sites such as *tolerance.org*, *antiwar.com*, *www.why-war.com* as well as watchdog organizations such as *Amnesty International*, *Human Rights Watch*, *Genocide Watch*, *Fairness and Accuracy in Reporting*, *PR Watch*, *Source Watch*, and *Media Matters for America*. These organizations maintain their independence from the pressure of corporate advertisers by sacrificing lucrative advertising revenues. We all benefit from their unbeholden voices. The writers and publishers of these magazines and websites have our wholehearted gratitude for bringing us the news we need to make sense of the world we live in and they deserve the support of subscribers that the mainstream media has forfeited.

Reading the insights of leading intellectuals is a valuable way to engage with the news but actually interacting with them in a forum to share knowledge and insights in pursuit of social justice is a profoundly democratic and empowering experience. ES is grateful for the opportunities and encouragement she gained by engaging with progressive social leaders through the opportunities created by the *Z Media Institute* and the *Boston College Media Research and Action Project*. The encouragement and direction of the leaders and alumna of the *Woodhull Institute* provided the essential road map to publishing this book.

Research support from Mount Allison University, the encouragement of colleagues, librarians, and academic administrators, and the energy and dedication of our undergraduate research assistants David Morse and Melissa Calvin, are sincerely recognized and appreciated. Freelance journalist Carole Pearson helped us communicate our vision of this book to our publisher. Artist Aidan Hughes created a powerful book cover image that has garnered the appreciative admiration of our undergraduate students.

Our friends and loved ones know who they are and we hope we make clear our profound appreciation for them in regular and meaningful ways.

Introduction

Let's begin with two pictures. One, a political cartoon, shows a grim-faced Uncle Sam as Dad behind the wheel of the family car. The license plate reads "USA." The windshield is splattered with dead bugs; look a bit more closely and the bugs are revealed as tiny turbaned men, wearing traditional Muslim garb and carrying machine guns. Some are squashed, plastered like mosquitos across the grille; others are still alive and running, trying to avoid being crushed by the advancing wheels. Inside the car, the children clamor in an insistent chorus, "Are we there yet?"[1] (See figure i.1) It's hard not to wonder where this road trip will end.

The second image shows a naked Arab prisoner at the end of a leash gripped by an American soldier. The soldier gazes not at the photographer but down at the prostrate body of her captive: there is a chilling impassivity in her expression as she looks down the length of the leash. This picture is familiar by now, part of the infamous series of photographs showing American soldiers torturing and humiliating enemy soldiers and civilians in Iraq's Abu Ghraib prison. The message of this image seems more immediate, more horrifying, and more easily understood than that of the political cartoon.

Why, then, juxtapose these two pictures? In many ways, they are crucially different: one is fictional, the other fact, part of a documentary record of torment and abuse. One is intended, in the tradition of political cartoons, to elicit amusement and encourage political analysis; the other is a photograph, an apparently more neutral chronicling of events. One is an individual artistic expression; the other portrays a collective action, captured by a viewer

Figure i.1.   Darryl Cagle. "Taliban Bugs Windshield." *MSNBC.com*. **October 30, 2001.**

whose mind was clearly far from questions of art. Yet these two images also share crucial similarities, and are, in fact, profoundly connected. In contrast to the notorious Abu Ghraib photograph, which has given rise to international shock and outrage, calls for war crimes trials and societal transformation, the political cartoon has largely been seen as harmless satire. Yet the images and metaphors used by the media to frame and shape our public discussion of the war on terror inform both photo and cartoon in profound ways, and in both artifacts require careful scrutiny. There is a crucial correlation between mainstream news media's readiness to repeatedly characterize opponents as insects or animals and what happened at Abu Ghraib, in which the metaphor of the animal is made horrifyingly literal. The slide from satirical insects to leashed humans, from cartoon to photograph, is all too easy. The human rights violations that emerged from Abu Ghraib are intricately connected to our war narratives, past and present, to our metaphoric systems, and to the kinds of stories we tell ourselves.

The images and language we use to discuss the war on terror have a powerful impact on the way we think about and treat other human beings. The metaphors we draw upon, often profoundly racist, increasingly threaten our chances of building a safe society. The language used by mainstream news media, politicians, military commanders, think tank scholars, religious leaders, pundits, columnists and bloggers in response to terrorism ironically makes us less safe by creating a world of discourse characterized by fundamental and insoluble divisions. We see this in both informal and official public speech: New York Republican Congressman Peter King refers to American Muslims as the "enemy living amongst us"; Illinois Congressman Mark Kirk comments: "I'm okay with discrimination against young Arab males from terrorist-producing states." Texas Congressman Sam Johnson brags to a crowd of veterans that he advised Bush to nuke Syria, and Colorado Congressman and candidate for the Republican nomination for President Tom Tancredo advocates wiping out Mecca in response to terrorist attacks. Former Secretary of State Lawrence Eagleburger states on CNN immediately after 9/11 that "There is only one way to begin to deal with people like this, and that is you have to kill some of them even if they are not immediately directly involved in this thing."[2] Daniel Pipes, a representative at the U.S. government-sponsored think tank *U.S. Institute for Peace*, exemplifies the discourses of dehumanization that allow and promote such talk of indiscriminate eradication. He figuratively links Muslims to disease, carriers of a religiously specific pathology. To Pipes, all Muslims are prey to a latent psychopathic contagion:

> Individuals may appear law-abiding and reasonable, but they are part of a totalitarian movement, and as such, all must be considered potential killers. . . . This is what I have dubbed the Sudden Jihad Syndrome, whereby normal-appearing Muslims abruptly become violent. It has the awful but legitimate consequence of casting suspicion on all Muslims. Who knows whence the next jihad? How can one be confident a law-abiding Muslim will not suddenly erupt in a homicidal rage?[3]

Pipes' pathological metaphor underlies, supports, and advances political calls to eradicate the enemy, a strategy justified as a cure for the "syndrome" of difference.

Many European leaders employ equally problematic language in statements about Islamic communities within their countries. Former Italian prime minister Silvio Berlusconi states that the superiority of western civilization entitled it to "occidentalize and conquer new people." Italian MP Roberto Calderoli flaunts his Muhammad cartoon T-shirt on TV, warning of an "Islamic attack on the West." Former French Interior Minister and now President of France, Nicolas Sarkozy, publicly labels Muslim immigrants "gangrene" and "scum," and Danish MP Pia Kjærsgaards calls Muslims "a cancer in Denmark."[4] Such recurring metaphors of disease, decay, and dehumanization are a frequent part of European and North American public discourse. While it is common to mock or dismiss the controversial statements of "shock talk" radio hosts, it is worth noting that the audience for these programs numbers in the millions; many of their hosts also reach thousands of readers through their best-selling books. American syndicated radio host Neil Boortz tells his audience of over 3.75 million listeners[5] that

> Islam is a creeping mold infestation. Islam is a virus. It is a deadly virus that is spreading throughout Europe and the West. We're going to wait far too long to develop a vaccine to find a way to fight this.[6]

Dehumanizing metaphor also flourishes in print: Steve Dunleavy, a columnist with the *New York Post*, the fastest growing newspaper in the U.S. with a readership of almost 800,000,[7] writes that "The response to this unimaginable twenty-first-century Pearl Harbor should be as simple as it is swift—kill the bastards. A gunshot between the eyes, blow them to smithereens, poison them if you have to. As for cities or countries that host these worms, bomb them into basketball courts."[8] The respected mainstream news source *The Washington Post* offers an editorial entitled "Terrorism as Virus."[9] Pulitzer Prize-winning columnist Maureen Dowd writes in the *New York Times*, the paper of record, that Al Qaeda is "replicating and coming at us like cockroaches." In the UK, the *Sun* tabloid runs the headline "Caught Like Rats in a Trap" alongside a photo of two bare-chested Arab suspects with their hands in the air.[10] In Canada, mainstream newspaper the *Calgary Sun* prints a headline reading "Britain Bitten By A Snake; Country Failed to Crack Down on Those Who Incited Hatred and Murder."[11] Internationally, the internet community is rife with such invective, such as this posting following the 2004 Madrid train bombings:

> It doesn't matter which batch of terrorists actually did it. If rats infest my house and one bites the baby in her crib, I'm not gonna fart around taking dental impressions to make sure I'm killing the right rat. I'm going to exterminate every rat from the helpless old granny rats to the little innocent baby rats until there are no more rats in my house.[12]

In the war on terror, mainstream news media headlines trumpet "Rat Trapped" at the arrest of an enemy leader, bloggers label ethnic minorities at home and abroad "cockroaches," and political pundits call for the extermination of entire countries. Military officials report on "cleansing" operations, and Islam is called a "cancer." Muslims are said to "infest" our communities, and Iraqis are called dune coons, sand niggers and camel jockeys. Turban-wearing men are called "diaper heads" by elected politicians.[13] There are regular calls for the arrest and deportation of non-white immigrants from European and North American countries. Most disturbing of all is the repeated call for the extermination and annihilation of entire countries that may or may not harbor suspected terrorists but which are certainly home to millions of peaceful families.

This is a war in which the deaths directly and indirectly attributable to the U.S. invasion and occupation of Iraq have neared one million people, a body count higher than the genocides in Rwanda and Sudan,[14] in which soldiers are implicated in the rape and murder of children at Al-Mahmudiyah, and in which civilians are massacred at Haditha. These very real phenomena are supported by sometimes subtle but equally real linguistic patterns. The dehumanizing metaphors employed in our public discussion of the war on terror have a powerful impact on the way we think and act; by systematically stripping humans of humanity, they provide a cultural platform for acts of war and a potent cognitive framework for interpreting such acts.

As the official reasons justifying the war in Iraq continue to erode under public scrutiny and investigation, many people have begun to ask "how did we get here?" This book explores the work of public discourse about the war in order to help to answer this question. Part I: Metaphor Matters, establishes the primacy of metaphor in speech, thought and cognition, arguing that the metaphors imported into the public discourse surrounding the war on terror have crucial consequences in that they frame the war's objects, enemies, and essential terms in ways that shape both perceptions and consequences. Chapter one makes a case for metaphor's individual and social influence and explores the implications and consequences of the framing of North America's encounter with terrorism through an apparently unavoidable martial metaphor. Chapter two examines propaganda's seizure of this metaphoric potency in its construction of an enemy Other, with particular attention to the role of race and Orientalism in this fabrication. The role of propaganda in creating an image of our enemies is examined, with particular emphasis on the racism of orientalist discourse in fabricating an alien Other. Chapter three discusses the dynamics of dehumanization and its contribution to civilian casualties and genocide, illustrated through historical examples of racist propaganda such as Nazi depictions of Jews, representations of the Japanese during WWII, and more recent examples from the first Persian Gulf War and Rwanda. Part II: Enlisting Discourse, extends the first section's premises to an analysis of how the historically resilient metaphors discussed in the first

section circulate through current media in ways both familiar and unex-
pected. Original case studies in this section focus on animal metaphors in
print media, extermination metaphors in political cartoons, and metaphors
of evolutionary debasement in talk radio in chapters four, five, and six respectively. These chapters interrogate a range of media practice that encompasses the written, the visual, and the oral, discovering a remarkable consistency of metaphor across the breadth of that spectrum. A similarly striking
metaphoric consistency is evident across another media spectrum, in that
case-study sources drawn from media outlets in varying degrees of legitimacy
and popularity all seem to evince almost identical metaphoric tropes within
the war discourse. From the "funny pages" to front page headlines, from
mainstream paper-of-record to supermarket tabloid, from radio phone-ins to
tirade-riddled shock-jock talk-show hosts, the same metaphors surface, circulate and resonate. Each case-study chapter in this section also investigates
some of the consequences of these metaphors, drawing a direct link between
dehumanizing tropes and figures and dehumanizing acts and practices: phenomena such as trophy-taking and "war porn," this section argues, find their
source in the pervasiveness and consistency of the damaging metaphors in
which even mainstream media continually re-invests itself.

   The book's final section, Part III: Dangerous Discourses, addresses the
contexts and constraints of media production that help account for the per-
petuation of these metaphors, metaphors which intensify and promote hate
speech and hate crimes in the U.S. and abroad. A critical and analytical
awareness of such contexts and the tropes they engender offers one way to
counter media hegemony. Only when we achieve a distance from these
metaphors that is tangible as well as critical, this final section argues, will we
be able to formulate more emancipatory metaphors. Chapter seven analyzes
the media filters that often disguise the workings of metaphor in discourse,
while allowing dominant agendas to appear neutral and uncontested. Chapter eight asserts that the consequences of failing to unpack the metaphors of
hate speech are not solely discursive, but have measurable consequences,
generating backlash, renewing violence and undermining both safety and the
possibility of resolution. Chapter nine suggests that the way we frame the war
on terror shapes and prohibitively limits the solutions we can develop in response. It observes that although our cultural lexicon of dehumanizing
metaphor has been remarkably enduring, it can also be made subject to a re-
visionary re-framing. By coaxing metaphor from the realm of the tacit into
the realm of the visible, as we do in this book, we may take a first necessary
step towards that revision.

As the work of scholars studying propaganda makes clear, the weapons of war are never solely physical.[15] Language itself, in the way it invites us to understand both the enemy and ourselves, becomes a potential weapon. But propaganda is found in more than the blatantly jingoistic WWII posters and martial sloganeering that the word conjures up. Because language embeds our values and assumptions, even in apparently calmer, more neutral discussion, language is always hard at work. In the war on terror, as in past wars, language serves the purposes of propaganda. It is language, rather than logic, that summons us through its emotional affect to a war we can no longer justify.

The way that we frame the war, in language, in public debate, and in metaphor, matters. Through selecting and reporting only certain facts, through overlooking or distorting others of equal relevance, through the associations we conjure to describe our opponents, we neglect or invalidate genuine discussion and debate, and promote instead public hysteria, panic, and witch hunts. We rally the public to a cause that is misrepresented or confused against an enemy who is never understood. Edward S. Herman notes that in the seventeenth century Daniel Dafoe reported that "there were a hundred thousand stout country fellows . . . ready to fight to the death against Popery, without knowing whether Popery was a man or a horse"; in our day, likewise, there are millions of stout-hearted fellows ready to fight to the death against terrorism without knowing anything of its real nature.[16]

The language of war, which includes the metaphors it draws on, does not simply hold a mirror up to the enemy. It does not reveal a clear, objective, or pre-existing image of what we fight. What is reflected in language is not reality but construct, something conditioned and assembled, put together from fragments of information and observation. Parts of these observations may very well be accurate, but they are always influenced and shaped by the processes and contexts of their assembly. In this sense, we really do, through the metaphors we choose and reiterate, "make" enemies. The mirror of language thus ultimately reflects back to us both the constructed image of the other and, also, something of ourselves.

And this, when it comes down to it, is why metaphors matter. When they are called upon to justify acts of violence that we would not normally endorse or tolerate, it becomes imperative to examine these metaphors with care, to unpack their freight of assumptions about race and culture, virtue and violence. We need to know not only whether the enemy is "a man or a horse," but more importantly, how representing that enemy as bestial shapes both our understanding and our response. There are many fertile examples of how enemies are made into the Other, dragged symbolically backwards down the evolutionary ladder until they, and the people who look like them, are no longer seen as human, but as insect or animal, germ or disease. This comes at a double cost. First, it fuels the kind of violence that has so horrified us at Abu Ghraib, furthering the cycles of offense and retaliation. Second, it binds our imagination into an adversarial pattern that works against the humanity and creativity required to break free of the kinds of cyclical violence central to the war on terror.

If metaphor is as crucial to our thinking as this suggests, we need to pay close attention to the patterns of metaphor at work in our public discourse. One such pattern is consistently to link terrorism to infestation, corruption, and spreading decay. Newspaper articles and broadcast news reports are infested with images of infestation, plagued by images of plague. These images are historically resonant, echoing the language used by the Third Reich to dehumanize its own hated and feared Others, those disenfranchised from citizenship and ultimately from humanity itself. Over and over, we discover in the voice of a supposedly neutral media a vocabulary that bypasses the objective and taps directly into the visceral. Even highly-charged or emotional language can be absorbed by and effectively disappear into the cool, dispassionate tones of a journalist or news anchor. If, however, we look beyond that neutral tone and scrutinize the language employed in these broadcasts, we often find a disconcerting degree of racism which permits terrorists to be consistently described as vermin, rats, snakes or cockroaches. Most importantly, this language expands in its application from encompassing individual agents to encompassing entire nations, entire peoples. This dehumanization of an entire group or race of people encourages an unconscious transformation in our minds and imaginations, a transference which is metaphor's key function, and in which entire populations are collectively stripped of their humanity and thus forfeit their claim to our empathy and compassion.

Images of infestation indirectly but inevitably call up a related solution: extermination. While we might shudder and protest if this were proposed directly, its indirect evocation through metaphor makes this solution start to seem natural—even clean, hygienic, and sterile. Extermination becomes more palatable when terrorists no longer have any currency as fundamentally human. This characterization, through repeated patterns of metaphor, removes any possibility that there could be legitimate grievances behind terrorist acts. Instead, the enemy is portrayed as beasts or insects that, unable to rationalize, act only out of primal, animal drives. All those sharing the same ethnicity and religious beliefs become part of the target group. As right-wing pundit Ann Coulter writes,

This is no time to be precious about locating the exact individuals directly in-volved in this particular terrorist attack. . . . We should invade their countries, kill their leaders and convert them to Christianity. We weren't punctilious about locating and punishing only Hitler and his top officers. We carpet-bombed German cities: we killed civilians. That's war. And this is war.[17]

The indiscriminate nature of the solution Coulter proposes is, far from be-ing a cure for terrorism, itself a form of terrorism. It promotes violent solu-tions, and re-directs and escalates levels of violence from single to multiple targets. She asks us to accept that our mission is fundamental and obvious enough to justify any methods, and dismisses any thoughtful resistance to the call to eradication as weakness. More importantly, her rhetoric, while claim-ing for itself the high moral ground of anti-Nazi efforts in WWII, itself par-ticipates in the kind of annihilationist language we are most familiar with in the kind of Nazi propaganda we now collectively abhor, language that shifts attention from the identification of "exact individuals" to "their countries," urging a movement away from discrimination to the broad and indiscrimi-nate retaliation of the exterminator.

Exterminationism, with its long and ugly history, is not a solution to ter-rorism. Indeed, across history such policies have triggered greater violence, as in the genocide in Rwanda, in which people were incited to conduct mas-sacres against different ethnic groups. By promoting extermination tactics as a way to eliminate terrorism, we contribute to increased violence. We only need consider the number of car-bombings against American-related targets in Iraq, increasing numbers of foreign fighters in Iraq and the bomb attacks in Bali and London in order to recognize that exterminationist ideas, and the mass killing of both combatants and non-combatants, have not served us well. Further, when extreme comments such as Coulter's are accepted as "le-gitimate commentary"[18] within North America and translated and reported outside North America as representative of Western attitudes toward Islam, the metaphorical binaries that perpetually divide "us" from "them" are solid-ified in both camps, fueling an ever-widening cycle of destruction.

The massacres and genocides that comprise our most painful historical mo-ments are characterized by a persistent dehumanization of the enemy. The lan-guage that has emerged in the twenty-first century as part of the public face of the war on terror has helped to fundamentally define that enemy, just as the metaphors we use reflect and reflexively shape our thinking. When we repeat-edly represent our enemies as essentially different in substance from us, as less than human, we extend ourselves permission to behave in ways that often echo the very violence we condemn. If metaphors affect the way we think and act, we must take extraordinary care, individually and collectively, with the metaphors we choose to adopt. We cannot break the cycle of violence by responding to physical violence with violence of speech or image. We may, however, begin to change that cycle by breaking down and examining the metaphors we employ, by working to understand the reverberations of race and propaganda that come to us from earlier historical conflicts, and by resisting those metaphors that urge us towards actions we would otherwise condemn. This resistance is profoundly important, not only for the sake of the enemy, but for our own. If we ally ourselves to a rhetoric that strips others of their humanity, it is inevitable that in the process our own will suffer. The multiple costs of the war on terror mask a broader expense of spirit and community: when we systematically reduce others, we are ourselves reduced. When we diminish others, we are diminished. It is important to analyze the metaphors that move us dangerously closer to solutions of eradication and extermination; in doing so, we can choose to change the direction of this movement through heightened critical awareness of metaphor's processes and power.

Notes

1. Darryl Cagle. "Taliban Bugs Windshield." *MSNBC.com*. October 30, 2001.

2. *Fairness and Accuracy in Reporting*. "Media March to War." *FAIR*. September 17, 2001. See www.fair.org/index.php?page=1853 (June 26, 2007).

3. Daniel Pipes. "Sudden Jihad Syndrome." *FrontPageMagazine.com* March 14, 2006. See www.frontpagemag.com/Articles/Read.aspx?GUID={730A921C-1FED-4DCD-9949 -D28A3390317D} (August 1, 2007).

4. Trish Schuh. "Racism and Religious Desecration as U.S. Policy: Islamophobia, a Retrospective." *Double Standards*. 6 May 2006. See www.doublestandards .org/schuh1 .html (June 26, 2007).

5. *Talkers Magazine*. "Top Talk Personalities," *Talkers Magazine*. Spring 2006. See www.talkers.com/main/index.php?option=com_content&task=view&id=17&Itemi d=34> (June 26, 2007).

6. *Media Matters for America*. "Boortz: Islam is a "deadly virus" and "we're going to wait far too long to develop a vaccine to find a way to fight this." *Media Matters for America*. October 18, 2006. See www.mediamatters.org/items/200610180005 (June 26, 2007).

7. *New York Post*. See www.nypost.com/mediakit/mk/index.php (June 26, 2007).

8. *Fairness and Accuracy in Reporting*. op. cit.

9. Paul Stares and Mona Yacoubian. "Terrorism as Virus." *The Washington Post*, August 23, 2005.

10. *The Sun* (UK). July 30, 2005.

11. *The Calgary Sun.* July 17, 2005.

12. *Baldilocks.* "Spain's the Target." March 11, 2004. See baldilocks.typepad.com /baldilocks/2004/03/spains_the_targ.html (June 26, 2007).

13. Joan Mckinney. "Cooksey: Expect Racial Profiling." *Advocate.* September 19, 2001.

14. David Goodner. "American Genocide in the Middle East: Three Million and Counting." CommonDreams.org. August 8, 2007.

15. Garth S. Jowett and Victoria O'Donnell, *Propaganda and Persuasion.* Thousand Oaks, CA: Sage Publications, 3rd edition, 1999.

16. Edward Herman. "Power and the Semantics of Terrorism," *Covert Action Information Bulletin*, Vol. 26, 1986:13.

17. Cited in Sheldon Rampton and John Stauber. "Trading on Fear." *The Guardian*, posted on *Commondreams.* Saturday, July 12, 2003. See www.commondreams.org/ views03/0712-01.htm (June 26, 2007).

18. Jim Ritter. "Muslims see a growing media bias." *Chicago Sun Times.* September 4, 2006.

PART ONE

METAPHOR MATTERS

CHAPTER ONE

Weaponizing Words:
Metaphor and War

The metaphor is probably the most fertile power possessed by man.

—José Ortega y Gasset

Metaphors matter. We choose our words from within a dominant system or frame of metaphor that offers us a specific lexicon of language, that defines words in certain specific ways, and that shapes both the "what" and the "how" of our communication. In this way, figuratively and often literally, through metaphor we make meaning. Our most common metaphors help us to understand problems and conflicts in certain ways, offering us certain available responses, and negating or obscuring others. Metaphor operates in the realm of thought, but its workings reverberate in concrete, active, tangible ways. Metaphor operates through the interplay of language's denotative value, what it says clearly and obviously, and its connotative value, what it evocatively and often subjectively calls up, its overtones, allusions, and associations. Public discourse, which relies on metaphors both obvious and tacit, can harness its power to shape opinion, set or justify policy, and direct action. Perhaps this is why, as the philosopher Ortega observes, metaphor is the most fertile power we know.

The literal meaning of the word *metaphor* is "to carry over"; metaphor symbolically transfers aspects of one object to another, even if the objects are originally in no way connected.[1] Through this transference, metaphor shifts ideas or meanings from one thing to another to achieve "a new, wider, 'special' or more precise meaning."[2] With repetition, this happens so adeptly that the transference is invisible and comes to seem inevitable. When the media repeatedly return, therefore, to similar patterns of image and language, these patterns begin to appear both familiar and natural. Instead of viewing Muslims as people who have been symbolically portrayed as animals, then, they begin in our minds to become animals, imaginatively transposed with the images that represented them. This transposition is one of the key effects of metaphor.

Linguistics, philosophy, and literature have all explored the power of metaphor in shaping our thinking. Once dismissed as largely decorative, something used to elaborate or "dress up" everyday language, metaphor has been seen by scholars since the 1970s as playing an important role in forming thought itself; it is now understood as "an essential aspect of cognition."[3] This understanding is crucial in times of war: persistent metaphors of beast or plague reduce individuals to categories and present these categories as innately dangerous to the human, linking the enemy with things beyond or beneath our own species. Further, they extend the violence of individuals to encompass an entire culture, a culture portrayed as inherently violent, uncivilized, empty of our values and our shared concern for the worth of human life.

In whatever ways metaphor has been understood over time, what Ortega described as its "fertile power" has always been acknowledged. Some rank it among the most essential forms of public speech: when famous orators like Cicero advised speakers to use a plain style and be sparing with rhetorical ornament, metaphor was exempted from this rule, since it was seen as common to everyone. Even simple "rustics," Cicero noted, use metaphor in speaking of their "thirsty" fields or "luxuriant" crops.[4] Metaphor was historically seen as appealing directly to the senses. Because of its visual appeal, it illuminates our ideas: Aristotle observed that metaphor "sets the scene before our eyes."[5] For Aristotle, metaphor enlivens and animates our ideas, making them more persuasive than if they were expressed plainly. But this very effectiveness of metaphor can be troubling; some are wary of metaphor's potent persuasiveness, seeing it as, at best, self-indulgent and over-wrought, at worst as a deliberate movement away from "pure" ideas and therefore always potentially manipulative or deceptive. Plato argued that an eloquent metaphor simply helped people to lie more effectively. The poet Paul Verlaine went further, passionately urging us to "Take eloquence and wring its neck."[6] The fact that this vigorous sentiment is itself expressed in the form of a metaphor exemplifies metaphor's pervasiveness and power.

Within a broad understanding of metaphor, it is simply a way to enrich or enhance our language, a way to make ideas more memorable, artful or attractive. Informally, outside the world of scholarship and the university, this is probably still the most widely used sense of metaphor. Thinking about metaphor solely as an embellishment or decoration to thought, however, overlooks a more complex and crucial function of metaphor. Metaphor does not simply decorate thought by providing an artful expression of pre-existing ideas. Nor, in a related premise, is metaphor solely the property of public discussion or discourse, used by speech-makers as a tool to make ideas more palatable, persuasive or compelling. Instead, metaphor enters and influences all our lives; it does not remain in the province of professional public speech but permeates individual and collective thought. Far from simply ornamenting or elaborating an idea, metaphor actively influences the thought it helps to articulate, giving it a form and shape that can define or alter it in fundamental ways.

How might this work? One way to understand this process is to compare the model of metaphor's *influential function* to the broader, popular model of metaphor's *decorative function*, in which metaphor is primarily seen as cosmetic or ornamental. This model has been both widespread and long-lived. Its roots go back to ancient Greece and Rome, to a period in which students were trained in rhetoric, the art of speech and persuasion, as an essential skill of citizenship. In Aristotle's codification of the arts of language, Terence Hawkes notes, metaphor is regarded as a "decorative addition" to literal language,[7] that is, language that says exactly what it means. Figurative language, in contrast, uses figures of speech, things which aren't literally or factually true, to express an idea. From the classical period to the days of the Romantic poets, literal language was regarded as the language of truth or fact; figurative language was in essence a "fancy" expression of that fact, bedecked with "extras" such as sparkling wit, gems of expression, or other such elegant baubles from the rhetorical arts.

Ordinary, everyday, non-figurative language was thus seen as distinct from metaphor, and was, in Aristotle's opinion, the home of clarity and real meaning. Metaphor elegantly clothed this workaday language, raising its diction to a level beyond the commonplace and familiar. A fine metaphor, in this model, is rather like a set of Sunday clothes for the clear language of ordinary communication. Like a suit of Sunday best, metaphor decorates only the surface. It's important to note that, in this model, the *idea* is seen as existing first, and the metaphor arrives later to serve that pre-existing idea, making it appear richer, more elegant, or more appealing, dressing it up and (in both the literal and the figurative senses) making it presentable. It does not change the nature of the body wearing it: it can't make the body taller or stronger, but it does affect the body's appearance, lending it an added beauty, charm or distinction. This analogy assumes that the way in which something is expressed does not influence or change what is being said; Aristotle said clearly that these decorative arts are really only "fanciful" and used to "charm the hearer"; they do not on any significant level change what he calls the "bare facts"—that is, presumably, the naked idea, the truths unclothed by the extra elegance of metaphor.[8]

The above paragraph employs a metaphor of its own in describing metaphor's relation to ideas. It speaks of "dressing up" an idea in the clothes of metaphor, of how metaphor helps to "flesh out," enliven, and animate. In this figure of speech, this metaphoric system or trope, an idea is clearly represented as a body. Related phrases like a "body of evidence" shore up this metaphoric connection, a connection that is invented rather than natural, between two things (bodies and ideas) that are not, in themselves, related at all, but which start to seem connected and, in fact, start to seem like a natural, even inevitable, way to understand each other. We might liken a debate to a body's skeleton, for example, when we speak of the "bare bones" of an argument. A solid argument might be called substantial or "meaty," adding flesh to this skeleton of ideas. If we are suspicious of an argument, we might resist it, keeping it out of our bodily system by finding it "hard to swallow," or we might expel it from our body of ideas, finding it "hard to stomach."

Why should we pay attention to such a metaphor? Is it really significant that this series of metaphors so clearly links thought to a physical body? If the answer is yes, then we need to pose another series of questions: what is this significance? What does it mean to conceive of thought as a body? Does employing such a consistent trope make any real difference to our thinking? Many scholars of linguistics, psychology, and philosophy argue that it does. In particular, those who analyze the gender, race and class aspects of such paradigms emphasize the significance of metaphor. For example, if we extend the body paradigm to include the state (as when we speak of the body politic, the head of state, the arm of the law), then those traditionally associated with the "higher order" qualities of the head are valued over those traditionally associated with the heart. When we speak of a "head" of state we simultaneously reflect and ratify what we value in a leader: reason and intelligence, for example, over intuition and empathy. Other parts of the body perform functions every bit as crucial to survival as those performed by the organs we venerate or romanticize, but we do not acknowledge them in our metaphors of bodily governance, which suggests the complex interactions between metaphors, ideas and, perhaps most importantly, values.

Lakoff and Johnson's influential book *Metaphors We Live By* discusses the ways in which metaphors influence both our thinking and behavior. They argue that our experience of the world is structured, not just described, by our "conceptual systems," and they contend that most of our conceptual systems are essentially metaphorical.[9] The concepts that govern thought are not just matters of the intellect; they also govern our everyday functioning, down to the most mundane details. Our conceptual systems structure what we perceive, how we get around in the world, and how we relate to other people, playing a central role in defining our everyday realities. If our conceptual system is largely metaphorical, then the way we think, what we experience, and what we do every day is very much a matter of metaphor.[10]

One of the most important reasons to pay careful attention to the relationship between metaphors and thought is that this relationship is often largely invisible. While some metaphors have an overt or obvious influence, the influence of others can be much more subtle and oblique. Our conceptual systems are "not something we are normally aware of. In most of the little things we do every day, we simply think and act more or less automatically along certain lines. Just what these lines are is by no means obvious."[11] Since the way we communicate emerges from the same conceptual systems out of which we think and act, an examination of our language becomes especially crucial in analyzing and interpreting that system.

Metaphorical concepts such as "argument is war," say Lakoff and Johnson, do not just influence the way we speak, they also govern the way we act. Our language is full of phrases that suggest the conflation of war and argument: we merge the two ideas, making them appear the same even though they are literally distinct. The barrage of linguistic correlations between war and argument gives ample evidence for this claim; we may speak of a good argument as "annihilating" an opponent, of "shooting down" ideas, of "defending" our points, or of finding a position "indefensible." We almost inevitably speak of "winning" or "losing" an argument or debate. And, of course, the previous sentence echoes this language, speaking of the list of examples as a "barrage," as if they were artillery instead of a series of observations, ammunition instead of illustration. This illustrates metaphoric transference or conflation: ideas and weapons are separate things, but the familiarity of this metaphor has so fused the two in our speech and imaginations that they begin, fundamentally, to merge.

The War Metaphor

The phrase "the war on terror" has been used so frequently that it is deeply entrenched in our thinking, so deeply that we might not realize that the phrase itself is not a description but a metaphor. The use of the war metaphor should be approached with caution, especially in the case of the war on terror. As with the influential phrase "The War on Drugs," widely used by the White House in the 1980s and 1990s, to say we are at war with something immediately invokes certain associations. It reduces an imposingly large, abstract, or disconcertingly complex problem to a well-defined, simplified, and ultimately manageable entity. It is difficult in a literal sense to be at war with something as opposed to someone, but by invoking the war metaphor, that "something," be it drugs or terror, is personified. Once the opposing idea is personified, metaphorically mutated into something approximating a human enemy, it appears possible to defeat that enemy, to achieve the clear triumph that would not be possible in battling either abstract concepts or complex and daunting social problems. The lure of such a promised victory proves almost irresistible; it calls up the feelings of triumph, clarity, and righteous response that so often elude us in considering hard-to-solve problems. Although war may evoke a range of horrific associations, it also has a compelling appeal; an "appropriate" war on an appropriately framed enemy can actually be more comforting than frightening. As Michael Erard notes, a phrase like "the war on terror" subtly "encodes a frame in which an intangible terror can be targeted or conquered." The success of this strategic frame depends on "the martial fantasy of inevitable victory."[12] It comes to seem almost ignoble not to answer the war metaphor's call to arms. The imagery around the figurative war often participates in a lofty range of speech, calling up, through images of flags, banners, and bands of brothers, the sentiments we feel for nation, community, identity, and other such potent values. Jayne Docherty and Frank Blechman, scholars in the field of conflict resolution, urge that the war metaphor should be used with caution: "Every metaphor is a way of seeing the world and every metaphor is also a way of not seeing the world. If we lock onto a single description of the problem and the appropriate response too early, we may not discover the most effective long-term responses to a crisis."[13] If we jettison the war metaphor in favor of another, new analogies might lead to new possibilities for response and resolution.

Why has the White House narrowed its metaphorical message so successfully that the war metaphor has largely over-taken all others? Why has the media echoed and replicated this metaphor in all its coverage? One answer to that question lies in the appeal, not of war itself, but of what the metaphor of war calls up. Erard notes that the phrase "war on terror" deliberately recycles a Cold War frame "in which we waged war on another intangible, Communism. And we won!" The promise of the phrase "the war on terror" is that "we can win this one, too." It invokes a national history of confident military strength: "America, after all, wins its wars."[14] Beyond the powerful appeal to a triumphalist history of the allusion to narratives of victory, the war metaphor promises something that is perhaps equally powerful: the simplification of the complex, the clarification of the subtle.

There is a certain clarifying quality to an extreme metaphor such as the metaphor of war that makes it potentially very attractive. War has the ability to focus issues, framing them definitively and inarguably. The public rage directed against those who questioned the war on terror in its early days is evidence of this: simply to question the appropriateness of this frame was seen as unpatriotic, even traitorous. One of the clearest examples of the war metaphor calling up the language of treason to brand sceptics is found in the response to an article penned by noted essayist Susan Sontag in the September 24, 2001 issue of *The New Yorker*. Sontag argued that the attacks of 9/11 needed to be understood within the broader context of decades of American foreign policy in the Middle East; in return, she was publicly denounced as a "quisling," a "fifth columnist," even a "pathetic ayatollah of hate." Political commentator Andrew Sullivan even invented a prize, the Susan Sontag award, for pillorying what he saw as the worst outpourings of the left.[15]

Similarly, John Edwards, candidate for the Democratic presidential nomination, was also called a traitor when he repudiated the notion that there is a "global war on terror," calling this metaphorical framing an ideological doctrine advanced by the Bush administration. In a May 2007 defense policy speech, Edwards called the war on terror a "bumper sticker" slogan used by Bush to justify everything from abuses at the Abu Ghraib prison to the invasion of Iraq. "By framing this as a war," Edwards said, "we have walked right into the trap the terrorists have set—that we are engaged in some kind of clash of civilizations and a war on Islam." His statements were immediately denounced: on the conservative web site Townhall.com a reader wrote "All you anti-war traitors should hang. We are at war because there is an enemy that initiated the war. After that any speech that gives aid and comfort and encouragement to the enemy should be hanged as a traitor."[16]

The war metaphor has also allowed the use of the term "Fifth Column" which disparages dissenters thought to pose an internal threat. Fifth columnists are traitors who act out of sympathy with the enemy to undermine a nation's solidarity from within. The term is currently being used by those on the political right to cast aspersions on academics and intellectuals who criticize the government by teaching the literature and politics of the Middle East. On the August 21, 2006, broadcast of his nationally syndicated radio show, Bill O'Reilly told his 3.5 million listeners[17] that "the Bush administration is in a war not only with the terrorists, but also with the far left in this country." Discussing the Bush administration's domestic surveillance program, which was recently struck down as unconstitutional by a federal district court judge, O' Reilly described the "far left" as the "fifth column in this country."[18] Once the conceptual structure of war has been evoked, it casts any dissent into a particularly negative, destructive light. Voices of difference are figured as dangerous, destructive, even traitorous: once we have war, it seems, we have traitors.

Just as wars involve two clearly defined sides, so the metaphor of war enticingly promises a clear narrative of aggressors and victims, winners and losers, soldiers and insurgents. Immediately after September 11, the war metaphor seemed, at first glance, to be reasonable: after all, the attack on the Pentagon was against a military target, the attacks were intended to challenge American economic and military power, and the level of damage made the south end of Manhattan look very much like a war zone, with all the attendant horror and chaos. However, other aspects of the attack do not fit this framing as well: The World Trade Center was not a military target; the attack vehicles were not military weapons; the attack was carried out entirely within this country; and, perhaps most importantly, the attackers did not represent the policy of another sovereign state. As events unfold, many commentators have cast doubts on the war metaphor, arguing that this is not (or should not be) a war against Islam, just against violent Islamic fundamentalists. These observers argue that the false clarity of the war metaphor effectively masks the many uncertainties and ambiguities of the War on Terror. For example, a sweepingly categorical term such as "enemy" can be used to obscure the fact that in this conflict the enemy is not a specifically national or a specifically religious one. As critics of the war on terror remind us, we need to beware of false logical propositions such as "All terrorists are Muslims therefore all Muslims are terrorists."[19] In the war on terror, the identification of the enemy has been increasingly difficult and problematic. Is the enemy terror itself? How is such an abstraction to be fought? What territory can be gained in such a hypothetical battle? What will be the front lines in this terrain of abstraction and symbolism?

In spite of its difficulties, the war metaphor has remained dominant. If we are in a war, then we have a specific lexicon or vocabulary to draw upon. Like the lexicon of any metaphorical system, this one does not simply describe things, but shapes the way we see them: our vocabulary guides our thinking, urging us to interpret events according to and within the frame of that language. The lexicon of war raises the stakes of the discussion and generates intensity: war, after all, is about our very survival. What is this lexicon? Its nouns crucially define identities: "our side" has "an enemy" who becomes "the enemy." We have "adversaries" and "antagonists." These nouns define the people and countries involved in conflict primarily in terms of opposition: we are defined by who we are against, and our opponents are defined as our opposites; both sides are thus locked into roles of essential difference and eternal opposition. The verbs in our lexicon of war also perform this kind of ideological work. In war, we "attack," "defend," "strike," and "engage" the enemy; we develop tactics and strategic objectives and employ "necessary means." The verbs of war allow for glorious activity: we are not passive but active, not acted upon but acting. The verbs of war are, frankly, rather exciting: they support a sense of progress and movement, while they negate any undesirable self-picturing of ourselves as hesitant, static, or uncertain. They replace the role of victim with the more potent role of aggressive defender. In this vocabulary, we are defined as hunter rather than prey, warrior rather than victim. Even the adjectives of war have a significant effect: soldiers are strong, active, powerful agents, while civilians are less than this: less experienced, less knowing, less involved in the conflict first-hand, and therefore less deserving of a voice.

The lexicon of war tacitly endorses the military's valuing of hierarchy and authority. Within this model, as citizens, part of the price of our recovered security is to defer to those in government and military who are seen as experts in the necessary deployments of war. This is significant because, in war, civilians have a limited importance relative to the martial arena: their job is to support the troops, not to question. The success of the war, we are told, requires singleness of vision and voice; a nation at war requires a harmonious chorus of support from its citizens, not a cacophony of dissenting voices. Any voice raised in protest, and thus out of tune with the prevailing chorus, is silenced, excoriated, or expelled. Voices of resistance or questioning are told, as the Dixie Chicks were famously told by an angry fan, to "shut up and sing."[20]

In this way the discourse of war enlists us into particular roles, and offers little space for the creative re-casting of these roles. The war metaphor offers the promise of victorious domination and protection: it implies we can so thoroughly defeat our enemies that we can keep them from ever hurting us again. This is a suspect promise, however; we have never successfully managed to fight the war to end all wars, and so clearly the closure and finality implicitly offered by the war metaphor is at least in part wishful thinking. Docherty argues that the war on terror will be no exception: the difficulties of identifying and locating the terrorist perpetrators will make a final reprisal difficult, and the very military attacks that create refugees will create new enemies emerging from the crowded refugee camps, perpetuating "the cycle of fear and terror for our children and grandchildren."[21] The war metaphor thus serves us poorly pragmatically and strategically as well as ideologically: we hamper ourselves if we assume we understand the nature and motivation of our enemies, or if we assume we can predict their response to our activities. We hamper ourselves further if we don't examine the contexts and conditions that have given rise to the world's escalating cycles of unrest and violence.

Another important aspect of the war metaphor is its inherent self-justification. It offers us a model that is reactive: our retaliation is right and, indeed, inevitable. We were given no choice in the matter, we might say to ourselves; we are in a war, this paradigm suggests, because others have declared war on us. Morally, the war metaphor risks everything a society builds by over-focusing resources on the war effort: "The great challenge of this metaphor is that it carries an all-or-nothing element. 'If you are not for war, you must be for doing nothing.' Without alternative models, critics of war do look weak and indecisive. Alternative metaphors are so badly needed."[22]

Many who urge a cautious, critical, or reflective attitude towards the war on terror emphasize not only the metaphor's ideological work, but its powerful political effect. Lakoff and Frisch argue that the war metaphor was primarily adopted for political reasons. Susan Sontag argues that because of its indefinite "enemy," the anti-terror war can never end, a "sign that it is not a war, but, rather, a mandate for expanding the use of American power."[23] The war metaphor allows for this expansion of power: when the government declares war on cancer or poverty or drugs it means the government is asking that new forces be mobilized to address the problem but when the government declares war on terrorism, it is giving itself permission to do what it wants. "When it wants to intervene somewhere, it will. It will brook no limits to its power."[24] The war metaphor negates any other non-military possibility as a way to defend the country. Since national security is inextricably tied to the war's success, to be against the war is to be against the nation's very survival, and therefore to be a national threat. Within the war metaphor, any hesitation to support the war becomes unpatriotic.

While the war metaphor encourages the government to "do what it wants" internally, an equally important feature is the war metaphor's repressive powers domestically. Lakoff and Frisch insist that the war metaphor puts dissenters on the defensive, since hesitation to give the President fuller authority opens critics and Congress to charges of defeatism, weakness, and lack of patriotism. Once the military extends the field of battle, the war metaphor creates a new literal reality, one that substantiates and reinforces the original metaphor. The war metaphor offers the President enlarged wartime powers and confers on him an "extraordinary domestic power" to fulfill the "agenda of the radical right" in moving resources away from social needs towards military needs in over-riding environmental safeguards, and in establishing systems of surveillance and intimidation to influence both enemies and citizens.[25] Since "war trumps all other topics," the war metaphor often expands powers not just in the international but in domestic arenas, granting the President a degree of power over political discussion as well as action.[26] Sontag's editorial echoes these concerns, arguing for the explicit connection of the war metaphor to the subjugation of free, open political debate. Framing America's post-911 foreign policy as "actions undertaken in war time," she says, acts as "a powerful disincentive" to critical discussion: in the aftermath of the attacks, individuals objecting to "the jihad language used by the American government (good versus evil, civilization versus barbarism) were accused of condoning the attacks, or at least the legitimacy of the grievances behind the attacks."[27] Because the war metaphor elevates virtues such as solidarity and unanimity, even a simple call to reflectiveness "is equated with dissent, dissent with lack of patriotism."[28] Within this model, reflection sides with the enemy, acting as a challenge to the "moral clarity" required to sustain a war.

The importance of how things are defined, then, cannot be underestimated. Frank Luntz advises right-wing organizations which words work best to sell their ideas to the public. He is credited with making estate taxes appear less palatable when he suggested they be re-named "death taxes." Through focus-group research, Luntz found that "estate tax" wasn't an objectionable concept to the majority of the public; it evoked a sense of wealthy people having to pay their fair share. The term "death tax," however, kindled voter resentment, calling up an image of government intruding into private family grief to snatch away the savings citizens wanted to pass along to loved ones. This word change had significant political impact: by provoking an outcry from a public who for the most part wouldn't be paying any significant amount in death taxes, the net result was a tax break for the wealthiest Americans. After the introduction of the new phrase, public support helped the Congress to repeal the tax. Economists observe that the repeal of the tax may cost more than a trillion dollars in lost revenue that could be used for much-needed social programs. Small words, then, clearly carry large consequences. In June 2004, Luntz wrote a memo for the Bush administration entitled *Communicating the Principles of Prevention & Protection in the War on Terror*, which offered guidance on specific language to use when talking about the war in Iraq. He notes:

> this document is intended to create a lexicon for explaining the policy of "preemption" and the "War in Iraq." However, you will not find any instance in

which we suggest that you use the actual word "preemption," or the phrase "The War in Iraq" to communicate your policies to the American public. To do so is to undermine your message from the start. Preemption may be the right policy, and Iraq the right place to start. But those are not the right words to use.[29]

His advice was to connect the war on terror to the war in Iraq by ensuring that "no speech about homeland security or Iraq should begin without a reference to 9/11." Luntz's recommended phrases such as "It is better to fight the War on Terror on the streets of Baghdad than on the streets of New York or Washington" and "9/11 changed everything," became staples of Republican rhetoric. Luntz acknowledged the influence of the war paradigm, and how essential it was to domestic political control, when he stated that invoking the war on terror would establish the conditions for Bush's electoral win in 2004. "If the public sees what the President's doing as a war on terror, he wins. If they see it as a war on Iraq, Kerry wins. What is the context of what the President is doing? Define it one way, you have one outcome; define it another way, you have a different outcome."[30]

Luntz's words suggest that governments may rise or fall on the meaning of a word, and that this meaning is determined by the context or frame in which the word circulates. The largest framing of the war on terror is a frame of race, and thus our most demeaning language and our harshest representations are reserved for those marked as racially Other. Evidence for this assertion can be found in the difference of language used to talk about internal voices of difference and those external Others who, as we draw them through our metaphoric language, are not just different but are *defined* by their difference. While the language used to denounce the "traitors" who publicly question the war on terror and American foreign policy is punitive, it still allows a basic humanity to those it denounces. "Quislings" are cowards, but they are cowardly persons; fifth columnists are dangerous and subversive, but dangerous and subversive people. These accusations attack groups' or individuals' actions, and the language of the accusations addresses these actions rather than the fundamental identity of the actor, who remains a fundamentally human agent. This goes against our historical sense that traitors are the worst kind of enemy because they destroy from within. Traditionally, traitors are seen as far worse than external enemies. But the language of the war on terror does not bear this out. Internal critics, while traitors, are allowed their humanity; the language and images associated with Arab terrorists, in comparison, relentlessly strips that humanity away. It achieves this by inextricably linking the "enemy other" with the animal—and not just any animal, but what we consider to be the lowest order of animal. War in general encourages imagery that debases the enemy, as following chapters will show; perhaps the most important reason to resist the war metaphor, then, is that it goes forward upon a sustained and seductive dehumanization of the enemy that, if we continue to indulge it, risks reducing our own humanity.

Notes

1. Terence Hawkes. *Metaphor*. London: Methuen. 1972: 1.

2. Terence Hawkes. *Metaphor*. London: Methuen. 1972: 1.

3. Ellen Winner. *The Point of Words*. Cambridge, MA: Harvard University Press, 1988: 17.

4. Brian Vickers. *In Defense of Rhetoric*. New York City: Clarendon Paperbacks. 1989: 299.

5. Brian Vickers. *In Defense of Rhetoric*. New York City: Clarendon Paperbacks. 1989: 299.

6. Paul Verlaine. "Art Poétique." *Aesthetic Realism*. See www.aestheticrealism.net/poetry/art-poetique.htm (June 26, 2007).

7. Terence Hawkes. *Metaphor*.

8. Cited in Terence Hawkes. *Metaphor*.

9. George Lakoff and Mark Johnson. *Metaphors We Live By*. Chicago: University of Chicago Press, 2nd edition, 1980: 4.

10. George Lakoff and Mark Johnson. *Metaphors We Live By*.

11. George Lakoff and Mark Johnson. *Metaphors We Live By*.

12. Michael Erard. "Frame Wars." *Texas Observer*. Posted on *Alternet*. November 18, 2004. See www.alternet.org/election04/20537/ (June 26, 2007).

13. Jayne Docherty. "Revisiting the War Metaphor." *Beyond September 11*. September 25, 2001. See http://www.emu.edu/ctp/bse-metaphor2.html (June 26, 2007).

14. Michael Erard. "Frame Wars."

15. Michael Bronski. "Brain drain: In defense of Susan Sontag, Noam Chomsky, and Gore Vidal." *The Phoenix.com*. September 19, 2002. See 72.166.46.24/boston/news_features/other_stories/multipage/documents/02441651.htm (June 26, 2007).

16. Peter Wehner. "John Edwards's irresponsible and revealing address." *Townhall*. May 24, 2007. See www.townhall.com/columnists/PeterWehner/2007/05/24/john_edwardss_irresponsible_and_revealing_address (June 26, 2007).

17. Project for Excellence in Journalism. "Annual Report on American Journalism, 2007." *The State of the News Media*. Spring 2007. See www.stateofthenewsmedia.org/2007/ (June 26, 2007).

18. *Media Matters for America*. "O'Reilly: The Bush administration is in a war not only with the terrorists, but also with the far left in this country." *Media Matters for America*. Aug. 23, 2006. See mediamatters.org/items/200608240001 (June 26, 2007).

19. Abdel Rahman al-Rashed. "Innocent religion is now a message of hate." *Telegraph* (UK). September 5, 2004.

20. Barbara Kopple. *Shut Up and Sing*. 2006. Videorecording.

21. Jayne Docherty. "Four Reasons to Use the War Metaphor with Caution." *Beyond September 11*. See www.emu.edu/ctp/bse-metaphor.html (June 26, 2007).

22. Frank Blechman and Jayne Seminare Docherty. "Frameworks other than war."

23. Susan Sontag. "Real Battles and Empty Metaphors." *New York Times*. September 10, 2002.

24. Susan Sontag. "Real Battles and Empty Metaphors."

25. George Lakoff and Evan Frisch. "Five Years After 9/11: Drop the War Metaphor."

26. George Lakoff and Evan Frisch. "Five Years After 9/11: Drop the War Metaphor."

27. Susan Sontag. "Real Battles and Empty Metaphors."

28. Susan Sontag. "Real Battles and Empty Metaphors."

29. Michael Erard. "Frame Wars."

30. Michael Erard. "Frame Wars."

CHAPTER TWO

Making Enemies:
Propaganda and the Making
of the Orientalist "Other"

Imagine for yourself "the enemy" as a man of resentment conceives him—and right here we have his action, his creation: he has conceptualized "the evil enemy," "the evil one," as a fundamental idea—and from that he now thinks his way to an opposite image and counterpart, a "good man"—himself!

—Friedrich Nietzche[1]

Propaganda

Propaganda is the fuel that feeds the machinery of war. It is key in generating the public support that is one of war's most essential requirements. If metaphor helps construct our reality, then propaganda is one of the chief materials in that construction. The frames through which we see the world are built from the language propaganda offers us, and that the media, echoing it, ratifies. Support for war is much more powerful when it is emotional or visceral than when it is logical or intellectual; likewise, the war on terror depends on our "feeling" more than our "knowing." This is made especially clear when we consider how much misunderstanding and outright error has surrounded the war. When, in January 2002, the Knight-Ridder newspaper company sponsored an opinion poll, it reported that while two-thirds of the respondents claimed they had a good grasp of the issues surrounding the war, "closer questioning revealed large gaps in that knowledge," including serious errors of fact. For example, fully half of those surveyed thought that one or more of the 9/11 terrorists were Iraqi when, in reality, not one of the terrorists was an Iraqi citizen.[2] The survey's results suggest that the more knowledge people possessed about events surrounding the war, the less likely they were to take a fierce, aggressive, or militaristic stance. Survey authors noted significantly that "Those who show themselves to be most knowledgeable about the Iraq situation are significantly less likely to support military action."[3]

Propaganda is not concerned with disseminating information but with rallying emotion. Information is a distraction from propaganda's fundamental work: it is not intended to enlarge our understanding of complex issues but to narrow it, so that we will be both focused and manageable. Propaganda's intent is not to educate but to generate and direct emotion, to boil the blood while it narrows the mind. Its most essential task, and its most dangerous, is to ensure that public emotion dominates public discussion.

Propaganda is the mechanism by which governments persuade the public of the evil of the enemy and the justness of its own cause. When propaganda spreads through public discourse, flowing from government spokespeople through the news media to the internet and television, re-articulated by news anchors and columnists, bloggers and talk show hosts, it inevitably influences public opinion. Influence, after all, is propaganda's purpose. The facts, for propagandists, merely confuse the issue, weakening the clarity required to create and sustain moral certainty. For the machinery of war to run smoothly, propaganda must be pure, distilled, and unpolluted by contaminants such as complexity or subtlety. While we may naturally associate clarity with knowledge, propaganda implicitly asserts the opposite: the more we know, the greater our confusion, hesitation, and ambivalence; the less we know, the more strongly and clearly we can feel.

We need, therefore, to be aware of the ways in which propaganda suppresses information, not overtly, as in policies of censorship, but subtly. The silencing effect is the same in both censorship and propaganda; the difference is that the censored generally know they are being censored, while those subjected to expert propaganda are often unaware of it. In the study of propaganda, scholars typically differentiate between how propaganda works differently in a controlled society than in an open society. Noam Chomsky states that "Propaganda is to democracy what violence is to totalitarianism."[4] In the controlled society, propaganda is obvious, and its very obviousness allows a stance of silent resistance or dismissal; it may be tolerated for fear of reprisal, but citizens recognize it for what it is. In contrast, in a more open society like America, says Nancy Snow, "the hidden and integrated nature of the propaganda best convinces people that they are not being manipulated."[5] For Americans, argues Snow, propaganda is something associated with dictators: "it is not supposed to be part of an open society."[6]

Evidence of propaganda at work in closed societies is easy to come by. Hitler's propaganda machine was legendary, and relied on one of the twentieth century's most influential practitioners of public relations, Edward Bernays. Bernays, the nephew of Sigmund Freud, merged Freud's work in individual psychology with his own brand of social psychology, using public opinion polls, advertising, and other means of persuasion to political ends. In his early books *Crystallizing Public Opinion* (1923) and *Propaganda* (1928), he spoke of constructing the "necessary illusions" that could be delivered to the public as reality in order to achieve what he famously called the "engineering of consent."[7] Joseph Goebbels used Bernays' work as the basis for his propaganda in the 1930s.[8] Herman Goering was blunt about how easy it is to control public sentiment about war, whether in a democracy or a dictatorship. Acknowledging that "of course the people don't want war," he added, "but it's always a simple matter to drag the people along whether it's a democracy, a fascist dictatorship, or a parliament, or a communist dictatorship. Voice or no voice, the people can always be brought to the bidding of the leaders." All that is necessary, said Goering, is to "tell them they are being attacked, and denounce the pacifists for lack of patriotism, and exposing the country to greater danger."[9]

The engineering of consent wasn't limited to European dictatorships. American President Woodrow Wilson relied on Bernays and influential journalist Walter Lippmann in 1917 to reverse America's reluctance to enter WWI. Bernays' famous slogan "Make the World Safe for Democracy" effectively reversed the tide of public opinion, creating a band-wagon effect so strong that to question it was seen as dangerously unpatriotic. The propaganda of the current war on terror remains equally effective in marshalling opinion, relying equally heavily on hired experts. PR consultant John Rendon, who has worked extensively for the Pentagon and CIA on supplying language for public discussions of Iraq, referred to himself in a 1996 speech as "an information warrior and a perception manager."[10] Managing perception included such tasks as supplying American flags for Kuwaitis to wave in televised scenes of U.S. Marines entering Kuwait City at the end of the Gulf War; these scenes, aired on news broadcasts all over the world, sent a strong visual message about the welcome of the marines as liberators.[11] "Did you ever stop to wonder," Rendon asked, "how the people of Kuwait City, after being held hostage for seven long and painful months, were able to get hand-held American flags? . . . Well, you now know the answer. That was one of my jobs."[12]

Propaganda speaks to two audiences. As misinformation, it is intended to confuse and mislead the enemy, supplying false facts and obscuring truth. This kind of disinformation has always been part of warfare; Alexander the Great purportedly left huge pieces of armour behind his retreating troops to "convince the enemy that his soldiers were giants."[13] But perhaps propaganda is most pernicious when directed towards a domestic audience. As Jacques Ellul observes, propaganda is always at its most effective when it is least noticeable.[14] Critics of the war on terror state that the American public has been manipulated and deceived by "a covert disinformation campaign" orchestrated by professional Public Relations consultants whose job is to "spin" the war and government messages to the public.[15] This is done in the name of the public good as a way of offering clarity; for example, in October 2001 Defence Secretary Donald Rumsfeld said that "we need to do a better job to make sure that people are not confused as to what this is about."[16] President Bush echoed this when, on May 24, 2005, he said, "See in my line of work you got to keep repeating things over and over and over again for the truth to sink in, to kind of catapult the propaganda."[17]

The interplay between clarity, confusion, and complexity in public discourse is important to observe in the language of propaganda. Most people are familiar with some of the phrases used by government representatives to downplay certain words' real meanings: the distant and technical-sounding "collateral damage" softens the harsh reality of "killed civilians," while the more benign-sounding "friendly fire" replaces the more brutal "shot down by his own side." Collateral damage, says Tom Engelhardt, is a phrase used to downplay slaughter and carnage; carnage "is always portrayed by the military as justified and the death of civilians, if finally admitted, invariably as 'accidental' in pursuit of the enemy; hence, 'collateral damage.'"[18] Even an apparently neutral term like "*non-combatant*," while apparently acting simply as a synonym for "civilian," suggests a very different connotation. The word civilian connotes a non-soldier, someone separate from the battle and therefore not a legitimate target. Civilians are the opposite of soldiers, but non-combatants are not the opposites of combatants, and could become combatants at any moment. The word *non-combatant*, looked at in this way, implies an activity rather than an essential condition, an activity that might suddenly change. The condition of not-fighting seems a more temporary state than the condition being a civilian. The term *non-combatants* seems to warrant less sympathy or compassion than the word *civilian* invites. This is reflected in the findings of a Pentagon survey of U.S. soldiers and marines in Iraq, based on interviews with 1,767 troops, in which only 47 percent of soldiers and 38 percent of marines felt Iraqi non-combatants should be treated with dignity and respect as required by the Geneva Conventions. Strikingly, only half of those polled said they would report a member of their unit for killing or injuring a non-combatant.[19] This is reflected in the events at Haditha, in which an internal military investigation determined that U.S.

marines killed as many as 24 Iraqis—including women and children—in the city of Haditha in November 2005 and then attempted a cover-up.[20] The victims included "a 76-year-old amputee in a wheelchair holding a Koran, a mother and child bent over as if in prayer," and children as young as one year old. Such brutalities are clearly linked to the ways in which enemies are constructed; as Engelhardt observes, it's a small step "from the knowledge that the enemy might be anywhere to the thought that the enemy is everywhere, and then to the feeling that every Vietnamese/Iraqi is an enemy." In the slaughter of civilians at My Lai, during the Vietnam War, one soldier on trial confirmed this perspective, noting that "even a baby sucking at its mother's breast" might "be helping to conceal a hidden grenade."[21]

This willingness to kill civilians without compunction is not just a feature of soldiers, produced by dangers of being in the field. It also finds a fierce echo in media commentators and columnists back home. An article by Ben Shapiro at TownHall.com highlights how the two terms are freighted with meaning. In an column entitled "Enemy 'civilian casualties' ok by me," Shapiro says he is "getting really sick of people who whine about 'civilian casualties.' Maybe I'm a hard-hearted guy, but when I see in the newspapers that civilians in Afghanistan or the West Bank were killed by American or Israeli troops, I don't really care. In fact, I would rather that the good guys use the Air Force to kill the bad guys, even if that means some civilians get killed along the way. One American soldier is worth far more than an Afghan civilian."[22] Shapiro goes on to argue that the term *non-combatant* is misleading, criticizing *The New York Times* and other papers as "disingenuous" for calling Afghan non-combatants "civilians," because, in doing so, they suggest that all civilians are somehow the same. Shapiro is clear that Afghan and American civilians are not at all equal: "American civilians are people who go about their daily lives without providing cover for terrorists or giving them money. Afghan civilians are not,"[23] so "frankly, it doesn't matter to me if some of their 'civilians' get killed for involvement with the enemy."[24] By this logic, Afghans can never be truly citizens nor can they be non-combatants, because they are fundamentally always "involved with the enemy." They are always guilty, therefore always fair game. This view is echoed by a blogger who posted this view:

> Hunt down every member of ETA, AlQ, PFLP, IRA and every other bunch of sonsabitches that ever sets off a bomb and kill them. Kill them until they fear us more than they love whatever twisted cause they serve. If it takes killing their families down to their goddamned pet hamsters that's fine with me.[25]

This sense of the fundamental and essential guilt of the enemy allows for the perpetration of atrocities both public and private. The infamous Abu Ghraib

photos of American soldiers torturing and humiliating Iraqis are one example
of private acts made public. While there has been public condemnation of
these photos, there have also been attempts to turn them back into private
acts. If they're private, after all, they can be distanced from national governments; they are not a product of deliberately racist rhetoric, but instead the actions of a few individuals, a couple of bad apples. In a speech to the U.S. House
of Representatives, Congressman Jim McDermott chronicles this process of
trying to limit damage and make the abuse a singular, anomalous event. "I have
been watching the hearings over in the Senate," said McDermott,

> the effort to limit this and say it is just seven or eight young people and per-
> haps a couple of lieutenants up the line but really it is a rogue operation, is sim-
> ply not true. It runs all the way to the top. The decisions here have to be signed
> off. Anybody who has been in the military knows about the chain of com-
> mand, and somebody does not sign off down at the lieutenant level and not
> bother to send it up to the captain or to the colonel or to the general. They all
> go up the line. They have all been signed off, one way or another, or somebody
> at the top said here is a blank check, do whatever you want.[26]

The attempt to make these actions appear to be those of private individuals
has been furthered by many media voices. A British Broadcasting Corporation
broadcaster described the photos as "merely mementos"—"Something one
would laugh about in the family and then paste in the family album."[27] The
family album is a private space, a catalogue of the domestic and personal; that
the Abu Ghraib photos can be treated as "merely" private, idiosyncratic "mementos" is a pernicious attempt to refute the systematic racism of current military policy. Ahdaf Soueif, a prominent Egyptian writer living in the UK,
writes scathingly in *The Guardian* that the news and photographs emerging
from Iraq show a progression of Western dehumanization of the Arab: "In the
past year the world has seen photos of many Iraqis stripped with their wrists
tied behind their backs with plastic cord. At first we could look into their eyes
and bear witness to what was happening. Then they were bagged. At no point
was there an outcry. We have grown used to seeing Arab men bound and
hooded."[28] Soueif tells another story of the "private" family memento, a personal souvenir photo of a young American soldier in Iraq. In this photo,

> There is no nakedness or torture, but it is no less nasty for that. The boys are
> holding a cardboard sign. They and the soldier are smiling and doing a thumbs
> up. He is pointing at the cardboard sign, on which he's written: "Lcpl
> Boudreaux killed my Dad. then he knocked up my sister!" Imagine the scene:
> Lance Corporal Boudreaux, a soldier on a liberating, civilizing mission, asks

the natives to pose for a "memento". He gives them the sign to hold. What lie did he tell them about its message? "Iraq is liberated", or "Mission accomplished"? And who, in this scene, is the more civilized?[29]

The contrast of the two families implied by this scene is poignant and horrifying; what idea does it inspire of the hypothetical American family back home, willing to find such a souvenir amusing, ready to be made proud of their boy for his exploits? The idea that anyone could speak of such photos as "mere" mementos, something to "laugh about in the family" suggests an intensely unflattering understanding of the families back home, believing in good faith in the moral value of what "our boys" are doing "over there." And what of that other family, that murdered father and "knocked up" sister? The always disturbing conflation of sex and violence aside, the image of the two Iraqi children flashing a thumbs-up at a sign celebrating the real or imagined devastation of their family is an apt illustration of what happens when we stop believing that anyone in the enemy nation can be a civilian. Even children, in this context, can in apparent glee be conscripted into the documentation of their own unknowing humiliation.

Perhaps the most startling linguistic disconnection shows up in the gap between the labels "freedom fighter" and "terrorist." In his essay "Media Spin Revolves around the Word Terrorist,"[30] Norman Solomon approvingly cites Reuter's policy of avoiding these and other "emotive words." Since these terms are intricately tied up with value judgments and political perspectives, to employ them is not simply to report events but implicitly to evaluate them. Reuters states that "we do not use terms like 'terrorist' and 'freedom fighter' unless they are in a direct quote or are otherwise attributable to a third party. We do not characterize the subjects of news stories but instead report their actions" so "readers can make their own decisions."[31] While many of the 160 countries from which Reuters reports have pressured the news agency to label their enemies as terrorists, an internal memo offered one reason to resist such pressure: "one man's terrorist," it observed, "is another man's freedom fighter."[32] It is often only when time allows a fuller picture of political, social, and cultural contexts to emerge that we begin to re-evaluate these terms; it was the development of just such a larger international picture that changed the label applied to Nelson Mandela, winner of the 1993 Nobel Peace Prize, from terrorist to statesman.[33]

Propaganda, however, rejects consideration of a conflict's more nuanced political, social, and cultural contexts as working against the clarity it promises. Propaganda values passion over reason. It implies that we already know everything we need to know to act. To distract from our fundamental lack of facts, it offers us information's seductive substitutes: hysteria, indignation, rage, and fear. These qualities are useful to the media, because they sell papers and make for sensational TV. They're useful to governments, because they allow us to be manipulated by carefully selected experts who know how best to play upon emotions in order to enlist us in approving their policies and powers. In wartime, passion trumps reason, and misplaced passion drives us eagerly forward where reason might urge reflection, care, measured speech and measured action.

Orientalism

The passion cultivated by propaganda in order to generate support for war emerges from a process that is neither accidental nor innocent. The sheer consistency of the narratives we tell ourselves about our enemies suggests this: these stories must be serving something or someone, or else they simply would not have such currency, such resilience, such extraordinary staying power. As thoughtful citizens, we are called upon to ask ourselves, as we should of all the dominant narratives that shape our consciousness and our lives: just what is it that these stories serve?

One of the most influential answers to this question has emerged from the work of Edward Said. In his widely studied book *Orientalism*, he argues that these narratives emerge from a history of imperial conquest but, more importantly, they also form the cornerstone of that history, supporting, enabling and justifying it. Said argues that the colonial and imperial projects depend upon the way we characterize those we see as deeply different from ourselves, as our opposite and our Other. Over time, these characterizations are systematized, grouped into an organized body of knowledge, a repertory of word and image so often repeated that it comes to seem like objective knowledge. Said calls the distorted and distorting lens created by this process Orientalism a framework through which the West examines and understands what it perceives as the foreign or alien. Said's work focuses on how the West, especially Europe and North America, has traditionally characterized the East, in which he includes the Middle and Far East. Through this lens, the East is always the West's opposite: if the West considers itself rational, progressive, and civilized, then the East is its inverse, superstitious, backwards, and barbaric. This characterization of the East is sometimes overtly hostile, as in the stereotype of the Eastern man as a violent primitive; sometimes, it is not hostile but infatuated, as in recurrent images of the Eastern woman as exotically sexual, sultry, pliable and tempting, or of the East as a sensuous place of mystery and marvels. Whether alluring or threatening, however, the Oriental

Other is inevitably seen as less than the West. It might be appealing or horrific, but it is eternally available to the West as an enemy to be conquered or a temptress to be ravished.

The West, in taking the Orient as its subject of study, comes to feel it knows and thus has mastered the East. Said argues that the distorting lens of Orientalism, the organized body of knowledge that creates our definition of the East, is ultimately intended to help us understand the "natives" so we may more easily conquer them. Because the West tells such consistent tales of the endlessly primitive East, it appears eternal, static, and unlike the developed West, can never really change or evolve. The West can justify its conquest as benign; within the Orientalist's metaphoric framework, conquest is for the good of the conquered, freeing them from their own barbarity. Said observes that, because of the politics of the Orientalist discourse, it ultimately tells us more about the West than about the East: how does the West act in gathering and ratifying its "official story" of the East? How does it create such stories, and how does it put them to work? These questions suggest that Orientalism is not an authentic body of knowledge but is instead "most valuable as a sign of European-Atlantic power over the Orient."[34]

The distorting lens of Orientalism masks a far richer, more complex reality. In sharp contrast to Orientalism's picture of the East as mystical, irrational and superstitious, a place of religious extremism and fanaticism, Said observes that in his experience, the East is actually an overwhelmingly secular society. It is the consistency and unanimity of media images which create the impression that the entire East is solely the birthplace of "villains and fanatics." It would be naive, says Said, to deny that there are terrorists in the East, "as there are everywhere."[35] The western media's exclusionary focus on a single aspect of Eastern experience when considering the East as enemy, however, has resulted in a picture of the Arab as essentially and exclusively fanatical, extremist, and violent. The stereotype has become, with repetition, an archetype.

The East covers an immense territory and encompasses many countries. These countries, while sharing some things in common, also have unique cultures, politics, and histories. In the same way that no single story could ever fully describe or account for all the multiple facets of life in the West, so the narrow story told by Orientalism cannot hope to capture the richness and range of the East's reality. The narrowed focus of Orientalism is both reductive and deceptive; it offers a false sense that this misleading picture has told the whole truth, and that we therefore can fully know the East, even if we've never traveled there, nor seen it in any guise except those which we in the West have constructed. Orientalism's illusion of comprehensiveness is dangerous enough when it causes us to misunderstand the East in the name of knowing it. It is even more dangerous when that false knowing occurs in the context of war.

The Fabricated Enemy

Since war demands an enemy, we must imaginatively construct one; propaganda furthers this construction. Orientalism allows us to fabricate an alien enemy effectively and dangerously. The more shadowy, unclear, or ambiguous the face of the enemy, the more urgently propaganda must fabricate an enemy that we can believe we know, so that we may in turn conquer it. Gene Knudson-Hoffman observes that "an enemy is a person whose story we have not heard."[36] In the face of the silence that exists when we have not heard that other story, our tendency is to race to fill that silence. Instead of listening to multiple stories, instead of using the investigative tools of our journalistic media and our critical minds to search out these stories, we rush to fill the silence with a story of our own: not the whole, complex truth but the story that war, to work, needs us to hear. Our most violent passions and our most dehumanizing metaphors seem to be directed towards those enemies that we ourselves most actively help to construct.

One of the defining features of the fabricated enemy, the enemy upon whom we have hung an artful mask, is that this enemy is both representative and indistinguishable. It is representative because the figure of this enemy stands in for the whole. In the study of metaphor this device is called metonymy. Synecdoche uses a part of something to represent or call up its entirety: we might talk of factory hands, for example, when by hands we really mean the whole body of the workers, not just their hands. While this is a straightforward example, the work of metonymy in constructing an enemy is anything but straightforward and has serious implications. When the terrorist comes to stand for all Arabs, for example, or religious extremists for all Muslims, then we generalize globally, broadening our target from immediate actors like the 9/11 suicide bombers to encompass all Middle-Easteners, as we see in blogs denouncing all Arabs as terrorists in sympathies if not in actions. Racism conspires in this kind of metonymy, whispering to us that "they're" really all alike any way, so it doesn't really matter if we retaliate specifically against the actual perpetrators or generally against everybody who happens to look like them. As Lori A. Peek points out, the process of defining the enemy and defining the Other have a lot in common: "the two are clearly similar processes that sometimes lead to devastating outcomes."[37]

Seeing the enemy Other as an indistinguishable mass is an essential strategy in the process of fabricating the enemy, especially since our technologies now allow us to kill so efficiently and indiscriminately. If a weapon cannot distinguish between a combatant and a civilian target, in order to live with our actions, we must train ourselves not to distinguish either: we must become as indiscriminate as our bombs. Wartime images stress this indistinguishability, as evidenced in Frank Capra's 1945 propaganda film, "Know Your Enemy—Japan," which told viewers that all Japanese resembled "photographic reprints off the same negative," a message visually re-inforced by repeated scenes of a steel bar hammered in a forge, and by scenes of regimented mass activity that confirmed the impression of a race lacking any individual identity.[38]

Racism at large works on this same principle, lumping together into a single mass all the variety of individual humanity. Said cites George Orwell's travel essay "Marrakesh" as an example of this; Orwell writes that, among the crowds of Marrakesh, there are so many people that " it is always difficult to believe that you are walking among human beings . . . the people have brown faces—besides, there are so many of them! Are they really the same flesh as yourself? Do they even have names? Or are they merely a kind of undifferentiated brown stuff, about as individual as bees or coral insects?"[39] Unlike the civilized citizens of the West, who are primarily identified with culture rather than with nature, the hordes of the East are as natural as insects, and as undifferentiated, simply an inseparable part of the hive or swarm. Orwell's essay links the citizens of Marrakesh with the dirt itself: "They rise out of the earth, they sweat and starve for a few years, and then they sink back into the nameless mounds of the graveyard and nobody notices that they are gone. And even the graves themselves soon fade back into the soil."[40] To say that these soiled beings, these people "with brown faces" who emerge from and return to the earth, die without anyone noticing is an extraordinary statement. Orwell, deeply invested in social critique, no doubt intended his words to evoke compassion, outrage, and a reforming zeal. As the product of an Orientalist culture, however, he had only a limited number of metaphors through which he was able to understand what he saw in the streets of Marrakesh. Conditioned by the dominant Orientalist discourse to think of those from the East as a seething, disorganized mass, how else could he interpret what he saw? Shaped by ongoing metaphors of the East as populated not by individuals but by aggregates, by chaotic masses of humanity, he was unable to imagine that even the poorest street beggar might possess family who would care about him, miss him, mourn his death. Instead, the Orientalist vision imagines that, because the West doesn't care about the individual Easterner, each must go into the ground not just unmourned but unnoticed. Orwell's words find a disturbing echo in our century in an email sent to peace activist Cindy Shee-han from someone describing himself or herself as a "patriotic American." The emailer claimed that Iraqi mothers and fathers captured on film scream-ing because their babies have been killed "are just acting for the cameras. They are animals who don't care about their children because they know they can produce another."[41]

When the seething mass portrayed by Orientalism is not perceived as threat, it is treated relatively benignly as the focus of our sympathy or our will to reform. When it becomes a threat, however, the metaphor of the mass be-comes murderous, justifying indiscriminate killing. It is within this metaphorical framework that a columnist like Ben Shapiro can call for the mass death of all Afghanis; every citizen of the enemy country becomes in-distinguishable, justifiable prey. When war is total, as current military strat-egy informs us it must be, no one is immune from attack. The metaphoric fabrication of an undifferentiated enemy endorses this approach; if one of them did it, then all of them must be guilty. Total war depends on con-structing an enemy that justifies such widespread hatred and wanton de-struction. The fabricated enemy becomes something broader, more perni-cious, and more insidious than an opponent in battle; the "entire population is viewed as a non-human Other."[42] Not only, in this framework, is it impos-sible to tell one indistinguishable lump of matter from another, it is equally impossible to distinguish them from the earth itself: they're all a part of the same big, brown pile of dirt.

Orientalism constructs its Other based on a series of oppositions or bina-ries, and when we fabricate an enemy through metaphor, we do the same. If we are one thing, we say, then they must be the opposite. These binaries are self-perpetuating, trapping us in an either/or framework. Each half or term of the binary holds the other term in place: if *they* are associated with nature, then *we* must be associated with nature's opposite, culture. Since *we* are as-sociated with culture, *they* will always be associated with nature. In a binary-driven discourse, it's hard to imagine a way out of these either/or formula-tions. Since wartime intensifies our public rhetoric, it is no surprise that the binaries invoked by our politicians in the war on terror and echoed by the media reflect that most fundamental of all oppositions, good versus evil. While our historical enemy might change over time, our metaphorical en-emy has never evolved: that eternal Other is always evil to our good, de-stroyer to our preserver, death to our life. Thus, while the specific adjectives we apply to our enemies may evolve from generation to generation, from conflict to conflict, the positive adjectives always belong to our side, and the negative ones are always assigned to the enemy other.

While the adjectives and images used in fabricating the enemy may alter, there are overlapping aspects they all share, metaphors of destructive difference that are common to all. The metaphors we use to give an evil face to a faceless enemy remain, over time, remarkably constant. Ann Burnette and Wayne Kraemer call this process of directing public fear and hatred onto a chosen target "putting a face on evil."[43] Historical analysis of the enemy image reveals that perceptions of the enemy tend to mirror each other—that is, each side attributes the same virtues to itself and the same vices to the enemy. In each case, "we" are trustworthy, peace-loving, honorable and humanitarian; "they" are treacherous, warlike, and cruel. Jerome Frank and Andrei Melville note that in 1942, when Germany and Japan were enemies of the United States, the first five adjectives used by Americans in opinion surveys to describe the enemies included warlike, treacherous, and cruel. None of these words appeared among the first five describing the Soviets, who at that time were American allies. In 1966, when the Soviet Union had become a threat, among the primary adjectives describing the Soviets were warlike and treacherous. These adjectives also were applied to the Chinese, but had disappeared from the lists applied to the Germans and Japanese, who by then were allies of the United States.[44] When the enemy is fabricated as representing everything that is evil, the nation is usually confirmed in its sense of its own identity. As David Kennedy observes, "while it may not be true that Americans *needed* an enemy image in order to define themselves, when they were compelled to construct the portrait of an enemy they did in fact reveal their sense of themselves."[45]

The binarized image of the enemy as our eternal opposite is not only dangerous for the stability of international relations but leads to serious consequences for the national domestic life. Frank and Melville note that this happens because

> the hysteria about the outer threat is often used as justification for secrecy and suspicion, covert actions, policies creating "mobilized" societies, artificial national unity, "witch hunts," and policies suppressing dissent, all ignoring domestic problems and distracting attention from them. By projecting the blame for these on the enemy, each side protects its own self-esteem from the realization that it has been unable to solve its own problems.[46]

The construction of enemy images is also, notes Debra Merskin, a "crucial part of the process of justifying an unjust war," and is necessary if "power elites want to move military and diplomatic policies forward without full disclosure but with maximum public support."[47] Such public support is easier to manipulate when the menace of our enemy-opposite is portrayed as comprehensive and fundamental. Rayan El Amine notes that the Islamic menace "has replaced the red menace, and the "evil empire" of the cold war has become the less eloquent, but just as deadly, "evil doers" of the Arab and Muslim world."[48] The intensity of the language and its archaic, almost biblical quality suggest that the war on terror is being framed as a new crusade, a holy war. George Bush made this framing explicit in a September 16, 2001, speech warning Americans that "this crusade, this war on terrorism, is gonna take a while."[49] The word *crusade* conjures up images of a spiritual war fought in the interests of Christianity over barbarism, bearing the imprint of a mandate that originates not with governments but with God. The crusades of the eleventh century also employed this strategy, calling soldiers to a war of divine liberation; looking back, historians now see such rhetoric as cover for a much more pragmatic conquest, a crusade not for saving souls but for a more earthly conquest. Bush's use of the word, says Grand Mufti Soheib Bensheikh, dangerously recalls "the barbarous and unjust military operations against the Muslim world" by Christian knights, who launched repeated attempts to capture Jerusalem over the course of several hundred years.[50] Bruce Lawrence notes that then as now, "there is no Muslim enemy. In the eleventh century the First Crusades constructed him to cover spurious conquests and wanton killings. In the twenty-first century, the New Crusades reconstruct him to cover global asymmetrics and moral blunders. Both sets of crusaders are zealots with feet of clay."[51] Emran Qureshi and Michael A. Sells point out that the fear, rage and ethnic and religious stereotyping seen in contemporary Western culture echo that found in the Middle Ages during the first Crusades. They suggest that, since the first crusades, the dominant perception of the relationship between Islam and the West has been one of a vast, unending, inevitable struggle. Propaganda gives a form to this struggle, presenting it as an unavoidable and unyielding battle between monolithic powers a "clash of civilizations."[52] The phrase "clash of civilizations," popularized by Bernard Lewis in "The Roots of Muslim Rage," articulates a particular way of understanding conflict in the post-Cold War world. Lewis' view is that Muslims exist historically and inevitably in a state of conflict with Judeo-Christian civilization. This view shapes and limits our understanding of history and conflict. Khaled Abou el-Fadl, a law professor at UCLA, recalls that Lewis, when asked in an interview what the West should do about "these problems with Muslims," said "in effect, 'Well, there's nothing we can do. They are just the way they are. They're just going to hate us and go after us.'"[53] Samuel P. Huntington expanded and popularized this theory in his best-selling 1996 book *The Clash of Civilizations and the Remaking of World Order.* Huntington argues that cultural and religious identities will overtake political allegiances as the main source of conflict in the post-Cold War world. In a 1993 *Foreign Affairs* article, he wrote:

> It is my hypothesis that the fundamental source of conflict in this new world will not be primarily ideological or primarily economic. The great divisions among humankind and the dominating source of conflict will be cultural. Nation states will remain the most powerful actors in world affairs, but the principal conflicts of global politics will occur between nations and groups of different civilizations. The clash of civilizations will dominate global politics. The fault lines between civilizations will be the battle lines of the future.[54]

Although the phrase "clash of civilizations" has a compellingly resonant sound, critics of the hypothesis point out its dangers. Abou el-Fadl notes that it locks both East and West into a state of irresolvable conflict by asserting that "Muslims have existed fundamentally and irreparably in a state of conflict with the Judeo-Christian civilization"; this "gives the Islamic threat a certain historical inevitability: 'Well, you know it was like that in history and will remain like that.'"[55] Once we are taught to see all Muslim-Western conflicts, no matter how specific or localized, as a titanic "clash of civilizations," then whatever these conflicts are really about is disguised, absorbed into a model that sees West and East as "two titans" always at war over fundamental differences of identity. The identity assigned by the West to Islam is, in this model, always hostile and alien, which means that there is no way out of the irreconcilable differences between the two combatants. Only by abandoning our long-standing construction of the Muslim world as intractably inimical can we hope to break free of the brutalizing binaries of the West versus East paradigm, which relies so heavily on the image of the monolithic Muslim other.[56]

The news media constantly re-circulate images and language that reinforce this characterization of the Muslim as fundamentally alien, as do scenes from countless movies and TV programs featuring Arabs almost solely in the role of zealots, fanatics or terrorists. News broadcasts repeatedly show scenes emphasizing this zealotry; moderate voices from Islam, and there are many, are ignored in favor of repeated images of extremity. Newspaper headlines echo the framing of the struggle in epic, eternal form. "This fanaticism that we in the West can never understand," says one such headline. "Praise to Allah—dancing with joy, the warrior race of fanatics born to detest the West" says another; "In the heart of London, demands for a Holy War" says a third.[57] Christopher Allen notes that these are not "the exception to the rule, nor are they a result of years of studying Islamophobia in the media. Instead these are just a small sample of many similar examples that have been prolifically emblazoned across front pages and shown across our screens since the atrocities in America."[58] Merskin notes that we didn't see "the end of enemy construction with the war in Iraq. The stereotype was carried from the Taliban, bin Laden, and terrorists to the axis of evil and Hussein. Since the occupation of Iraq, the evil Arab image shifted to Shiite Muslim cleric Muqtada al-Sadr and 'crazed' Iraqis opposed to U.S. occupation."[59] Such images are not, Merskin argues, "simply an issue of imbalance and unfair representations," but speak to larger, more fundamental questions of why such images are so necessary and prevalent."[60]

It is this founding of enmity in identity, rather than in circumstance, that causes critics like Said to observe that Muslims are hated not for what they do, but for who they are. In *Covering Islam*, Said writes:

> Much of what one reads and sees in the media about Islam represents the aggression coming from Islam because that is what 'Islam' *is*. Local and concrete circumstances are thus obliterated. In other words, covering Islam is a one-sided activity that obscures what 'we' do and highlights instead what Muslims and Arabs, by their flawed nature are.[61]

To protect the simplicity of enmity required to sustain a war, we might not actually want to know more about our enemies; it is enough that we can identify them and claim to know them. We want to very clearly mark our enemy as other, and this marking is not always figurative: sometimes we want literally to mark them, to stamp them clearly with the sign of their alien identity. Nazi Germany infamously did this with its enemy Others, forcing Jews, homosexuals, Jehovah Witnesses, and Gypsies to wear yellow stars, and pink, violet, or brown triangles for easy identification, so that they could be effectively rounded up, imprisoned and executed under the visible banner of their Otherness. We might think we are, in a more liberal democracy, far from that kind of marking, yet a recent American talk-radio show on the AM station 630WMAL featured listeners enthusiastically endorsing the show's suggestion that all Muslims living in the U.S. should be identified with an armband or crescent-shaped tattoo. Reuters news agency reported on December 2, 2006, that radio host Jerry Klein received many calls in support of his modest proposal; one caller said, "Not only do you tattoo them in the middle of their forehead but you ship them out of this country . . . they are here to kill us."[62] Demonstrating the link between identifying and punishing the Other, another said that simply marking Islamic American citizens' documents wasn't enough. "'What good is identifying them?' he asked. 'You have to set up encampments like during World War Two with the Japanese and Germans.'" After an hour-long discussion "rich with arguments on why visual identification of 'the threat in our midst' would alleviate the public's fears," Klein revealed his proposition was a hoax, intended to make public the xenophobia always just below the surface in post 9/11 America. He expressed shock and disbelief that anyone agreed with his mock proposal: "For me to suggest to tattoo marks on people's bodies, have them wear armbands, put a crescent moon or their driver's license on their passport or birth certificate is disgusting. It's beyond disgusting. Because basically what you just did was show me how the German people allowed what happened to the Jews to happen. . . . We need to separate them, we need to tattoo their arms, we need to make them wear the yellow Star of David, we need to put them in concentration camps, we basically just need to kill them all because they are dangerous."[63] Klein confessed himself surprised by the degree of acceptance of his tattoo plan: "There were plenty of callers angry with me, but there were plenty who agreed."[64]

As Klein's hoax shows, fabricating an enemy is a social process with profound consequences. When the enemy is not immediately apparent, we must provide one in order to generate a rationale and an impetus for war—and, as Said points out, in order to justify the money and resources diverted to the military and away from other national needs. As a social process, making an enemy begins with governments and is crystalized in expertly managed PR campaigns, furthered by a news media no longer able to perform its necessary work of objective investigation, and absorbed and continued by a public deprived of the full picture, too harried by propaganda-fed anxieties and restrictive metaphoric frames to do its own key, citizenly job of critical thought.

Notes

1. Friedrich Nietzsche. *On the Genealogy of Morals*. 1887. Oxford University Press, Revised edition, 1998: 186.

2. Survey cited in Sheldon Rampton and John Stauber. "How to Sell a War." *In These Times*. April 8, 2003. See www.inthesetimes.com/comments.php?id=299_0_1_0_M (June 26, 2007).

3. Sheldon Rampton and John Stauber. "How to Sell a War."

4. Noam Chomsky. "Propaganda, American-Style." Z. September 17, 2001. See www.zpub.com/un/chomsky.html (June 26, 2007).

5. Nancy Snow. *Information War: American Propaganda, Free Speech and Opinion Control since 9-11*. New York: Seven Stories Press, 2003: 23.

6. Nancy Snow. *Information War*.

7. James Sandrolini. "Propaganda: The Art of War." *Chicago Media Watch*. Fall 2002. See www.chicagomediawatch.org/02_3_artofwar.shtml (June 26, 2007).

8. James Sandrolini. "Propaganda: The Art of War."

9. Gustave M. Gilbert. *Nuremberg Diary*. New York: Farrar, Straus and Co., 1947.

10. Sheldon Rampton and John Stauber. "How to Sell a War." *In These Times*. April 8, 2003. See www.inthesetimes.com/comments.php?id=299_0_1_0_M (June 26, 2007).

11. Sheldon Rampton and John Stauber. "How to Sell a War."

12. Sheldon Rampton and John Stauber. "How to Sell a War."

13. Sheldon Rampton and John Stauber. "How to Sell a War."

14. Jacques Ellul. *Propaganda: The Formation of Men's Attitudes*. New York: Vintage Books, 1973: 64.

15. Sheldon Rampton and John Stauber. "How to Sell a War."

16. Normon Solomon. "War Needs Good Public Relations." *FAIR*. October 25, 2001. See www.fair.org/media-beat/011025.html (June 26, 2007).

17. Trish Schuh. "Racism and Religious Desecration as U.S. Policy: Islamophobia, a Retrospective." *Double Standards*. 6 May 2006. See www.doublestandards.org/schuh1.html (June 26, 2007).

18. Tom Engelhardt. "Collateral Damage: The "Incident" at Haditha." TomDispatch .com June 7, 2006. See www.tomdispatch.com/post/88850/the_real_meaning_of_ haditha (August 1, 2007).

19. Thomas E. Ricks and Ann Scott Tyson. "Troops at Odds with Ethics Standards." *The Washington Post*. May 5, 2007. Posted on *Truthout*. See www.truthout.org/ docs_2006/050507Z .shtml (June 26, 2007).

20. Thomas E. Ricks. "Probe Into Iraq Deaths Finds False Reports." *The Washington Post*. June 1, 2006.

21. Tom Engelhardt. "Collateral Damage: The "Incident" at Haditha."

22. Ben Shapiro. "Civilian Casualties OK By Me." *TownHall*. July 25, 2002. See www.townhall.com/columnists/BenShapiro/2002/07/25/enemy_civilian_casualties_ ok_by_me (June 26, 2007).

23. Ben Shapiro. "Civilian Casualties OK By Me."

24. Ben Shapiro. "Civilian Casualties OK By Me."

25. *Baldilocks*. "Spain's the Target." March 11, 2004. See baldilocks.typepad.com/ baldilocks/2004/03/spains_the_targ.html (June 26, 2007).

26. Jim McDermott. "Rhetoric of the War Crusade." Speech to the U.S. House of Representatives. May 11, 2004. See www.house.gov/mcdermott/sp040511a.shtml (June 26, 2007).

27. Jim McDermott. "Rhetoric of the War Crusade."

28. Ahdaf Soueif. "A profound racism infects the U.S. and British establishments." *The Guardian* (UK). May 5, 2004. Posted on www.arabworldbooks.com/arab/ ahdaf3.htm (June 26, 2007).

29. Ahdaf Soueif. "A profound racism infects the U.S. and British establishments."

30. Norman Solomon. "Media Spin Revolves around the Word Terrorist." Z. October 4, 2001. See www.zmag.org/solorerr.htm (June 26, 2007).

31. Norman Solomon. "Media Spin Revolves around the Word Terrorist."

32. Norman Solomon. "Media Spin Revolves around the Word Terrorist."

33. Blair Shewchuk. " Terrorists and Freedom Fighters."CBC News Online. October 18, 2001. See www.cbc.ca/news/indepth/words/terrorists.html (June 26, 2007).

34. Edward Said. Orientalism. New York: Vintage Books, 1979: 6.

35. Edward Said. On Orientalism. 1998. [Videorecording]. Media Education Foundation.

36. Gene Knudsen Hoffman. "Taking it from the personal to the global via Compassionate Listening." Peace Heroes. January 2002. See www.peaceheroes.com/Peace Heroes/jeanknudsenhoffman.htm (June 26, 2007).

37. Lori Peek. "Constructing the Enemy during Times of Crisis: America after 9/11." Divide: Journal of Writing and Ideas. 1(2), 2004: 26–30.

38. John Dower. War without Mercy. New York: Pantheon Books, 1986: 19.

39. Cited in Edward Said. Orientalism.

40. Edward Said. Orientalism.

41. Cindy Sheehan. "A New World Is Possible." Truthout. January 26, 2006. See www.truthout.org/cgi-bin/artman/exec/view.cgi/48/17252 (July 17, 2007).

42. Lori Peek. "Constructing the Enemy during Times of Crisis."

43. Ann E. Burnette and Wayne L. Kraemer. "Putting a Face on Evil: The Rhetorical Creation of an Enemy in the U.S. War on Terrorism." Presentation to the National Communication Association Convention 2003.

44. Jerome D. Frank and Andrei Y. Melville. "The Image of the Enemy and the Process of Change." In Anatolii Andreevich Gromyko and Martin E. Hellman (Eds). Breakthrough: Emerging New Thinking, Beyond War Foundation, online edition, 1988.

45. David M. Kennedy. "Culture Wars." Enemy Images in American History. Edited by Regnhild Fiebig-von-Hase and Ursula Lehmkuhl. New York: Berghahn, 1997: 355.

46. Jerome D. Frank and Andrei Y. Melville. "The Image of the Enemy and the Process of Change."

47. Debra Merskin. "Post-9/11 Discourse." Bring 'em On: Media and Politics in the Iraq War. Lee Artz and Yahya R. Kamalipour (eds). Lanham, MD: Rowman and Littlefield, 2005.

48. Rayan El-Amine. "The Making of the Arab Menace." Left Turn Magazine. May 1, 2005. See www.leftturn.org/?q=node/345 (June 26, 2007).

49. Peter Ford. "Europe cringes at Bush 'crusade' against terrorists." The Christian Science Monitor. September 19, 2001. See www.csmonitor.com/2001/0919/p12s2-woeu.html (June 26, 2007).

50. Peter Ford. "Europe cringes at Bush 'crusade' against terrorists."

51. Bruce Lawrence. Review of The New Crusades: Constructing the Muslim Enemy. Emran Qureshi and Michael A. Sells (Eds). New York: Columbia University Press, 2003. Posted on Columbia University Press website. See www.columbia.edu/cu/cup/catalog/data/023112/0231126662.HTM (June 26, 2007).

52. Emran Qureshi and Michael A. Sells (Eds). The New Crusades: Constructing the Muslim Enemy. New York: Columbia University Press, 2003: 3.

53. Haroon Siddiqui. "Four telltale Themes: Anti-Muslim bigotry 'spreading like wildfire'." *Scholar Of The House*. November 24, 2002. See www.scholarofthehouse.org /fourtorstar1.html (June 26, 2007).

54. Edward Said. "The Clash of Ignorance." *The Nation*. October 4, 2001. See www .thenation.com/doc/20011022/said>. (June 26, 2007).

55. Haroon Siddiqui. "Four telltale Themes: Anti-Muslim bigotry 'spreading like wildfire'."

56. Emran Qureshi and Michael A. Sells (Eds). *The New Crusades*.

57. Christopher Allen. "Islamophobia in the Media since 911." *Forum against Islamophobia and Racism UK (FAIRUK)*. September 29, 2001. See www.fairuk.org/docs /Islamophobia-in-the-Media-since-911-ChristopherAllen.pdf (June 26, 2007).

58. Christopher Allen. "Islamophobia in the Media since 911."

59. Debra Merskin. "Post-9/11 Discourse."

60. Debra Merskin. "Post-9/11 Discourse."

61. Edward Said. *Covering Islam: How the Media and the Experts Determine How We See the Rest of the World*. Revised Edition, New York: Vintage Books, 1997: xxii.

62. Bernd Debusmann. "Radio Hoax Reveals U.S. Anti-Muslim Sentiment in U.S., fear and distrust of Muslims runs deep." Reuters. December 1, 2006.

63. Bernd Debusmann. "Radio Hoax."

64. Bernd Debusmann. "Radio Hoax."

CHAPTER THREE

Rallying Racism:
Dehumanization and Genocide

In the scale of dehumanization, we drop from the midpoint of the sub-
human barbarian to the nonhuman, from the savage to the animal. . . .
The lower down in the animal phyla the images descend, the greater
sanction is given to the soldier to become an exterminator of pests.

—Sam Keen[1]

Dehumanization as a Process

The object of warfare is the death or destruction of the enemy. In total war,
that destruction must be total. But who is this enemy who must be obliter-
ated? Almost all military texts, observes Sam Keen in *Faces of the Enemy*,
speak of the enemy in strangely oblique terms. We are obsessed with the idea
of the enemy and yet we avoid deep or sustained thought on the subject,
gleaning our ideas from headlines, sound bites, and other forms of truncated
information. We are reluctant to think too deeply about the enemy because
to do so might weaken our simplicity and moral clarity, replacing it with complexity and nuance. To resist this, in times of war we go in the opposite direction, creating images of the enemy that simplify and reduce. We are per-
suaded that we're on the right side; metaphors that represent our side as
righteous and the enemy as demonic reinforce this conviction. The most potent images are those that not only portray enemies as straightforwardly vil-
lainous, but also go further to deny their basic humanity. These images are
part of verbal and visual metaphoric systems linking the enemy to objects or

animals, dirt or germs, things that require domination, cleansing or elimination. This dehumanization allows for acts of violence that would usually be forbidden to be celebrated. It also allows us, in the face of these acts, to protect our image of ourselves, since by killing the constructed enemy we are being intrinsically virtuous. When our enemy is inhuman, especially when metaphorically figured as toxic, spreading, insidious, and contaminating, it becomes a civic, even a moral duty to inhibit its pernicious spread. Eradication of the enemy within this framework becomes a paradoxically humane task, taking on the very aspects of humanity we have removed from our dehumanized enemy.

Metaphors creating and reinforcing the enemy's lack of humanity permit us to confirm our own humanity, allowing acts of war to be imaginatively transposed. As we transform the human enemy into the sub-human, our humanly motivated wars, driven by tangled complexes of motivation, are themselves transformed. They become something simpler, clearer, and more monolithic. They also re-cast us, whether we see ourselves as aggressors or respondents, as both heroic and necessary. The less human the enemy, the more insidious and pervasive it appears, the louder the call to extermination. Metaphors of extermination allow us to perform what, in other circumstances, we would see as grossly inhuman acts, all in the name of a threatened and beleaguered humanity. In doing so, we can reassure ourselves that we are serving not just ourselves but the world: cleansing it; making it safe; ridding it of the noxious, the poisonous, the verminous, or the infectious. In the process, we preserve our identities as doers of good; we are performing necessary acts of eradication, protection, even hygiene. Only by creating a consistent textual body of such dehumanizing metaphors can we surmount individual and community inhibitions against killing, inhibitions that are long-standing and deep-seated. It is not easy to kill another human being, so our propaganda ensures that we don't see our enemies as human, telling ourselves instead persistent stories about their animal, diseased, or indistinguishably conglomerate nature.

Keen observes that the categories by which we dehumanize the enemy have a remarkable coherence. After studying wartime propaganda from many periods and nations, he observed that the posters and cartoons, whatever their origins, were in key ways so similar that "it's as if [the propagandists] all went to the same art school."[2] Keen categorizes these images into "archetypes" characterized by dominant themes depicting different aspects of their otherness and alienness. These archetypes act as key mechanisms in progressively reducing the figured and fabricated enemy.

For Keen, most human societies are organized around principles of profound distrust and paranoia and solidified by the tribal mind's "basic antagonism between insiders and strangers."[3] Race is crucial to this process. The visible distinctions of racial difference offer a central locus around which this antagonism gathers. Our hostility to strangers is most reserved for those who look least like us. We can, with our flexible and resilient metaphoric imaginations, make an enemy of anyone once we perceive ourselves under threat; our varied campaigns against those of different sexual orientations, economic classes, even ages demonstrate this. However, race and its potent visibilities of difference is fundamental to our most virulent processes of enemy construction. Identifying a sub-human enemy based on racial characteristics offers us seductive ways of dealing with the threat. If they are beasts, for example, we have greater opportunities for control: we can "round them up," "herd them," or "ship them out," maintaining a pure space reserved for the humans who look like us. Systematic racism is central to the belief that we can isolate or corral these animals, decreasing our risk of future disaster. The race-related metaphors of purity and pollution work to limit miscegenation within a society, to keep bloodlines pure and prevent dilution, while anxieties around issues of national borders work to limit incursion from without. The "hostile imagination," its hostility fed by paranoid anxieties about an encroaching other, creates a repertoire of images of the enemy.[4] These images reflect and consolidate our sense of the enemy's fundamental difference from us. Keen broadly identifies several common categories by which this difference is conferred: the enemy is portrayed as the eternally alien stranger, as aggressor, faceless, barbarian, greedy, criminal, torturer, rapist, death, enemy of God, and animal or germ. This final metaphor is distinctive in that, unlike the other categories, it explicitly treats the enemy as sub-human. The stranger, barbarian, rapist, and so on, are profoundly troubling images, tapping into some of our most primal fears, but they still grant a human status to the enemy; the rapist is still a human agent, and as such can be dealt with within the sphere of human agency, such as a criminal trial. Even rapists, we acknowledge, possess some basic human rights, and criminal guilt does not entirely abrogate those rights. For those seen as outside the realm of humanity, however, and therefore outside the scope of ideas like law and justice, these rights are irrelevant: "the concepts of deserving basic needs and fair treatment," says Susan Opotow, simply "do not apply."[5]

The categories identified by Keen powerfully and primally stigmatize the enemy. The expressions of the hostile imagination are often ingenious and compelling, which is part of their power and their effectiveness. Beyond simple stigma, however, lies dehumanization. Like other forms of propaganda, dehumanization repeatedly portrays the enemy as less than us; it goes further, however, in the extent to which it strips away humanity through the consistency of its metaphoric links with the bestial, the verminous, and the microscopic. Tropes of animal, insect, germ and disease are so important to our construction of the enemy in the war on terror, so linked to larger discourses of racism, that they require concentrated attention.

Dehumanization creates an enemy that not only allows for but demands cruel treatment; such cruelty is seen as requisite to the larger task of extermination. Dehumanization allows us to re-cast cruelty and violence as something else; after all, if an enemy is so far down the evolutionary ladder that it cannot feel pain, then how can inflicting pain be cruel? One of the most striking historical examples of this comes from WWII: the Japanese military performed medical experiments on human prisoners who they called "*maruta*"—literally, "logs of wood."[6] Once made not only inhuman but inanimate, the bodies of feeling beings could be brutalized without compunction or regret.

Dehumanization also allows us to blame the victims by eliminating their basic human attributes and thus their claims to protection. Hanan Ashrawi argues that "Blaming the victim has been the common resort of the guilty in rationalizing and distorting the horror of the crime."[7] Within this metaphoric framework, the fault lies in the nature of the sub-human enemy, and those faults are perceived as so hideous and dangerous that obliterating them is both necessary and noble: like the cancerous cell, if simply left alone, the encroaching enemy will spread and replicate. Obliteration is therefore the only safe, rational, even the only moral response.

A History of Dehumanizing Practices

One of the most important reasons for developing a critique of how metaphors dehumanize the enemy is the gravity of dehumanization's consequences. One of its most devastating roles is in mass killings and genocide. Gregory H. Stanton has influentially argued that dehumanization is a necessary precursor to genocide, a prerequisite for genocide's comprehensive violence. The first three stages leading to genocide, Stanton argues, are classification, symbolization, and dehumanization. Our metaphors of the enemy accomplish in one gesture all three of these steps, powerfully conflating them into a single process that simultaneously identifies, marks, symbolizes and profoundly devalues the Other.

For Stanton, genocide is not a product but a process. It may appear sudden but is actually linked to a series of separate stages, each progressive and each integral to the "genocidal process." Classification, symbolization, and dehumanization are followed by organization, polarization, identification, extermination, and finally denial of the genocidal act. Stanton argues that every genocide is followed by denial. The mass graves are dug up and hidden. The historical records are burned, or closed to historians. Even during the genocide, those committing the crimes dismiss reports as propaganda. Afterwards such deniers are called "revisionists." Others deny through more subtle means: by characterizing the reports as "unconfirmed" or "alleged" because they do not come from officially approved sources; by minimizing the number killed; by quarreling about whether the killing fits the legal definition of genocide ("definitionalism"); by claiming that the deaths of the perpetrating group exceeded that of the victim group, or that the deaths were the result of civil war, not genocide.[8]

Before there can be an act of genocide to deny, however, there must be a number of conditions in place to allow genocidal violence to occur. Stanton argues that classification, the first condition or stage, is fundamental and deeply encoded in human language. All languages require classification, a "division of the natural and social world into categories."[9] All cultures have categories to distinguish between "us" and "them," between members of our group and others. While all language may make this distinction, it is when we add symbolization to "name and signify" our classifications that what Keen calls the "paranoid culture" begins to assert itself, making certain physical characteristics (such as skin color or facial features) symbols for racial or ethnic classifications.[10] In the later stage of the genocidal process, these markers may become abstract and externalized, as with the yellow star forced on the Jews of Nazi Germany or the blue-checked scarf used by the Khmer Rouge in Cambodia to identify, marginalize, and deport people from the Eastern Zone.

Classification and symbolization are widespread human practices that are part of our national identity and cultural self-awareness. When joined by dehumanization, these qualities move a society significantly further down the grim road to genocide. Dehumanization relegates the classified group to a category of sub-humanity, making it easier to overcome an aversion to killing. Instead, killing becomes something to be celebrated; thus, in a notorious tape recording of an interview with members of the elite Canadian Airborne Unit in Somalia, a soldier is heard telling the interviewer that their "peacekeeping" mission "sucks, man. We ain't killed enough n____ yet."[11]

In the later stages of the genocidal process, polarization intensifies difference, as moderates are silenced or killed. Often, the first casualties of genocide are moderates within the killing groups, voices raised in objection over the escalating violence. Extremists target moderates so that only the extremes will be left in conflict, with no milder middle to slow the cycle of descent into genocide. Once moderate voices have been suppressed, individual deaths escalate into mass killings, in which the rhetoric of extermination is invoked. Genocide is always organized, says Stanton, usually by the state and through the deployment of the army or militias. This can set off retaliatory or revenge killings, creating a "downward whirlpool-like cycle of bilateral genocide."[12]

Dehumanization and Slavery

Where dehumanization does not lead to genocide, it often leads to enslavement. Here again, people are seen as animals: just as Aristotle called the ox the "poor man's slave," the inversion of that equation links the dehumanized Other to the laboring animal. In fact, it's often theorized that the domestication of animals that began during the Neolithic Revolution provided the model and inspiration for human slavery. Collars, chains, prods, whips, and branding irons were employed to domesticate and control animals just as similar tactics were used on slaves to ensure they remained docile, subservient and unable to escape. In ancient Mesopotamia, slaves were not only branded as if they were domestic animals, but were priced according to their equivalent in cows, horses, pigs, and chickens. This laid the groundwork for later European and American racial theories that called for the conquest and exploitation of the "lower races," who continued to be regarded as animals and treated accordingly.[13]

The first African slaves shipped to Lisbon in the mid-1400s were marketed and priced like livestock. Black Africans were portrayed as more akin to animals than humans because of their "beastlike sexuality and brutish nature."[14] During the 1600s and 1700s, the rising growth of the slave trade reinforced this image of Africans; they were rounded up and given work similar to that of laboring animals. Entirely commodified, slaves were chattel that could be "bought, sold, traded, leased, mortgaged, bequeathed, presented as a gift, pledged for a debt, included in a dowry, or seized in bankruptcy."[15]

By the 1800s, European scientists had developed theories promoting the superiority of the white race. In their hierarchical structure, their inferiors were, in descending order, non-Europeans, women, and Jews. Africans remained at the bottom of this ladder. Like the Japanese scientists who experimented on people they called "logs of wood," American scientists proclaimed that African slaves could endure without undue suffering levels of brutality no human could sustain. Some medical doctors argued that the bodies of black Africans possessed fewer pain receptors and therefore could be flogged without feeling it as a white body would.[16] Scientific and medical discourses were both regularly called upon to justify brutality to African and African-American slaves. In one widely distributed 1905 broadsheet, a caption declares confidently "Scientists Say Negro Still in Ape Stage," followed by the assertion "Races Positively Not Equal"[17] (see figure 3.1). In a quasi-scientific illustration clearly designed to look like it was taken from a medical textbook, hand-drawn figures of "The Ape" and "The Negro" are juxtaposed in identical postures and are nearly indistinguishable. To reinforce the clear visual message that "the Negro" is really just an ape masquerading as a man, elaborate anatomical labelling delineates, limb by limb, the identical features of the two figures; both have "big hands," "weak lower limbs," a "small brain," an "animal smell," the "ape groove" in the skull, and a "black ape color." As late as the 1970s, this pamphlet was still being distributed as part of white supremacist literature, confirming the resilience and endurance of the animal metaphor as a key mechanism in supporting systematic oppression.

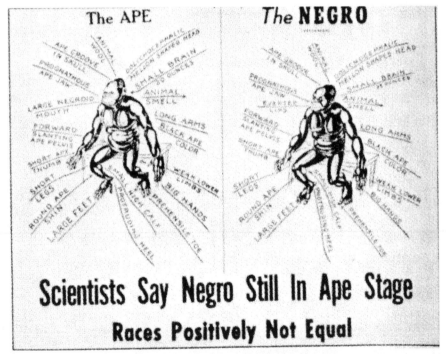

Figure 3.1. *"Scientists Say Negro Still in Ape Stage."* **Klu Klux Klan, 1905.**

Dehumanization and Native Peoples

The European explorers and colonists who came to America regarded the native people they encountered there as "dark, sinful, inhuman, and dangerously close to animals."[18] Members of Christopher Columbus' voyage were contemptuous of those they encountered, calling them "beasts" because they slept on mats instead of beds. Just as herds of wild buffalo came to be reck-lessly decimated so, too, were native people; as non-human, neither group was valued, protected, nor, in their destruction, mourned. Settlers, descen-dants of the first wave of Europeans, largely saw them as a hindrance to fur-thering colonization and spent the next three hundred years fighting them.

As in the progressive stages of annihilation outlined by Stanton, dehu-manization preceded destruction. Indians were vilified in order to justify their extinction. As David Stannard writes in *American Holocaust: The Con-quest of the New World*, Indians were considered "nothing more than a half-filled outline of humanity whose extermination was a logical and necessary final solution to the problem." European settlers described "Indians as 'ugly, filthy, and inhuman beasts,' [and] newspapers commonly characterized them as swine, snakes, pigs and baboons."[19]

From formal public discourse to informal mythical folklore, these charac-terizations persisted. The legendary Davy Crockett, iconically portrayed in popular culture as the man in the coonskin cap, was in the nineteenth cen-tury best known as a noted frontiersman, politician, and martyr. Crockett was one of the most famous people in America when he was killed at the Alamo in 1836. His fame was exploited in the *Davy Crockett Almanacs*, a series of inexpensive books published after his death but filled with advice, anecdotes and aphorisms attributed to Crockett. Valued as examples of early American folklore, they have also been called "a pornography of racism and vio-lence."[20] In the *Crockett Almanacs*, Indians are called "red niggers," "a pesky set of heathens," "red skin varmints," "pesky cowards," and "injun savages." The comic anecdote called "Crockett Boiling a Dead Indian For His Sick Bear" demonstrates the use of the "injun" as a vehicle for humor, excluding any possible consideration for the Indian as human. It contains comments that were, at the time, considered quite acceptable: "So I went out an shot an injun, an sauced him up with tender varmits, sitch as toads, lizards, a croc-odile's tail, and other spurious vegetables, that was calculated to set well on a delicate stumack and I biled 'em together, with directions to give the pa-tient half a peck every two hours."[21] The narrator concludes complacently that "the bare got well directly."[22]

Animal metaphors placed Indians beyond the reach of moral obligation or legal protection. In 1823, U.S. Supreme Court Chief Justice John Marshall wrote that "The tribes of Indians inhabiting this country were fierce savages, whose occupation was war, and whose subsistence was drawn chiefly from the forest."[23] In such circumstances, he said, the law need not be applicable; no prosecution was needed for killings which could not, since the victim was in-human, be considered murder. According to Richard Drinnon, "In times of trouble, natives were always wild animals that had to be rooted out of their dens, swamps, jungles."[24] Until the conquest of the natives was complete, the message was always the same and almost always voiced through metaphors of natural animality. The most fitting end for "the animals vulgarly called Indians," as Hugh Brackenridge, an eighteenth century jurist and novelist wrote, was extermination.[25] Within this animal metaphor, the "injuns'" inability to be civilized confirmed the idea of their bestiality, which could thus be seen as fundamental, pernicious, and stubbornly resistant to improvement. In this way, they were blamed for their extermination: by being beyond the reach of the civilizing impulse, they brought their end upon themselves.

Because of their resistance to absorption, acculturation, and conformity to European models of civilization, natives were constructed as wild, a threat to culture, and an obstacle to western progress. Their removal therefore was not only necessary, it was also inevitable, natural and morally desirable. The efficacy of the American Indian genocide garnered some international notice; according to his biographer John Toland, Adolf Hitler was impressed with its scope. Toland writes that the Nazi leader "Often praised to his inner circle the efficiency of America's extermination—by starvation and uneven combat—of red savages who could not be tamed by captivity."[26]

Propaganda and Japanese Foes in WWII

During World War II, animal and insect epithets were used by the military, media, and the American public to describe the Japanese. They were labelled "reptiles," "insects," "rats," "cockroaches," "vermin," and "baboons," setting the stage for the war that followed and justifying any tactics necessary for victory by the western allies. Historian John Dower describes in *War without Mercy: Race and Power in the Pacific War*, the "attachment of stupid, bestial, even pestilential subhuman caricatures on the enemy, and the manner in which this blocked seeing the foe as rational or even human facilitated mass killing. It is, at least for most people, easier to kill animals than fellow humans."[27] Dower notes that bestial metaphors do not emerge solely in wartime: they are widely present already in the culture but intensify in times of conquest or contest. The images from which these metaphors are drawn have been in place since moments of first encounter and are not the exception but the rule, "part of a rich symbolic world" developed and relied upon by white Europeans and Americans "over the ensuing centuries to put others in their place."[28] Dower notes that as early as the sixteenth century, traveling Spaniards were characterizing the Japanese as "wild beasts and animals." One Spaniard wrote to his European audience that "In wisdom, skill, virtue and humanity, these people are as inferior to the Spaniards as children are to adults . . . there is as great a difference between them as between savagery and forbearance, between violence and moderation . . . [as] between monkeys and men."[29]

This image of the Japanese as monkey was remarkably persistent, showing up repeatedly in political cartoons, along with the other dominant images of rats and bats; all three animals prominently featured pinched faces, squinty eyes, and protruding teeth. An American poster with the banner "Jap Trap" shows a rat wearing round spectacles and a Japanese soldier's cap caught in a mousetrap, its slanted eyes shut in pain, its giant buck teeth clamped to the wood of the trap. A U.S. Navy poster depicts Alaska as "Death-Trap for the Japs": a mousetrap with springs labelled "Army," "Navy" and "Civilian" is shown ready to snap shut on a buck-toothed, bewhiskered rat wearing a cap marked with the insignia of Japan. Another poster warning "Don't Talk. Rats Have Big Ears" shows a rabid-looking rat standing astride Japan, wearing a soldier's cap and spectacles. The rat is clenching pointed teeth and wiping blood from a huge, samurai-style sword, while its grotesquely outsized ears, larger than the country the rat straddles, are pricked to catch careless whispers. The cover of the popular *Colliers* magazine from December 12, 1942, shows another familiar image, the Japanese enemy as an epauletted vampire bat aloft over Pearl Harbor, with devilish-looking slitted eyes, metallic-looking hooks at each wing tip, and giant fangs (see figure 3.2).[30] This representation is particularly interesting in that the bat clutches both a very traditional-looking, decorative sword and a very modern-looking bomb in its prehensile, elongated, monkey-like fingers. A primitive with tools, an animal with access to modern weaponry is clearly seen as a particularly horrific image.

Anthony V. Navarro notes how frequently these images recur: the U.S. "fixated," he notes, "on the dehumanized depiction of the Japanese, presenting them as monkeys and gorillas."[31] European foes, in contrast, were not animalized in the same way, largely because most Americans were of European descent, so "to dehumanize the Europeans would be to dehumanize themselves."[32] This difference is reflected in a comment made by a Marine to war correspondent John Hersey in 1942: "I wish we were fighting against Germans. They are human beings, like us—But the Japanese are like animals."[33] With the Japanese enemy, the majority of Americans felt no such genetic or ethnic ties, so an ethnic hatred for the alien Other could easily be incited as the Japanese government did to its American enemy: "Both countries realized the importance of eliciting an ethnic hatred for the enemy as well as creating a subhuman image of them. It is much easier to kill a big hairy white mongrel or vine-swinging, gun-wielding monkey than it is to kill another human being."[34]

Figure 3.2. Cover of *Colliers Magazine*, December 12, 1942.

These images were regularly reinforced in popular culture. John Wayne's 1944 film *The Fighting Seabees* offers just one example: in the film's climatic final combat, American soldiers come upon a valley in which Japanese soldiers are hiding. The Americans flood the valley with oil and then set it alight. As they run from the flames, the Japanese are machine-gunned down, even though they offer no resistance. The film reinforces the comment made by one of Wayne's fellow soldiers: "we're not fighting men now, we're fighting animals."[35] As Celia Roy observes, when Wayne declares in the movie that he can't "wait to 'begin killing the bug-eyed monkeys of Tojo,' he is not just hurling a racist epithet, he is voicing the belief system of an entire nation."[36]

These images did their work effectively, removing a sense of Japanese humanity so that it became possible to coldly calculate which Japanese cities would be most advantageous to bomb: should it be the city with the most intellectuals (Kyoto) or the city surrounded by hills which would make the bomb have the greatest effect (Hiroshima)? An estimated 214,000 Japanese civilians were killed immediately or died within months after the U.S. dropped atomic bombs on Nagasaki and Hiroshima. The loss of lives was justified as necessary to bring a swift end to the war, saving lives on both sides. "Among the many things that warfare does," writes Stannard, "is temporarily define the entire enemy population as superfluous, as expendable—a redefinition that must take place before most non-psychopaths can massacre innocent people and remain shielded from self-condemnation."[37]

The extent of this redefinition in the Pacific war is made clear in comments by American journalist Ernie Pyle; in one of his first reports from the Pacific, Pyle wrote that "In Europe we felt that our enemies, horrible and deadly as they were, were still people. But out here I soon gathered that the Japanese were looked upon as something subhuman and repulsive; the way some people feel about cockroaches or mice."[38] Images of insects, pests, and vermin surface repeatedly in public discourse about war and the enemy. Among "subhuman" and "repulsive" beings, vermin clearly rank high (or low) in the collective conscious. It is not surprising, then, that the rat is a popular animal metaphor for characterizing enemies. A poster frequently found in American West Coast restaurants during World War II proclaimed, "This restaurant poisons rats and Japs."[39] *The Nation* ran a story in 1945 describing a Japanese soldier's death on Iwo Jima as "a rat's death, defiant in a corner until all else fails."[40]

Dehumanization and Vietnam

The Nation's description of the Japanese soldier's death as "a rat's death" finds a disturbing echo decades later in Lt. William Calley's language as he defended the massacre by American soldiers of as many as five hundred un-armed Vietnamese civilians, including old men, women, children, and in-fants in My Lai and neighboring villages. In the initial psychiatric report fol-lowing the massacre, Calley's army psychiatrist noted that he did not believe he was killing fellow humans, but "rather that they were animals with whom one could not think or reason."[41] As Norman Nakamura wrote in "The Na-ture of GI Racism during the Vietnam War," for many soldiers in Vietnam "there are no Vietnamese people. To them the land is not populated by people but by "Gooks," considered inferior, unhuman animals by the racist-educated G.I."[42] One Vietnam War veteran observed that in basic training, "The only thing they told us about the Viet Cong was they were gooks. They were to be killed. Nobody sits around and gives you their historical and cul-tural background. They're the enemy. Kill, kill, kill. That's what we got in practice. Kill, kill, kill."[43] Joe Allen argues that My Lai, although the most publicized example of this mentality, was not remotely its sole example. My Lai "was not an aberration," writes Allen; "smaller, unreported My Lais hap-pened throughout the war."[44] This claim is reinforced in the testimony of James Duffy, testifying at the "Winter Soldier" investigation in 1971. Duffy reports "opening fire on what he thought was a group of peasants," a group that turned out to be a work party hired by the U.S. government: "I just saw gooks and I wanted to kill them . . . [there was] the unwritten code that you can do anything you want to as long as you don't get caught. That's, I guess that's what happened with the My Lai incident. Those guys just were fol-lowing the same pattern that we've been doing there for ten years, but they had the misfortune of getting caught at it."[45]

In Duffy's words we can see the brutal consequences of a sustained pattern of dehumanizing imagery; war's metaphors perform dangerous acts of transla-tion and mutation, discursive and imaginative acts that precede the physical act of massacre. Keen argues that animal images of the enemy survive from conflict to conflict, noting that in WWII, as Glenn Gray recounts, veteran soldiers spoke of "flushing" a Japanese soldier from his hiding place as if they were hunters; in telling the story of such a hunt, one veteran "emphasized the similarity of the enemy soldier to an animal." None of the American soldiers, who found the enemy soldier's attempt to escape "uproariously funny," ap-parently "ever considered that he may have had human feelings of fear and the wish to be spared."[46] In Vietnam, the dominant metaphor of the hunt continued. One soldier recalled that

We had this one dude who would go out shooting people, then yell "Snake." Like, don't worry, I just killed a snake next to the trail. We come across this old papa-san dying in the dirt in a hooch. Mama-san is there leaning over him. The dude walks up, pulls out that .45, and blows the fucker's brains out. Says to me, "I was just helping the fucker out." Then he turns around and shoots this mother and her baby. Steps outside the hooch and says, "Snake."[47]

Once a population is successfully translated into the non-human through the operations of metaphor, then anyone, including children, necessarily become merely prey, always "fair game." Keen suggests that successfully dehumanizing an enemy is effective because it allows soldiers to kill without guilt, but is also double-edged. It

> allows the warrior-become-exterminator little sense of dignity or pride in his skill in battle. There is little emotional purgation gained from the slaughter of such an enemy—no heroic sparring with a worthy opponent, no cosmic drama of a battle against enemies of God, no wrestling with barbarian giants. Only an escalating brutality and insensitivity to suffering and death.[48]

However, the glee exhibited by many soldiers in recounting their kills, and the collection of grisly mementos of these kills suggests that we might reconsider this claim in light of a different kind of "dignity and pride." The tropes of the epic warrior or the knightly warrior may be made irrelevant by the use of animal metaphors, but they are replaced by the equally potent trope of the soldier-as-hunter. The hunter-soldier experiences risk equal to that of the knightly warrior riding against a human foe, so the level of perceived glory can be just as high; in fact, because the enemy is viewed as treacherous, pestilential, and insidious, the hunter-soldier might be seen as at even greater risk: he is always vulnerable to the low attacks of the snake in the grass. In the name of extermination he performs a task that is absolutely necessary, and his collection of symbolic trophies attests to this necessity and to his success at the task. The narrative of the great hunt and the mighty hunter simply replaces one variety of paradigmatic pride with another, equally potent kind.

Dehumanization and the Nazi Representation of Jews

When the persecution of the Jews began in Nazi Germany in the 1930s, Jews were consistently characterized in terms of disease or parasites; Hitler talked repeatedly of the "Jewish bacilli." This metaphoric language was essential to the Nazi project of extermination.[49] As Richard Grunberger points out, "the incessant official demonization of the Jew gradually modified the consciousness even of naturally humane people" so that the populace became indifferent to Jewish suffering, "not because it occurred in wartime and under conditions of secrecy, but because Jews were astronomically remote and not real people."[50] Siegfried Bork's research shows that Nazi publications consistently described Jews as infection, poison, parasites, tumours, bacilli, vermin, leeches, bacteria, maggots, and malignant ulcers.[51] Intensifying their deliberate linking of Jews with the micro-organic and the verminous, Nazis created propaganda films that interspersed scenes of Jewish immigration with shots of teeming rats.

The most famous of these films is *Der Ewige Jude* (The Eternal Jew), produced under the supervision of Joseph Geobbels. It depicts Jews as "corrupt, filthy, lazy, ugly, and perverse: they are an alien people which have taken over our world through their control of banking and commerce, yet which still live like animals."[52] The film's visuals explicitly link the Jews of Poland to vermin and insects: an early scene follows a crowd shot of Jews packed tightly in the streets of a Polish ghetto with swarms of flies on a wall. The voice-over narration says that "Jewish houses are dirty and neglected," but the visual correlation is much stronger and more immediate: it clearly suggests that Jews do not just attract flies but *are* flies.[53] The film's conflation of Jews with rats is even more overt and transparent. A shot of a world map marking the spreading global immigration of Jews "like an irresistible tide," as the narrator says, is followed by a shot of seething rats. "Whenever rats appear," continues the narration, "they bring ruin, by destroying mankind's goods and foodstuffs. They are cunning, cowardly, and cruel, and are found mostly in large packs. Among the animals, they represent the rudiment of an insidious and underground destruction—just like the Jews among human beings."[54]

Less well-known than *Der Ewige Jude* are a series of picture-books for children that carry the film's message to a young audience. Ernst Hiemer published storybooks such as *Don't Trust a Fox in a Green Meadow Or the Oath of a Jew*. Heimer's books, says Mary Mills, capitalized on children's interest in the natural world to schematize Germans as good animals and Jews as bad animals: Hiemer constructs stories centered on what are generally considered to be despicable traits in certain animals and insects and concludes each story by transferring the undesirable characteristics to the human world via the Jews. For example, Mills observes that Jews are likened to insect drones because they do not work but live from the labor of others:

> Like the cuckoo, Jews are depicted as stealing other people's homes. They are the foreigners who threaten to displace the Germans from Germany. As hyaenas strike disabled animals, Jews are portrayed as preying upon disadvantaged Germans/Christians. Other animals included in these comparisons are the chameleon (the great deceiver), the locust (the scourge of God), the bedbug (the

blood sucker), the sparrow (good-for-nothings), the poodle-mops-dachshund-pincher (an inferior race created by cross-breeding various types of races), the poisonous snake (the viper of humanity), and the tapeworm (the parasite of humanity).[55]

In German folklore Jews were compared to mongrel dogs, insects and parasites in statements such as "in the case of Jews and lice, only a radical cure helps."[56] By constantly describing Jews as disease-bearing vermin, germs, or pigs, the Nazis were able to convince the German public that it was necessary to destroy them.[57] This is explicit in a Danish cartoon poster, likely produced by the Danish Nazi Party, showing the head of a Jewish man atop the hunched body of a rat. The rat, drawn in painstaking detail down to the individual scales and bristles on its long tail, sits in the dark behind a wall, peering out avariciously into the light through a jagged hole. The message of threat and invasion could not be more clear: they're in there, crouched in the dark behind our walls, ready to leap out and get us. The oversized banner reads "ROTTEN," which means rat, and in smaller letters "udryd den," urging viewers to wipe out or exterminate it (see figure 3.3).[58]

In his examination of the role of metaphor in racial prejudice, Musolff argues that the Nazis' anti-Semitic metaphor system is a powerful demonstration of how stigmatization and dehumanization lead to genocide, a warning about "the horrific cost of misunderstanding metaphor as mere rhetoric." He argues that

the source imagery of Hitler's world-view consisted in the conceptualization of the German nation as a *human body* that had to be *shielded from disease* (or, in case of an outbreak, *cured*). Jewish people, who were conceptually condensed into the super-category of "the Jew" and viewed as an *illness-spreading parasite*, represented the danger of *disease*. Deliverance from this threat to the nation's *life* would come from Hitler and his party as the only competent healers who were willing to fight the *illness*.[59]

The persistent military metaphor of cleansing brings together this trope of the nation as a body that must be purified of the infection with the trope of the enemy as a parasite that must be eliminated in the name of safety, purity, and hygiene. Since cleanliness is one of the binary opposites to both metaphors of infestation and metaphors of infection, the two notions of pestilence as germ/disease and as rodent/plague are inextricably conflated. In the paranoid discourse of propaganda, bodily infection by disease, cultural invasion by the encroaching enemy, and national infestation by the corrupting enemy become one and the same thing, a single, resonant, three-sided trope that demands the totalizing cure of elimination, eradication, and hygienic cleansing.

Figure 3.3.   Danish Nazi Party Propaganda, W.W.II.

Dehumanization and Rwandan Genocide

The trope of cleansing and purification also supported the genocidal process as it unfolded in Rwanda. The massacre of 800,000 Rwandans in April 1994 provides evidence of international and institutionalized racism and the effectiveness of hate propaganda. The international community ignored ample, even frantic, warnings about the impending genocide, failing to intervene as nearly one million Rwandans were massacred in a month-long frenzy. The Rwandans who organized and executed the genocide, says Human Rights Watch, must bear full responsibility for what happened. However, it goes on to say, "genocide anywhere implicates everyone; to the extent that governments and people elsewhere failed to prevent and halt this killing campaign, they all share in the shame of the crime."[60]

Genocide is neither spontaneous nor random; however complex the historical and cultural conditions from which it emerges, it is always at root linked to perceptions of hostile difference. International response (or lack of it) to genocide is often deeply implicated in elaborate structures of racism. Because of Orientalism's lens, telling us there is something fundamentally alien, interchangeable and indistinguishable about certain races, we become almost complacent in the face of mass killings of black- or brown-skinned people; after all, within the imperial or colonial mentality, as Orwell's essay highlights, "there are so many of them!"[61] Racist metaphors of non-human mass, non-human volume, non-human indistinguishability underlie the comments made by American broadcaster Michael Savage on his nationally syndicated radio show, during which he told his audience that "intelligent people, wealthy people . . . are very depressed by the weakness that America is showing to these psychotics in the Muslim world. They say, 'Oh, there's a billion of them.'" Savage continued: "I said, 'So, kill 100 million of them, then there'd be 900 million of them."[62] Since Americans historically prize individuality and individualism, to emphasize the presumed collective nature of the enemy-Other, framing them repeatedly as interchangeable members of a dark multitude is intrinsically to devalue it. Being both dark and "billions," as the "psychotic" Muslims are in Savages's extended logic is enough to invite and justify the impulse to thin the herd. "So, kill a million of them" can only be a defensible statement within a racist metaphorical frame that sees population density as de facto evidence of inhumanity. The lack of international intervention in the Rwandan massacre, while not as actively murderous in tone as Savage's comments, like them arose from and was permitted by the operation of the metaphor of indistinguishable mass.

Over a period of three years the groundwork was laid by ruling party officials to turn Hutus against Tutsis for the purpose of political gain. In March

1993, a rabidly anti-Tutsi article in the Hutu extremist newspaper *Kangura* presented readers with examples of evil committed by the Tutsi. "We are not wrong in saying that a cockroach gives birth to another cockroach," the article says. "The Tutsis represent an evil that will reproduce itself for as long as Tutsis exist. Future generations of Tutsis will not be any better than their predecessors because a cockroach cannot give birth to a butterfly."[63] The word *"inyenzi"* or cockroach was explicitly applied to the Tutsi population; in the months before the outbreak of genocidal violence in April, hate propaganda and inaccurate news reports were broadcast over *Radio Television Libre des Milles Collines*, depicting Tutsis as snakes, animals, and most insistently, cockroaches. Government leaders urged the massacre to continue by using euphemisms for killing, telling citizens to "clear the bush," "get to work," or "clean around their houses." Listeners readily understood these as encouragements to slaughter their Tutsi neighbours.[64] The hate propaganda within the country fomented hostility towards Tutsis and the resulting murders led to retaliatory killings of Hutus, a genocidal spiral resulting in the death of nearly a million people, grim evidence for the effectiveness of race-based metaphor in fueling violence.

Dehumanization in the Persian Gulf War

The first Gulf War in 1991 was launched by Coalition forces to force Iraq to withdraw its troops after invading Kuwait in August 1990. Douglas Kellner claims that "The U.S. public have widely viewed Iraqis and Arabs as less than human since the Gulf War."[65] In the Gulf War, the U.S. forces' overwhelming technological superiority won a quick, decisive victory, resulting in civilian deaths now estimated at over 100,000. Following the war, some in the media quietly acknowledged they had been under pressure "to produce sanitized coverage which almost entirely ignored the war's human cost."[66] In the final forty-eight hours of the Persian Gulf War, defeated Iraq called for a cease-fire and announced its forces were retreating from Kuwait. Thousands of soldiers, foreign workers and civilians headed home on the highway towards Basra in Southern Iraq. This escape route became known as the "Highway of Death" when, on February 26, American pilots bombed both ends of the highway, then systematically strafed and firebombed the stranded columns for hours without resistance. American Pfc. Charles Sheehan-Miles said, "It was like going down an American highway—people were all mixed up in cars, in trucks. People got out of their cars and ran away. We shot them. . . . The Iraqis were getting massacred."[67] In a *Washington Post* interview, one pilot complained that the Air Force was unable to reload cluster bombs fast enough to kill all the retreating "targets."[68] Estimates suggest that more than

2,000 vehicles were destroyed and tens of thousands of people killed on the highway.[69] On some planes, as bombs were dropping, the PA system blasted Rossini's "William Tell Overture," famous to Americans as the *Lone Ranger* theme.

Racist metaphor again accomplished its dehumanizing task: the word "cockroach" appeared as a label for Iraqis while pilots in attack planes likened the campaign to "shooting fish in a barrel." Veterans of Desert Storm described the massacre on the road to Basra as "the turkey shoot." American soldiers described the attack in hunting terms such as "clubbing seals." Pilots flying over groups of Iraqi troops reported that the Iraqis "ran like ants" when the bombs were dropped, commenting "It's like someone turned on the kitchen light late at night, and the cockroaches started scurrying."[70] Reports indicated that many of those retreating from Kuwait City put white flags on their vehicles, which were visible to pilots. Consequently, there were claims that the slaughter of retreating Iraqis and others constituted a war crime, violating "the Geneva Conventions of 1949, Common Article III, which outlaws the killing of soldiers who are out of combat."[71]

Joyce Chediac reports that even within the military there was horror at the mass killing. She cites army intelligence officer Major Bob Nugent who said "Even in Vietnam I didn't see anything like this. It's pathetic." Nugent goes on to note that the "one-sided" carnage and "racist mass murder of Arab people" happened while the U.S. and its coalition partners had promised that they would not attack Iraqi forces retreating from Kuwait. "This is," he said, "surely one of the most heinous war crimes in contemporary history."[72] Media crews traveling with the Allied forces in Kuwait came upon the attack's aftermath by chance. In his book *Hidden Agendas*, veteran investigative journalist John Pilger describes the media coverage of the massacre.

> In a memorable report for BBC radio, Stephen Sackur described the carnage in such a way that he separated, for his listeners, ordinary Iraqis from Saddam Hussein. He converted the ducks, turkeys and fish to human beings. The incinerated figures, he said, were simply people trying to get home. Most newspapers, however, preferred a front-page photograph of a U.S. Army medic attending a wounded Iraqi soldier. Here was the supreme image of magnanimity and tenderness, a "lifeline" the Daily Mirror called it, and the exact opposite of what had happened.[73]

When large-scale ethnic or nationalist violence occurs, people rarely cite hate propaganda as one of its main causes. "Instead, they think of age-old hatreds between groups as the root cause of these conflicts. Or they blame the atrocities on the culture of the perpetrators, which is assumed to be inherently violent," says Jonathan Belman, who also notes that "While hate propaganda is a common element in conflicts, it is often not a symptom of hatred between groups. Rather, it is the cause of that hatred."[74]

Dehumanization, Atrocity and the Military Identity

In *Journalism in the Gulf*, Jim Naureckas writes, "The way wars are reported in the western media follows a depressingly predictable pattern: stage one, the crisis; stage two, the demonization of the enemy's leader; stage three, the demonization of the enemy as individuals; and stage four, atrocities."[75] In applying Naureckas' outline to the current war on terror, it is easy to find examples identifying each stage. The demonization of Saddam Hussein and the personification of all Iraqis as terrorists are characteristic of stages two and three. In the final stage, people find it acceptable, even enjoyable, to degrade and torture others. Committing atrocities becomes officially or unofficially sanctioned by those in command in the name of the necessities of war. Dehumanization makes such actions permissible. Sociologists and historians see this process as central to all types of wars. According to Naureckas, throughout history, in times of domestic and international conflict, state-organized dehumanization tactics asserting the inferiority of another group have been directed against racial or ethnic groups, nationalities, immigrants or "foreigners," religious groups, sexes, sexual minorities, disabled people as a class, economic and social classes, and many other groups.

In times of war, soldiers are sent into battle to subdue enemy forces. Motivated by retaliation or the desire for conquest, armies are seldom content to simply capture opponents or drive them out. The most effective tactic is to kill as many of their people, soldiers and civilians, as possible. Yet there is something psychologically unnatural about people killing their own kind. This is not simply an ethical comment: scientific studies have shown that killing, even in war, involves forcing soldiers to overcome powerful mental barriers, which normally create resistance to the idea of taking the life of another human. "In war, you are crossing a line you never expected to cross," says Lt. Col. Spencer Campbell, an expert on combat stress at Fort Bragg, N.C. "So you question, 'If my wife knew what I was capable of, would she show affection for me? And having done what I have done, how do I nurture my children?'"[76]

Dr. Dave Grossman, a professor of military science at Arkansas State University, conducts scholarly studies on the destructive acts of war. This field of study, known as "killology," suggests that when soldiers are placed in high-pressure combat situations, they stop thinking with their forebrain, the part of the brain which makes us human, and begin thinking with the mid-brain, or mammalian brain, which is generally indistinguishable from that of an animal. Military leaders throughout history have gone to great lengths to train soldiers to suppress or override resistance to violence in order to enable them to kill on command. This response was observed in human combat by Brigadier-General SLA Marshall, an American military historian who studied the behavior of soldiers from 1943 to 1945. He discovered that during World War II, only 15 percent of riflemen ever fired their weapons on enemy soldiers. Even in elite and battle-hardened units, this figure rarely rose above 25 percent. The soldiers held their positions or advanced conscientiously; they simply exhibited a clear reluctance to open fire on enemy soldiers. Marshall concludes, "when left to their own devices, the great majority of individual combatants throughout history appear to have been unable or unwilling to kill."[77]

Once this discovery was made, military programs were created to overcome this innate reluctance. Special psychological conditioning was used to make shooting other humans easier and more reflexive. By the Korean War, the firing rate by soldiers had been increased to 55 percent; it reached up to 95 percent at the height of the Vietnam war. Grossman points out a corresponding increase in exposure to violence in society during this time. He argues that the "breakdown of American society, combined with the violence depicted in the media and interactive video games, is conditioning our children to kill in a manner similar to the army's conditioning of soldiers."[78] According to Grossman, "We are reaching that stage of desensitization at which the infliction of pain and suffering has become a source of entertainment: vicarious pleasure rather than revulsion. We are learning to kill, and we are learning to like it."[79] Grossman's comments detail the ways in which the reluctance to kill other human beings can be effectively overcome through psychological manipulation and training. While this may make what some consider to be a better soldier, we might question the emotional cost of overriding these instincts.

Part of the cost comes to the psyche of those conditioned to resist such instincts. Army suicides are at their highest rate in 26 years. The suicide rate represents more than 17.3 soldiers per 100,000 troops, compared with 9.1 per 100,000 in 2001.[80] The suicide rate in the military is traditionally lower than that of the general population; the fact that, following Iraq, it is now higher indicates that something, somewhere, is going badly wrong.

Suicide is only one expression of the damaged psyche; the Iraq conflict was replete with many others. *The New England Journal of Medicine* reports 19.5 percent of troops who served in Iraq had moderate or severe mental health problems. If milder symptoms such as anxiety are included, the number rises to 27.9 percent. By December 2003, the majority of the 8,581 medical evacuations from Iraq that were unrelated to combat were mental health evacuations. The impact on soldiers is reflected in rising suicide rates, high percentages of low personal and unit morale and the number of troops sent home for emotional disorders. Soldiers have been changed irreparably by their experience. They, too, are dehumanized and diminished when they inflict suffering and death upon others, and this is even more true when a feeling of enjoyment is associated with the killing. Marshall concludes, "It is, therefore, reasonable to believe that the average and healthy individual—the man who can endure the mental and physical stresses of combat—still has such an inner and usually unrealized resistance to killing a fellow man that he will not of his own volition take life if it is possible to turn away from the responsibility. . . . At a vital point he becomes a conscientious objector, unknowingly."[81]

Even if this objection happens solely in the individual consciousness, it can create guilt or unease. Stan Goff, a Vietnam veteran, admits that he changed in Vietnam and "they were not nice changes either."[82] He speaks of craving other people's pain and becoming someone "who desired the rush of omnipotence that comes with setting someone's house on fire just for the pure hell of it, or who could kill anyone, man, woman, or child, with hardly a second thought. We had to dehumanize our victims before we did the things we did."[83] Not surprisingly, the torment of dealing with these conflicting emotions takes a toll that lingers long after the conflict has ended. Herold Noel, Private First Class in the U.S. Army, said "The things we had to do over there . . . we left our souls in Iraq."[84] Individual soldiers are often left with guilt and grief. Ronald W. Maris, a professor emeritus of psychiatry at the University of South Carolina, says that "World War I and World War II seemed a little more righteous in that there was an initial aggression by an enemy that we didn't start"; this did "not apply to Vietnam and not to Iraq."[85] He adds that public debate over the war can cause soldiers to further question themselves. "When troops first start out," explains independent journalist Dahr Jamail in an interview with David Barsamian, "they believe their mission is to help the Iraqi people. They believe their presence is linked to maintaining American security. But after three to four months, that's gone," he says. "They realize they're in the heart of a brutal guerilla war, which they are losing, where anyone, anywhere can attack them. They begin indiscriminate shooting. That cycle continues as they further dehumanize Iraqis because they don't have the help they need to deal psychologically with the situation."[86]

In an effort to reduce the guilt of non-combatants back at home, knowledge of atrocities is often suppressed. The American government has made extraordinary efforts to conceal the horrors of war from the public. In an attempt to "sanitize" the war, President George W. Bush gave assurances that American "high tech weaponry" only strikes "the really bad guys."[87] Other measures by the government to limit public exposure to war images include buying up all rights to satellite photographs of battle fields and banning photos of the caskets of dead U.S. soldiers, lest the public be reminded that war involves the death of other human beings. It also carefully refrains from counting enemy dead ("We don't do body counts")[88] to hide death tolls that human rights agencies say could range up to a three-quarters of a million Iraqi men, women, and children.[89]

Despite this level of control exercised over the media, modern technology foiled these efforts with the release of photos of U.S. soldiers abusing Iraqi prisoners at Abu Ghraib prison. Thanks to cell phone cameras and electronic mail, some of the most graphic and shocking evidence of the dehumanization and brutalization of Arabs and Muslims by American soldiers have eluded censorship and became public. A friend of U.S. Private Lynndie England, who was shown grinning in several of the Abu Ghraib photo and was eventually convicted for her role in the abuse, told a media conference that the "country boys" in their West Virginia hometown "feel that if you are of a different nationality or race, you are subhuman."[90] This attitude is not limited to "country boys"; Seymour Hersh, who broke the Abu Ghraib story in the *New Yorker*, quotes a U.S. Army military policeman who, in describing an act of abuse on an Iraqi prisoner, referred to the prisoner as "it" rather than "he." These attitudes provide insight into the mentality of people capable of degrading other human beings through physical and psychological torture. It is the almost inevitable result of what happens when people are conditioned to regard an enemy as something less than human. "What is common between the images of American soldiers laughing at naked and humiliated Iraqi prisoners, the video of a terrorist group in Iraq slaughtering an American civilian, and the photos of an Iraqi mob desecrating and hanging the bodies of four American private commandos on March 31st in Fallujah?" Abdul Malik Mujahid asks rhetorically in "Demonization of Muslims Caused the Iraq Abuse." "It is the hatred and inhumanity of the people doing it."

When we consider the uses of race in fomenting war, dehumanizing the enemy and rallying hatred, our minds might readily leap to Nazi Germany, one of the most analyzed and documented genocide attempts in history. Nazi propaganda was, Stig Hornshoj-Miller says, by today's standards "both crude and transparent."[91] Yet the persistence and resilience of even the most obvious of its metaphors demonstrate that our current propaganda is not entirely different in kind. While we might have moved a long way from the crude manipulations, low-tech effects and often bizarre narration of Nazi propaganda films, we still employ racist fears and racist discourse to catalyze the systematic dehumanization of the enemy. The infamous rallies at Nuremberg during Hitler's rise in power drew thousands of people to propaganda events designed to showcase the power of the Third Reich and rally racist hostility against non-Aryans. The rallies could not have existed without the earlier, more potent, more systematic rallying of race accomplished by the Nazi message of hatred and difference. What we must require of ourselves now is a counter-measure to the protocols of dehumanization we have seen endure across time. In the name of both our own humanity and our enemy's, we must now rally a thoughtful, critical energy to examine, resist and refuse collaboration in the ongoing rhetoric of hate.

Notes

1. Sam Keen. *Faces of the Enemy: Reflections of the Hostile Imagination*. New York: Harper Collins, Reprint edition, September 1991: 60–61.

2. Sam Keen interviewed in Bill Jersey and Jeffrey Friedman. *Faces of the Enemy* [Videorecording]. California NewsReel, 1987.

3. Sam Keen. *Faces of the Enemy: Reflections of the Hostile Imagination*.

4. Sam Keen interviewed in Bill Jersey and Jeffrey Friedman.

5. Susan Opotow. "Aggression and Violence." In *The Handbook of Conflict Resolution: Theory and Practice*. Morton Deutsch and Peter T. Coleman, eds. San Francisco: Jossey-Bass Publishers, 2000: 403–27.

6. Sam Keen. *Faces of the Enemy: Reflections of the Hostile Imagination*.

7. Hannan Ashrawi. "Anatomy of Racism." Z. October 18, 2000. See www.zmag.org/meastwatch/anatomy_of_racism.htm (June 26, 2007).

8. Gregory H. Stanton. "The 8 Stages of Genocide." *Genocide Watch*. 1996. See www.genocidewatch.org/8stages1996.htm (June 26, 2007).

9. Gregory H. Stanton. "The 8 Stages of Genocide."

10. Gregory H. Stanton. "The 8 Stages of Genocide."

11. Barbara Rudolph. "Racism in the Ranks." *Time Magazine*. January 30, 1995.

12. Gregory H. Stanton. "The 8 Stages of Genocide."

13. David Stannard. *American Holocaust: The Conquest of the New World*. Oxford: Oxford University Press, 1993: 185.

14. Darold Wax. "A People of Beastly Living: Europe, Africa and the Atlantic Slave Trade. *Phylon*, Vol. 41, No. 1. 1980: 12–24: 14.

15. David Brion Davis. "The Problem of Slavery." In *Slavery, Secession and Southern History*, Robert Louis Paquette and Louis A. Ferleger (eds). Charlottesville, VA: University Press of Virginia, 2000.

16. Marie Jenkins Schwartz. *Birthing a Slave: Motherhood and Medicine in the Antebellum South*. Cambridge, MA: Harvard University Press, 2006.

17. University of Mississippi Libraries. "Scientists Say Negro Still in Ape Stage." *Inventory of the Klu Klux Klan collection*. See www.olemiss.edu/depts/general_library/files/archives/collections/guides/latesthtml/MUM00254.html (June 26, 2007).

18. David Stannard. *American Holocaust*.

19. David Stannard. *American Holocaust*.

20. Catologue entry for *Crockett's Almanac*. Philadelphia, New York, Boston, and Baltimore: Fisher & Brothers, 1841, 1847, and 1852. The Theodore H. Koundakjian Collection of American Humour. See bancroft.berkeley.edu/Exhibits/nativeamericans/10.html (June 26, 2007).

21. *Crockett's Almanac*. Philadelphia, New York, Boston, and Baltimore: Fisher & Brothers, 1841, 1847, and 1852. The Theodore H. Koundakjian Collection of American Humour. See bancroft.berkeley.edu/Exhibits/nativeamericans/10.html (June 26, 2007).

22. *Crockett's Almanac*.

23. Maureen Konkle. *Writing Indian Nations: Native Intellectuals and the Politics of Historiography, 1827–1863*. Chapel Hill, NC: University of North Carolina Press, 2003.

24. Richard Drinnon. *Facing West: The Metaphysics of Indian-Hating and Empire-Building*. Norman, OK: University of Oklahoma Press, 1997: 53.

25. Hugh Brackenridge. Quoted in *The Literature of Justification*. Lehigh University Digital Library. See digital.lib.lehigh.edu/trial/justification/about/soundbites/ (June 26, 2007).

26. David Stannard. *American Holocaust*.

27. John Dower. *War without Mercy: Race and Power in the Pacific War*. New York: Pantheon Books, 1986.

28. John Dower. *War without Mercy*.

29. John Dower. *War without Mercy*.

30. Colliers, December 12, 1942. Reprinted in Keen, *Faces of the Enemy: Reflections of the Hostile Imagination*.

31. Anthony V. Navarro. "A Critical Comparison between Japanese and American Propaganda during World War II." Posted on website of *Michigan State University*. See www.msu.edu/~navarro6/srop.html (June 26, 2007).

32. Anthony V. Navarro. "A Critical Comparison between Japanese and American Propaganda during World War II."

33. John Hersey. *Into the Valley: A Skirmish of the Marines*. New York: Knopf, 1943: 56.

34. Anthony V. Navarro. "A Critical Comparison between Japanese and American Propaganda during World War II."

35. Celia Roy. "The Bug-eyed Monkeys of Tojo: Using Animal Metaphors to Widen Racial Schisms." See journals.iranscience.net:800/mcel.pacificu.edu/mcel.pacificu.edu/jwasia/reviews/seebeesCR.html (August 27, 2003).

36. Celia Roy. "The Bug-eyed Monkeys of Tojo."

37. David Stannard. *American Holocaust.*

38. Ernie Pyle cited in John Dower. *War without Mercy: Race and Power in the Pacific War.* New York: Pantheon Books, 1986: 78.

39. Douglas Linder. "The My Lai Courts-Martial" posted on website of *University of Missouri-Kansas Law School.*1999. See www.law.umkc.edu/faculty/projects/ftrials/mylai/mylai.htm (June 26, 2007).

40. Douglas Linder. "The My Lai Courts-Martial."

41. *Socialist Worker.* "The American way of war crimes." *Socialist Worker Online.* June 9, 2006. See www.socialistworker.org/2006-1/592/592_06_AmericanWay.shtml (June 26, 2007).

42. Norman Nakamura. "The Nature of GI racism during the Vietnam War." *Gidra,* June/July 1970. Posted on *Model Minority.* See modelminority.com/modules.php?name=News&file=article&sid=74 (June 26, 2007).

43. *Socialist Worker.* "The American way of war crimes."

44. Joe Allen. "Vietnam: The War the U.S. Lost." *International Socialist Review,* January/February 2004. See www.thirdworldtraveler.com/Asia/Vietnam_War_US_Lost.html (June 26, 2007).

45. James Duffy cited in Joe Allen. "Vietnam: The War the U.S. Lost." *International Socialist Review,* January/February 2004. See www.thirdworldtraveler.com/Asia/Vietnam_War_US_Lost.html> (June 26, 2007).

46. Sam Keen. *Faces of the Enemy.*

47. Sam Keen. *Faces of the Enemy.*

48. Sam Keen. *Faces of the Enemy.*

49. Wolfgang Mieder. "Proverbs in Nazi Germany: The Promulgation of Anti-Semitism and Stereotypes through Folklore." *The Journal of American Folklore.* Volume 95, Issue 378, 1982: 435–64.

50. Richard Grunberger, *Twelve-Year Reich: A Social History of Nazi Germany.* New York: Holt, Rinehart & Winston, 1971.

51. Cited in Kathryn Ruud. "Liberal Parasites and Other Creepers." In *At War with Words.* Mirjana Dedaic and Daniel Nelson (eds). New York: Mouton de Gruter. 2003.

52. Stig Hornshoj-Moller. "On the Eternal Jew." *Holocaust-History,* 1999. See www.holocaust-history.org/der-ewige-jude/ (June 26, 2007).

53. Stig Hornshoj-Moller. "Still Images from the Eternal Jew." *Holocaust-History,* 1999. See www.holocaust-history.org/der-ewige-jude/stills.shtml (June 26, 2007).

54. Stig Hornshoj-Moller. "Still Images from the Eternal Jew."

55. Mary Mills. "Propaganda and Children during the Hitler Years." *The Nizkor Project.* See www.nizkor.org/hweb/people/m/mills-mary/mills-00.html (June 26, 2007).

56. Wolfgang Mieder. "Proverbs in Nazi Germany."

57. Andreas Musolff. "What role do metaphors play in racial prejudice? The function of antisemitic imagery in Hitler's Mein Kampf." *Patterns of Prejudice.* Volume 41, Issue 1. February 2007: 21–43.

58. Danish WWII, Propaganda. Reprinted in Keen *Faces of the Enemy: Reflections of the Hostile Imagination.* op. cit.

59. Danish WWII, Propaganda.

60. *Human Rights Watch*. Leave None to Tell the Story: Genocide in Rwanda. *Human Rights Watch*. April 1, 2004. See www.hrw.org/reports/1999/rwanda/ (June 26, 2007).

61. Cited in Edward Said. *Orientalism*. New York: Vintage Books, 1979: 252.

62. *Media Matters for America*. "Savage advocated "kill[ing] 100 million" Muslims." *Media Matters for America*. April 19, 2006. See mediamatters.org/items/20060 4190001 (June 26, 2007).

63. Jonathan Belman. "A Cockroach cannot give birth to a butterfly and other messages of hate propaganda."*Peace, War and Human Nature*. May 2004. See www.gse .harvard.edu/~t656_web/peace/Articles_Spring_2004/Belman_Jonathan_hate_prop aganda.htm (June 27, 2007).

64. Jonathan Belman. "A Cockroach cannot give birth to a butterfly."

65. Kellner, Douglas. *The Persian Gulf TV War*. San Francisco: Westview Press, 1992.

66. John Stauber and Sheldon Rampton. *Toxic Sludge Is Good for You*. Monroe, ME: Common Courage Press, 1995.

67. Mike Buckingham. "1991 massacre of thousands of fleeing Iraqi troops was part of U.S. 'total war.'" *Hartford Web Publishing*. February 8, 2003. See www.hartford-hwp .com/archives/27c/069.html (June 26, 2007).

68. Michael Albert. "After the "Turkey Shoot." Z. See www.zmag.org/zmag/articles /albertold19.htm (June 26, 2007).

69. Ramsey Clark. "War Crimes: A Report on United States War Crimes against Iraq." *War Crimes: A report on United States War Crimes against Iraq*. New York: Maisonneuve Press, 1992.

70. Kellner, Douglas. *The Persian Gulf TV War*.

71. Joyce Chediac. "The Massacre of Withdrawing Soldiers on The Highway of Death." In *War Crimes: A report on United States War Crimes against Iraq*. Ramsey Clark et al. New York: Maisonneuve Press, 1992.

72. Joyce Chediac. "The Massacre of Withdrawing Soldiers on The Highway of Death."

73. *Daily Mirror* (UK), March 2, 1991. Cited in John Pilger, *Hidden Agendas*. New York: The New Press. 1998.

74. Jonathan Belman. "A Cockroach cannot give birth to a butterfly."

75. Jim Naureckas. "Journalism in the Gulf" in Janine Jackson and Jim Naureckas (Eds). *The Fair Reader: An Extra! Review of Press and Politics in the '90s*. Boulder, CO: Westview Press, 1996.

76. Lt. Col. Spencer Campbell cited in Ann Scott Tyson. "The other battle: coming home." *The Christian Science Monitor*. July 9, 2003. See www.csmonitor.com /2003/0709/p01s03-usmi.html (June 26, 2007).

77. *Killology Research Group*."Psychological Effects of Combat." *Killology Research Group*. 1999. See www.killology.com/art_psych_resistance.htm (June 26, 2007).

78. Dave Grossman. *On Killing: The Psychological Cost of Learning to Kill in War and Society*. New York: Little Brown, 1998.

79. Dave Grossman. *On Killing*.

80. *Associated Press*. "Army Suicides Highest in 26 years." August 16, 2007.

81. Andy Newman. "US Army feels the strain." *Socialist Unity Network*. September 2004. See www.socialistunitynetwork.co.uk/news/strain.htm (June 26, 2007).

82. Stan Goff. "Hold On to Your Humanity: An Open Letter to GIs in Iraq." *Military Families Speak Out*. See www.mfso.org/article.php?id=225 (June 26, 2007).

83. Stan Goff. "Hold On to Your Humanity."

84. Cited in Patricia Foulkrod. *The Ground Truth: After the Killing Ends*. [Video-recording]. 2006.

85. Theola Labbé. "Suicides in Iraq, Questions at Home Pentagon Tight-Lipped as Self-Inflicted Deaths Mount in Military." *Washington Post*. February 19, 2004.

86. David Barsamian. "Dateline Baghdad: An Interview with Dahr Jamail." Z. December 2005. See zmagsite.zmag.org/Dec2005/barsamian1205.html (June 26, 2007).

87. George W. Bush cited in Norman Solomon. "Picture-perfect killers: Military weapons are often technological marvels but always instruments of death." *San Francisco Chronicle*. June 19, 2005.

88. Edward Epstein. "How many Iraqis died?" *San Francisco Chronicle*. May 3, 2003.

89. John Tirman. "Study: More Than 600,000 Dead in Iraq." *AlterNet*. October 11, 2006. See www.alternet.org/waroniraq/42867/ (June 26, 2007).

90. Marina Hyde. "This Week." Guardian. May 8, 2004.

91. Stig Hornshoj-Moller. "On the Eternal Jew."

PART TWO

ENLISTING DISCOURSE

CHAPTER FOUR

Rats in the Trap:
Animal Metaphors in the News

Words are loaded pistols.

—Jean Paul Sartre

Symbolism of the Animal Metaphor

The historically resonant metaphors of dehumanization discussed in Part I retain a striking and consequential currency today. The three case studies that comprise Part II focus on how these dehumanizing metaphors continue to circulate through our contemporary media, in print journalism, political cartoons, and talk radio, respectively. In each case, there is a connection between the remarkably consistent and sometimes overlapping metaphorical frames that figure the enemy-Other as animal and disease, and some of the most horrifying practices that have surfaced in the war on terror. Examining the symbolism of the animal metaphor in detail provides a useful point of departure.

Across wars and across cultures, animal metaphors have persisted as a central component in representing the fabricated enemy. Within the metaphorical frames constructed by our public discourses, animals operate as recurring symbols, offering us a condensed cognitive code that allows a single image to call up complex emotional and intellectual associations. Kenneth Burke has suggested that the generation of symbols is part of what defines us as human; "Man," he states, "is the symbol-using animal."[1] Like metaphor, symbolism so saturates our culture that it is often effectively invisible; it permeates our everyday language as well as art, poetry, religion, legal customs, and advertising. Single icons or images can evoke extraordinarily complex symbolic intersections, rooted in lengthy and evolving traditions. Over time, symbols can simplify or broaden, accreting new, expanding meanings. Hans Biedermann notes that "many traditional symbols are ambiguous: they cannot be explained as having a single, constant meaning. Not every dragon in every culture is an evil enemy; the heart does not always stand for love."[2] Indeed, say Biedermann, "real symbols, at different stages, are sources of very different, but always relevant, 'information.'"[3] The rose, for example, as a symbol that has survived for centuries in art, literature, and religion, has collected around itself many layers of meanings, some of which contradict or challenge each other. As associated with the Virgin Mary, the rose symbolizes chastity and purity, while as associated with sexuality in medieval romance literature, it symbolizes carnality and sensual bliss, its tightly furled bud a favorite symbol of female virginity, its full-blown blossom a symbol of sexual passion.

Multiple meanings may jostle for dominance around a symbol, or, in contrast, a symbol may over time, come to possess a single, fixed sense. Symbols, therefore, can enrich language by bringing it an array of different possible meanings, or they can reinforce a single meaning, as with images that consistently dehumanize. Both kinds of symbols are woven into almost every level of our public discourse; whenever a signifier communicates something beyond its literal or concrete sense, we find the workings of symbolism, and its potential for linking together distinct or unalike things. As with metaphor, this powerful conjunction of dissimilar things lies at the heart of symbolism; it is, Arnold Whittick notes, "a bringing together of ideas and objects, one of which expresses the other. The symbol is either an object that stands for another object, or an object that stands for an idea."[4] Even very pragmatic, apparently literal activities may be carried out by means of symbolism; what is money but an elaborate, consensual symbolic system, in which almost identical pieces of paper can be "worth" either one or one hundred dollars? What is a dollar but a collectively agreed-upon symbol in which something (a bill, a check) stands in for something else (the sum it is valued at)? Alfred North Whitehead, in fact, observes that society is held together by its shared acceptance and reverence for its symbolic systems;[5] the symbolic system of currency could not operate without such a consensus.

Through symbols and symbolic rituals we make our everyday actions more resonant by linking them with larger systems. Harvesting a field, for example, is both a material act and, as part of a larger symbolic system, a transcendent activity in which the harvest is figuratively linked to life itself and celebrated with an appropriate iconography. Symbols thus have the effect of making some aspects of our life larger and more abstract; they allow us, Lewis Mumford argues, to bring into our lives not just the visible but the invisible.[6] Similarly, the symbols commonly called to the fore in wartime, such as the flag, crown, or throne, often bring a sense of enlargement to the activities of war by suggesting noble causes and necessary protections. Biedermann points out that the Aztec civilization's ritual symbolic trinity of "sacrificial blood, heart, sun" allowed for human sacrifice, just as the symbols of "Flag, *Fuhrer*, blood and soil" have allowed for human slaughter.[7] Such symbols typically touch us in particularly emotional ways: the symbols most associated with the natural world, such as light and dark, touch us at the most primal levels. In the study of symbol analysis, animal images are seen as potently compressed codes that call up rich associations with a single word, phrase, or image. These compacted messages ideally suit the purposes of war propaganda.

George Lakoff anatomizes the metaphoric systems in which animal symbols have such currency in relation to the war on terror. He notes that immediately after the attacks of September 11, George W. Bush referred to the terrorists as "cowards," but that this description seemed at odds with the attackers' willingness to sacrifice their lives in the service of their ideals. The descriptors quickly changed from coward to animal: Bush has spoken of "smoking them out of their holes," drawing on our symbolic associations with rodents, and Defense Secretary Donald Rumsfeld has spoken of "drying up the swamp they live in," an odd choice of metaphor considering the desert landscape from which the attackers originated. The swamp metaphor, then, is not grounded in logic or geography, but is based instead in the labyrinthine but powerful symbolism of the swamp. The swamp has a particularly rich symbolic geography: in the popular imagination it is a landscape more primitive and more deadly than others, teeming with dangerous things that hide beneath the brackish waters' surface and emerge without warning. In popular film, the swamp is generally portrayed as dark and over-run, choked with entangling vines, full of the mysterious sounds—plops and slithers and susurrations—that mark it as a site of threat and secrets. The shadowy swamp potently suggests secrecy, corruption and fetidity, and is the home of an animal life usually regarded with equal distaste: rats, alligators and, especially, the serpent. The snake as symbol calls up a variety of associations ranging from corrupting evil (the Devil in Eden) to sexuality and penetration (Freud's phallic associations). The conceptual metaphors common to both Bush and Rumsfeld's comments, says Lakoff, rest on the assumption that "Moral Is Up; Immoral Is Down (they are lowly) and Immoral People Are Animals (that live close to the ground)."[8]

The symbolic landscape of lowliness is one found regularly in discussions of the war. Many news reports draw on the landscape of the low, describing the hiding places of the enemy as holes, burrows, or lairs, suggesting the subterranean and threatening, a dark place treacherously hiding the fleeing enemy and eroding away the safety of our own "high ground." Like the Nazi cartoon showing the Jew as rat-in-the-walls, the symbolism of the burrow suggests not only the presence of the abhorrent rodent, but the rodent's potency as a threat: it can penetrate and navigate places where humans can't; it can survive in such places invisibly, so that we aren't aware of its threat; it can penetrate our world of light, open spaces any time it wants, corrupting the places we imagined safe. When images of swamps and burrows are repeatedly used in public discussion, they cultivate an almost irresistible sense of threat and incursion, emphasizing the presence of creatures beneath us that are insidiously and invisibly weakening our strong, safe surfaces.

The language of lair and burrow is found frequently in newspaper headlines. The condensing effect of symbol, in which a large emotional content can be compressed into a single word, phrase, or picture, makes symbolism ideal for newspapers. There has been a remarkable similarity in the symbolic vocabulary used by the news media since the start of the war on terror. Reporters lead their stories with "Raid Zaps Iraqi Rat,"[9] "Suspected al-Qaida Nest,"[10] "The Vermin Have Struck Again,"[11] and "Viper's Nest of Terrorism."[12] Examining media sources and public discussions of the war on terror reveals a pattern of using not just animal symbolism but related metaphors of the hunt. Reports concerning the war on terror are filled with terms implying the pursuit and capture of an animal, using verbs such as "hunt," "trap," "snare," "net" and "corral." The much-used phrase "hunt for terrorists" has widely replaced more neutral verbs like "search" or "look for." When the "hunt" is successful, terrorists are "caught in a trap"; the enemy is described as "scurrying for cover" or "slithering out of our grasp." The danger in such depictions is the way in which they represent their subjects as animals to be captured and eliminated. The proliferation of such language has the effect of justifying it; such phrases come to seem like simple, natural descriptions, rather than motivated, deliberate, symbolic choices that perform significant ideological work. These phrases, constantly reiterated, take on a collective force, shaping the conceptual frameworks by which we understand the war on terror.

The collective force of these reiterated allusions to hunting makes it difficult to conceive of the war on terror in any other terms and limits the imaginative possibilities open to us as we search for solutions. In this way, our symbols, while they allow for certain actions, actively preclude others. One of the reasons we must pay heightened attention to our symbolic language is that such language can actually foreclose on our own autonomy; if we insistently figure ourselves as hunters, it becomes increasingly difficult to choose a different role for ourselves. The hunter seems to possess the autonomy and control in the hunt, but in many ways the actions open to the hunter are limited: the hunter may stalk, chase, track, snare, wound, kill, or bag, but cannot, by his nature and that of his prey, negotiate, confer, settle, or otherwise alter the circumstances. Symbolic roles endlessly recirculated through our language thus lock us into positions that can be surprisingly stringent and limiting. Within the structures of the hunter-prey diad, the hunter's role is also largely responsive and reactive; his actions are largely determined by what the prey does, where the prey goes. While the image of the Great Hunter has traditional symbolic associations with courage, triumph, testing the limits of the self, and so on, it also carries within it some inherent limits to freedom of choice and autonomy of action.

Despite these limits, media sources have seized eagerly and almost unanimously on the hunt motif. The headlines below and throughout this chapter come from a range of newspapers with a range of political affiliation; papers from tabloid to venerated, from left to right of center, have all chosen to echo the language of the hunt throughout their publications, as have television, internet, and other broadcast media in their coverage of the war on terror. Consider the consistency of the hunt symbolism in these sample news media headlines:

As British close in on Basra, Iraqis scurry away[13]
Terror Hunt Snares Twenty-five[14]
Exhausted Saddam Snared[15]
Coalition Forces Corral Dozens of Insurgents[16]
Net Closing Around Bin Laden[17]
Efforts to Trap Terrorists Ensnare Illegal Workers[18]
Iraq Braggart Bagged[19]
Pentagon aims to smoke [Saddam] out[20]

This imagery is reinforced when terrorist hideouts are described as animal habitats. Common examples describe such places as "underground terrorist lairs" and "nests of terrorists" instead of as human-constructed hideouts, bunkers or training camps. A few examples include:

Pakistanis Give up on Lair of Osama[21]
Terror Nest in Fallujah Is Attacked[22]

Britain 'Is Breeding Ground for Terror'[23]
Draining the Swamps of 'Homegrown Terrorism'[24]
US forces launch major raid on Fallujah insurgency den[25]

The language of the hunt is not limited to headlines. Indeed, once alert to it we discover it throughout news media's coverage. It is spread widely across different newspapers, writers, and types of writing, from the content of news articles to editorial opinion, from columnists to letters to the editor. The headlines here represent only a sample of the evidence documenting the persistence of the hunt motif; in fact, the language employed in the headlines shown here is reflected in literally tens of thousands of hunt-metaphor and animal-metaphor phrasings found in newspapers and broadcasts since the events of September 11. Although they are only a small percentage of what is publicly said and written about the war on terror, it is worth paying special attention to headlines because they are, for a large part of the population, a main source of information; many people glean their knowledge from scanning headlines rather than reading whole articles. George W. Bush acknowledged in the question-and-answer period of a press conference that while he glances at headlines, he "rarely" reads the articles.[26] Bush is not alone in this; David Ogilvy, successful advertising executive and author of *Confessions of an Advertising Man*, has claimed that four out of five people read only news headlines. Whether in headlines or articles, it is remarkable to consider that so many different voices have so collectively echoed such a restricted and repetitive body of images. It is also remarkable to consider how broadly these words are reaching us: millions of citizens, many avid and eager for "pure" information about the war so they can develop their own ideas about it, are receiving their news entirely through invisible conduits of metaphor. The shape of these conduits, with the enemy consistently portrayed as beast and the retaliator as hunter, pre-fabricates for us certain understandings of the war and our role within it.

Animal symbols can be broken down into different types, and within propagandistic discourse special categories of animal emerge. The term "animal" in general is often broadly applied to individuals who have committed acts we find particularly loathsome or heinous; domestically, murderers of children or child pornographers are typically labeled animals. In the war on terror, however, the construction of the enemy often occurs through calling up particular themes of animal symbolism. After all, the word "animal" can call up benign associations: animals can be useful, they can be our companions, they have laws to protect them from cruelty, and they have active, energetic, vocal public advocates such as PETA and the SPCA working on their behalf.

It is worth noticing, then, that when government and media draw upon animal metaphor systems, they call up specific versions of the metaphor, versions that come with a particularly and exclusively negative connotation. One such version is the "beast," which we find in multiple headlines:

Chained Beast—Shackled Saddam Dragged to Court[27]
Death of "wild beast" Dadullah hits Taliban campaign[28]
Beast who gloried in massacre and torture[29]
These beasts must pay for sick cruelty[30]
War in Iraq: a U.S. Walkover in Beast's Heartland[31]
Iraq Beasts Hang Kids; Children Butchered in Front of Parents for Talking to Soldiers[32]

The word *beast* connotes a particular kind of animal, excluding most benign or even neutral meanings. We might think of the beast as an intensified animal symbol; a beast is an animal that is wild, fierce, dangerous, brutish, often repugnant (in England, "beastly" is a synonym for nasty or horrid) and ungovernable. An animal might be tamed, but in the more intense, often mythical associations surrounding the beast, taming is much less possible. The bestial and the mythical come together in a headline such as "The beast with many heads strikes again—Terror in Jakarta."[33] This headline suggests a related strand of intensified animal imagery, the monster. The monster appears over and over in news media headlines:

Arab world created this suicidal monster[34]
The Terrorism Monster[35]
Revolving-Door Monsters [36]
Iraqi Monster's Head Ripped Off; Horror at Execution[37]
Monster Set to Be New Dad[38]
Throw out These Monsters Who Prey on the Innocent[39]
The Terrorism Monster[40]
These Monsters Are No Freedom-fighters[41]
Of Monsters and Muslims[42]
Spare Us the Righteous Tears at the Death of Another Monster[43]
Monsters Slaughter 24 Children in Iraq[44]

Monsters have their own rich mythic and pop-culture traditions; they are hard to kill and, once killed, are often able to return, usually in a more dangerous form. Headlines such as "Bin Laden's hunted monster has simply grown more heads"[45] reinforce these mythic associations. Even independent scholars, consultants, and pundits may use and reinforce these intensified animal symbols; when the ONASA news agency of Bosnia-Herzegovnia publishes a headline proclaiming "Al-Qaeda Metamorphoses into International Islamist Monster: Experts,"[46] we might wonder for a moment what monster experts are being called upon to comment.

At the other end of the spectrum of animal metaphors are vermin. While monsters and beasts carry an imposing mythical freight, evoking ideas of largeness, power, and ungovernability, vermin evoke the opposite. Monsters may be individual; vermin rarely are. Vermin are characterized by plurality and mass: where we find one rat or roach, says common wisdom, there will be a hundred or a thousand more. Relatively harmless in the singular, they can be deadly *en masse*: their sheer numbers make them a threat. We do not speak of a singular vermin; rather, as in this lead line from the *NY Daily News*, vermin are inevitably "they": "And so the vermin have struck again—as all knew they surely would. Does today there remain any safe haven on this Earth from beasts who slither out of their murderous holes to wreak their havoc?"[47]

Within the category of vermin, rats are seen as particularly loathsome. In many cultures, rats are equated with destruction, disease, and the spread of plague. The rat is also associated with untrustworthiness, slyness and ruthless self-interest; an informer is a "rat"; to "rat" on someone is tantamount to betraying them. In both East and West, the rat is seen as unclean; as a denizen of earth's bowels, it "has distinctly anal connotations."[48] While rats are physically most common in places of poverty, they are sometimes figuratively associated with wealth, especially through images of money-grubbing, sinister greed, and destructive appetite.

When the media labels suspected terrorists, enemy military and political leaders, and ultimately an entire population as "rodents," it conjures up a spectrum of negative cultural associations. It transforms people into vermin, whose capture and extermination becomes justified and necessary. These headlines again repeat and solidify the equation of enemy with rat:

Troops Grab 50 in Raid on Afghan Rat's Nest[49]
Rats in a Trap: How Feds Snared Fort Dix Terror Plotters[50]
Hussein's Rat Hole[51]
Out of a Rat-hole[52]
Americans Cleared out Rats' Nest in Afghanistan[53]
Fallujah: 'It's a Rats' Nest'[54]
This Rat's Better off Dead[55]

In 2003, the UK's BBC broadcasting described souvenir T-shirts, available for purchase at the American military detention site in Guantánamo Bay, Cuba, depicting a rat wearing a turban, orange jumpsuit and shackles, with the words *Guantánamo Bay: Taliban Lodge* inscribed around it. Another depicts six shackled rats in orange jumpsuits, surrounded by the caption *Al Qaeda six-pack—Guantánamo Bay, Cuba, Home of the Sand Rat*.[56]

There is one significant exception to the general aversion to rats; for a troop of soldiers with the long-standing nickname of the Desert Rats, the label is a venerable one. The British 7th Armoured Brigade, or Desert Rats, is considered to have "one of the proudest histories in the British Army."[57] Formed in 1940, it was charged with stemming the Axis advance in North Africa and protecting the vital Suez Canal, and fought a dogged campaign against Rommel's forces at the battle of El Alamein in 1942. The troops adopted the nickname after the emblem on their shoulder badge, a small desert creature called a jerboa. After the war, they continued wearing the jerboa insignia. In October 1990 the Brigade was deployed to the Gulf War, and in 1994 to Bosnia–Herzegovnia. They are currently serving in Iraq.[58] The Desert Rats are "our" rats, perhaps more affiliated with the cute, clean white rats sold by pet stores than with the filthy, insidious, threatening enemy-rat. As Biedermann observes, "not every dragon" is "an evil enemy"[59]; likewise, not every rat is vermin. Significantly, however, the rats that are symbolically most loathsome are those consistently identified with the enemy. The jerboa on the soldier's badge is drawn in a remarkably different mode than the rat images employed in images of the enemy Other. Enemy-rat images emphasize the rat's grim-looking jaws, replete with prominent fangs and razor-sharp teeth; in the Desert Rat pennant, no teeth at all are visible. In two different insignias designed by Edward Mooney and Todd Mills, in fact, the jerboa featured is standing quite adorably on its hind legs, tiny paws positioned like those of a pet taught to beg on command. The upright posture of the jerboa in both images provides a clue to how different good rats are from bad, enemy rats. It suggests forthrightness: these rats are not a subterranean threat; they don't scurry along in swamps and sewers, wearing away our firm footing. Instead, they are charmingly human in their posture, far from the lowly squirmer beneath the ground or deep in the walls. It's also worth noting that the badge and pennant depict a single rat, not the teeming masses interspersed with Jewish faces in *Der Ewige Jude*. C. Douglas Lummis observes that when the terrorist is shown as a rat, it is most often the gutter rat: "Not the white rat or the brown country rat, but the plague rat, the one that is never displayed in zoos and that no one (ex-cept witches) ever keeps as pets. The plague rat, like the cockroach, exists in popular imagination . . . as an animal to be killed on sight, and exter-minated if possible."[60] In "our rat" headlines, "good rats" are treated affec-tionately, in marked contrast to the enemy-rat:

Desert Rats' leader warns on risk of armed uprising in Basra[61]
Desert Rat becomes 99th to die in Iraq[62]
Desert Rat to meet the Queen[63]
My Dad, the Desert Rat[64]

Another suggestive application of rodent symbols to enemies who are not racially othered is evident in the labeling of opponents to Bush's war on Iraq and Afghanistan as weasels. While seen as neither as destructive nor as loathsome as the rat, the weasel still has an unsavory reputation: it combines perceived qualities of treachery, sneakiness, and cowardice. With its long, sinuous body, it can worm its way into narrow spaces; it lives on the surface but can crawl underground using other creatures' tunnels; it can back its way out of very tight places. According to Jose A. Carillo,[65] on of the scale of treachery the weasel ranks above even carrion-animals like the jackal or vul-ture: a "weasel" is an untrustworthy, deceitful person; to "weasel out" means to escape commitments or responsibilities. Even words that are perceived as weak or slippery are called "weasel words."

When politicians and media label the leaders of Western countries op-posing the war on terror weasels, these associations of cowardly vacillation, betrayal, and deceptive self-interest are effectively called up. The U.S. pres-ents itself as betrayed by those "weaseling out" of their foreign policy obliga-tions. The evocative symbolic connotations of the weasel imply a lack of in-tegrity in these leaders and the country they represent. The *New York Post*, especially, seems to delight in characterizing opponents of the war this way. In huge, tabloid-style black letters, its various headlines declare:

Axis of Weasel: Germany and France Wimp out on Iraq[66]
It's Showdown Time at the UN as Powell Takes on the Euro-weasels[67]
Stop! Goes the Weasel as Euros Back Bush[68]
McCain: Be Nice to Weasels[69]
Weasels Paid Thugs Ransom[70]

Other newspapers echoed this language:

Mexico gets free pass despite behaving like weasel in war debate[71]
Sniffing Profits; with Iraq's Fall Imminent, the Axis of Weasels Want a
	Piece of the Action[72]
Axis of Weasels Must Not Profit from the Reconstruction of Iraq[73]

This persistent symbolization seems to suggests the dangers of dallying too closely or too sympathetically with rats; such proximity might not make you a rodent, but it certainly rubs off, lowering you in others' eyes and in the metaphoric landscape.

Another significant animal symbol is the snake, especially the viper. In western culture, the serpent is commonly a symbol of evil; Satan famously took the form of a serpent to trick Eve into offering Adam forbidden fruit. Popular culture has enthusiastically played with the snake as a primal fear, from horror movies about giant snakes to snakes on a plane. In Western cultures, it's difficult to find positive models for the snake; the West has largely forgotten or suppressed the traditional association of the snake with healing present in many non-Christian cultures. The symbolic snakes twined around the caduceus in the ancient sign for physician is perhaps our last surviving link to this benign association. Whittick argues that in western art and ecclesiastical design, the snake shows up as "the Christian typification of the forces of evil, opposing and vanquished by the godly forces of righteousness."[74] The snake's malevolent role is most strikingly depicted in conjunction with the eagle, the latter representing righteousness overcoming evil. This image was employed as early as in Homer's *Iliad*, in which an eagle carrying a bleeding snake in its talons appeared before the Greek heroes as an omen of their success over the Trojans.

Vipers, particularly treacherous serpents, also have a rich symbolic history: young vipers, gnawing though the belly of their mother, symbolized children plotting against their parents. In the 16th century, the viper signified "a common woman or harlot" ready to "sting men with lust."[75] The symbolism of snake and viper communicates the idea that our opponents possess a drive to poison us that is, like a snake's, instinctive, natural and irresistible. The serpent will strike simply because that is its nature. There is no arguing with a snake, no reasoning with it; its deadliness is fundamental and inarguable. When confronted with an aroused and lethal snake, the only rational response is a deadly counterattack. These symbolic associations are repeatedly reflected in headlines identifying the enemy with snake, serpent, and viper:

Brave Brit Smashes Vipers' Nest[76]
US Report Calls for War on 'Principal Nest of Terrorist Vipers'[77]

Port City of 14 [million] Harbours Viper's Nest of Terrorism[78]
The Viper Awaits[79]
The Snake Leaves the Desert[80]
Snake with a Taste in Scandinavian Models-Hussein's Greed[81]
Former Arab Power Is 'Poisonous Snake'[82]
Britain Bitten By A Snake; Country Failed to Crack Down on Those Who
    Incited Hatred and Murder"[83]

Like the symbol of the snake as a natural enemy, the spider is also a symbolically primal foe. The spider archetype has a long history and is traditionally associated with Fate, a teacher, destroyer, or trickster. Perhaps it is this trickster image that allows such a strong link to be made between Saddam Hussein's hiding place and a spider hole. A media content analysis of the words "spider hole" results in lists of stories about the capture of Saddam. When Lt. General Ricardo Sanchez, the top U.S. commander in Iraq, informed the media about the conclusion of the search, he said Saddam "was caught in a spider hole." The phrase was quickly adopted in the media and employed in almost every subsequent article about the capture. Something about this image clearly captured the attention of the public: the term "spider hole" rapidly entered widespread use and was named one of the ten top phrases of 2003.[84]

The term has a specific military history; during the American Civil War it referred to a hastily-dug foxhole. In WWII, it came to refer to a one-person foxhole, a hole in the earth used for stealthy attack by Japanese forces in many Pacific battlefields. Usually deeper than a foxhole, spider holes are covered over and used in ambushes. In her article "Spider Hole: the Origin of the Species," *Washington Post* journalist Libby Copeland addresses the metaphor directly. She writes that "the phrase conjures the lair of a sneaky, ugly, menacing creature, a thing so dumb and degraded it lives only to kill and be killed. On the food chain, the arachnid is below the dog, the pig and even the rat, the most popular subhuman beings we use to label folks we don't like."[85] In an interesting twist in the discussion, Linda Rayor, an assistant professor of entomology at Cornell University, took umbrage over the connection between the spider and Saddam Hussein. She told the *Washington Post* that references to Saddam Hussein's hideout as a spider hole was "an insult to spiders."[86] The public adopted the phrase readily, as in the joke "your self-esteem is lower than Saddam Hussein's spider hole."[87] The joke hearkens back to Lakoff's conceptual metaphor of lowliness: we are high and the enemy is low; the worse the enemy, the lower the place he occupies.

Like the spider hole, the spider web is common to media and political language. "Web of terror" is now the dominant phrase used to describe possible or actual terrorist networks. The web as a symbol for terrorism calls up potent associations of entrapment going back to childhood: Miss Muffet's spider; spiders put down the back of playground victims; the nursery rhyme spider that fatally invites the fly to "Come into my parlor." Calling up the spider's resonant images of threat, the Charleston, South Carolina, *Post and Courier* ran the headline, "Attacking al-Qaida's terror webs," and reported on a "spider's web of Islamic radicals."[88] This language frequently accompanies exhortations to "wipe out" or "exterminate" these "spider webs of terror." We can find further spider references in headlines such as,

Saddam Caught; U.S. Troops Find Tyrant Hiding in a Spider-hole[89]
Saddam's "Spider Hole" Could Be Destroyed[90]
"Spider Hole" Fits Saddam[91]
Saddam Captured; Nine-month Search Ends in 'Spider Hole'; Hussein
    Loyalist's Tip Led to Dictator[92]

Sub-human images of the enemy also take the form of other kinds of insect life; newspaper accounts draw on a repertoire of creepy-crawly symbols, all of which consistently emphasize the enemy's toxic, noxious, or pestilential nature. This is especially true in the equation of the enemy to a cockroach, an insect largely considered to be the "least loved of all non-humans."[93] Cockroaches are associated with filth and disease and are often shown as natural enemies in horror and science fiction films. Some examples of cockroach and other insect symbolism appear in the following headlines:

Operation Desert Pest[94]
Terrorists, like rats and cockroaches, skulk in the dark[95]
A Washington homecoming for a cockroach[96]
Taking Military Advice From The Cockroach Conqueror[97]
U.S., Iraqi forces find "hornet's nest" in Fallujah[98]
American troops kill 40 in "hornet's nest"; Battles around Najaf as rebels
    come under fire[99]
Killing of protesters stirs up Sunni hornet's nest[100]
In Fallujah; Push South Greeted By "Hornet's Nest"[101]

Such language is repeated in the words of a political commentator who recommends that Americans leave the "hunt" for Osama bin Laden to Pakistani forces because Pakistanis would be less conspicuous to locals. The writer refers to this as "using one evil to end another evil." The article explains, "Sending in over-equipped and over-confident Marines and Green Berets to catch bin Laden would be like sending in an army of elephants to catch a cockroach. One must use a cockroach to catch a cockroach."[102] These persistent symbols have logical linguistic extensions; once we have confirmed that our enemy is a cockroach, we seem to move inexorably to a corollary discussion of extermination and eradication. Like bugs, our enemies are there for the squashing; we need have no more compunction about wiping them out than we have in wiping out a roach colony from under our kitchen sink or a hornet's nest from our back porch.

There is one other recurring low-animal metaphor in the rhetoric surrounding the war on terror. Within this metaphor the enemy is not only inhuman, he is not even a mammal, not even a visible organism. Instead, in this representation, the enemy is something utterly alien: the microbial, the bacterial, the viral, or the cancerous. These metaphors are invoked in headlines such as:

Al Qaeda Mutating Like a Virus[103]
Like Cancer Cells, Terrorist Organizations Are Proliferating[104]
Stop Sectarian "Cancer" in Iraq, Urges UN[105]
The Terrorist Virus Is No Lightweight Matter. We Must Contain Its Spread[106]
Al-Jazeera Notes Blair's Warning of "Virus of Islamic Extremism"[107]
Headscarf Is a Cancer in Turkey[108]
Root out This Cancer of Evil[109]
Ridding Islam of the Cancer Within[110]

When the enemy is a disease-bug, as when he is an insect-bug, extermination and eradication become the logical, responsible, even humane response. In normal circumstances, when applied to humans, these words evoke historical memories of genocide, and we have an inbuilt resistance to them. When, within the intensified rhetoric of wartime, the humanity of the enemy-Other has been systematically compromised through such insistent metaphors and such highly charged symbolism, we are more willing to annihilate: we seek not just to vanquish the enemy but to erase him utterly. When we speak of eradicating terrorists, we employ a word most commonly used when speaking of wiping out diseases or infestations. In the eradication model, we don't scruple to kill the whole colony; it would be ludicrous to try to separate out the individual bugs which have harmed us. When we extend the eradication model to the fabricated enemy, we likewise don't distinguish between those who harm us and those who seem indistinguishably like them. When racist metaphor dehumanizes an entire population, we may come to see them as so different from ourselves that it is no longer possible to see ourselves mirrored in their suffering.

That we have already slipped into a widespread public metaphor of extermination is clear from news media language such as this:

> The purpose of engagement is not to win friends and popularity. It is instead to find and utterly annihilate the enemy—in this case all those secular and Islamists dedicated to our own destruction.[111]
>
> Good progress is certainly being made in the extermination of dispersed Saddamite opposition.[112]
>
> Live with terrorism or go all-out to eradicate it.[113]

Newspaper headlines also echo this language:

> Cleansing of Foreign Evils a "Good Thing"[114]
> Kuwait Vows to Exterminate Terrorists[115]
> The extermination of Saddam Hussein[116]
> Exterminating the [Iraqi] regime[117]
> Iraqi PM Vows to "Annihilate" Terrorist Groups[118]
> Saudi King Vows to Annihilate Al-qaeda[119]
> Iraq Premier Forms Security Service to "Annihilate" Terrorists[120]
> Allies "Wipe out Iraqi Division"[121]

In the world of blogs, the low-animal metaphor is used with even more vehemence than in traditional forms of media; particularly disturbing is the way in which many bloggers extend the idea of the enemy from terrorists to all of Islam. When the disease metaphor is invoked in the following examples, it is applied not just to those suspected of terrorism but to the whole religion: "A little bit of Islam is like a little bit of cancer;"[122] "Islam, America's cancer;"[123] "Islam is the cancer, nukes are the answer;"[124] "Like a cancer spreading over the body, the beautiful 'peaceful' religion of Islam is spreading all over this earth;"[125] "Islam is a hideous, hairy-warted cancer."[126]

The symbolism of serpent, vermin, and rodent is also invoked in many voices from the blogosphere. The snake metaphor is very deliberately called upon to necessitate extermination in this quotation: "Once the rattlesnake has bitten your child and killed it, you are unlikely to allow it and its family nest to continue to exist. And the analogy is a perfect one because we have the ability to exterminate Islam from the face of the Earth."[127] Other examples include:

> Terrorism is only the poison the snake spits. The snake itself is the rise of Islam as a force in the modern world.[128]
>
> You can talk as sweet as you want to a snake but never turn your back on it.[129]
>
> I believe that Britain has fed a snake at its bosom and has been bitten by the snake.[130]
>
> It will only be a matter of time before it becomes open season on Muslim extremists around the world and we will be able to just exterminate you like the rats that you are.[131]
>
> It is time for Americans to unite—and for us to help root out every last one of these vermin hiding within our country,[132]
>
> Why don't we expel all of the Muslim vermin currently infesting this great country. [133]
>
> Drive the Islamist terrorist vermin into the sea.[134]
>
> If folks simply shoot spit wads of lard at Islamic items, tomb stones, crescents, vermin pits (aka mosques), korans and other public islamic vermin symbols[135]
>
> Shame about all the muslim vermin that have infested Britain.[136]
>
> I really hope we exterminate these al-Qaida vermin as quickly as possible. [137]
>
> I fully agree with the comments about terrorists whatever their beliefs or religion exterminate them.[138]
>
> Who will be our Adolf and bring extinction to the Islamic beast?[139]

This startling call for "our Adolf" reinforces and makes explicit the link between genocide and the public use of dehumanizing metaphor. While the internet offers a forum for extremities of hate speech that most of us would decry and distance ourselves from, the fact that these bloggers so consistently employ metaphors identical to those we find in much more mainstream and representative media such as newspapers is extremely telling.

Is it any wonder, given this consistency of metaphor, that we see photos such as those from Abu Ghraib, which literalize the figurative language of metaphor by treating humans as animals? Although the Red Cross estimates that between 70 and 90 percent of the Abu Ghraib prisoners were innocent and eventually released, while detained they endured treatment that made their less-than-human status very clear, including being leashed and being ridden like animals.[140] Hussein Mohssein Mata Al-Zayiadi, detainee No. 19446, one of the hooded prisoners shown in the infamous Abu Ghraib photographs, told military investigators that he and other prisoners were forced to crawl on their hands and knees with guards "sitting on our backs riding us like animals."[141] Amnesty International reports that Abu Ghraib detainee Nori gave a sworn statement to military investigators on January 17, 2004, alleging that "They treated us like animals, not humans. They kept doing this for a long time. No one showed us mercy. Nothing but cursing and beating. After that they left us for the next two days naked with no clothes, with no mattresses, as if we were dogs."[142]

It was not just prisoners at Abu Ghraib who were vulnerable to such treatment: in 2004, U.S. soldiers detained an elderly Iraqi woman in her seventies, placed a harness on her, made her crawl on all fours and rode her like a donkey. British Prime Minister Tony Blair's human rights envoy to Iraq, Ann Clwyd, said she had investigated and believed the claims of the woman: "She was held for about six weeks without charge," Clwyd told the UK's *Evening Standard* newspaper. "During that time she was insulted and told she was a donkey. A harness was put on her, and an American rode on her back."[143]

Accusations of prisoner abuse also abound at the U.S. military base in Guantánamo Bay, dubbed "Camp X-Ray" by military authorities, where "enemy combatants" are illegally held for years without trial. The term "enemy combatant" has historically referred to the armed force of an enemy state. Enemy combatants in the present conflict, however, come from many nations, wear no uniforms, and use unconventional weapons. Enemy combatants in the war on terrorism are not defined by readily apparent criteria such as citizenship or military uniform; the power to name a citizen as an enemy combatant is therefore extraordinarily broad.[144] But questions of how to define combatants are only subsidiary questions in a much larger issue of the systemic racism underpinning the war. As twenty-three-year-old Josh Middleton of the 82nd Airborne division bluntly observed after a four-month tour in Iraq, "A lot of guys really supported the whole concept that if they don't speak English and they have darker skin, they're not as human as us, so we can do what we want."[145] "What we want," when we perceive our enemy as less than human, is to perform that inhumanity in ways both literal and symbolic. Thus prisoners at Guantánamo Bay are kept shackled and caged, as legal counsel and former captives affirm. Amnesty International confirms that prisoners are kept inside their wire cages "sometimes up to 24 hours a day with little exercise time out of their cells."[146] Former detainee Mamdouh Habib made his animal status clear when he told human rights workers "I never see the sun, I never have shower like a human being, I never have soap, I never have a cup to drink, I never treated like a human being."[147] Fellow detainee Sayed Abbasin told Amnesty International after his release in 2003 that the Guantánamo prison camp was "like a zoo."[148] British prisoner Tareq Dergoul said that he was interrogated for up to ten hours at a time while chained like a dog to a ring in the floor. In a sworn statement, he said he had been tied up "like a beast" and beaten.[149] Riasoth Ahmed, whose son Rhuhel was released after being held for questioning for 790 days, echoes this consistent language of the bestial when he observes: "They have treated my son like an animal. He has been held in a cage in Cuba for two years without any charge and with no access to a lawyer."[150] Rhuhel Ahmed was one of the "Tipton Three," the name given to three young Muslim men from the English town of Tipton who were arrested when visiting Pakistan and turned over to the American military on suspicion of terrorist activities, accusations that have never been proven. The Red Cross investigated their claims of torture and abuse at the hands of the U.S. military and reported that "some of the abuses alleged by the detainees would indeed constitute inhuman treatment. Inhuman treatment constitutes a grave breach of the Third Geneva Convention and these are often also described as war crimes."[151] The American administration's position that the Guantánamo detainees should be denied the opportunity to challenge the lawfulness of their detention led U.S. Supreme Court Justice David Souter to point out that U.S. law at the Naval Base "even protect[s] the Cuban iguana,"[152] while detained humans are left with no protections.

Persuading prisoners that they are merely animals is a recognized interrogation strategy taught by those like Geoffrey D. Miller, a retired U.S. Army Major General who commanded American detention facilities at Guantánamo Bay and Abu Ghraib. Miller told military intelligence officers that, to control the interrogation, "You have to treat the prisoners like dogs"; "If you treat them differently or if they believe that they're any different than dogs, you have effectively lost control of your interrogation from the very start."[153] To this end, at Abu Ghraib naked prisoners were forced to crawl like dogs and, as part of the prison's curriculum of "dog tricks," were forced to bark like dogs; "if we didn't do that," one prisoner reported, "they start hitting us hard on our face and chest with no mercy."[154] When Military Working Dogs (MWD) arrived at the Abu Ghraib site in November 2003, they were used to threaten and bite detainees, both for interrogation purposes and for entertainment. Alex Danchev writes that

> Two Army dog-handlers had a competition to see who could make a detainee urinate or defecate on himself, if sufficiently terrorized by Marco and Duco, dogs with better names than detainees [who were known only by numbers]. Other soldiers came to watch. Soon "doggy dances" were all the rage. These

antics appear to have been regarded as just that by almost everyone who participated in them, or witnessed them, or heard about them, a sizeable constituency. Far from being concealed, they were a commonplace of prison conversation.[155]

Danchev notes that like the " routine sexual humiliation" and "pervasive nakedness" used to cow and demoralize prisoners, the use of dogs was "accepted practice" at Guantánamo Bay.[156] In fact, the "dog tricks" were often filmed and used as screen-savers on soldiers' personal computers.[157]

The use of films and photos of such abuse as personal mementos highlights another important element of dehumanization. When animal metaphors are joined to metaphors of the hunt, we inevitably find the phenomenon of the war trophy. Like the hunter's trophy, the soldier's war trophy testifies both to the hunter's prowess and the prey's utter abjectness. It is not enough, within the hunt metaphor, for the enemy to be an animal; he must also be a defeated animal, stilled, stuffed, and mounted for the eternal glorification of the hunter. The enemy's weakness must be confirmed by the completeness of his defeat, his subhuman nature confirmed by the extraordinary degree to which he can be brought to heel.

Dangerously, this message is spreading to both combatants and non-combatants around the world. Columnist Bob Wing of the *War Times* describes a conversation between a friend and his Egyptian father, a man who originally supported the war. Speaking of the notorious photograph showing a female U.S. soldier holding a leashed Iraqi, White's friend said, "What is the message of that photo? It's that the Iraqi is a dog." "No," said his father: "The message is that he's *my* dog."[158]

War Trophies

For many years, soldiers in war have collected trophies of their military conquests, such as weapons, valuables, photos, ordnance, medals, and other keepsakes. Soldiers in many previous wars have taken photos of dead enemy soldiers and sent them home to family and friends with triumphant notes attached. Often these photos would be passed around from soldier to soldier like playing cards.[159] By soldiers' accounts, the commemorative taking of ears, fingers, even heads was not out of the ordinary in previous wars.[160]

Trophy hunting is likewise very much part of the war on terror. During the initial invasion of Iraq, reports described soldiers taking rugs, crystal, copies of the Koran, and other artifacts from Saddam's palaces during the invasion and selling them online on eBay.[161] Journalists were also criticized for taking valuables, art, weapons, and artifacts from Iraq. When charged by U.S. customs agents for being in possession of stolen property, Jules Crittenden of the *Boston Herald* stated in open letter to American journalists:

> I understand and share the world's concern about the disappearance of legitimate Iraqi national treasures that are in fact treasures of human civilization [but these] are matters separate from the time-honored tradition among soldiers of bringing home reminders of some of the most intense experiences of their lives.[162]

Especially troubling is the way many of these trophies do not simply memorialize but celebrate these "intense experiences." Keeping mementos, from diaries to souvenirs, is a long-standing tradition, but the symbolism of the trophy explicitly glorifies the hunt and its triumphs. In one of the most disturbingly literal versions of the hunt metaphor, there have been eyewitness accounts of American soldiers in Fallujah tying the dead bodies of resistance fighters to their tanks and driving around with their trophies like hunters with an animal carcass tied to their hood.[163] Such trophy-taking is often more symbolic than literal, however, as in the case at some detention camps where, according to the Pentagon, military leaders established a ritual for departing personnel who "did a good job" by presenting them with a detainee's hood.[164] It's difficult not to see this as more than a simple reminder of the camp experience; it seems also to suggest a symbolic possession of the enemy-Other, presented in the most abstracted, anonymous, interchangeable form possible, the blank, black, obscuring mask. Now the departing soldier can possess, pack up and take home the face of the enemy, in its most materially fabricated form. If it were not for the largely unchallenged domination of the prevalent metaphors that, as they circulate and re-circulate through the media, consistently diminish and de-humanize the enemy figuring him as beast and prey, then such trophy-taking would surely be harder to justify by the actors and observers of the practice. Since the headlines' insistent metaphors collectively figure the war as hunt, these trophy-taking activities offer a grotesquely appropriate concretization of the hunt metaphor, in which the "beasts" of the newspaper headlines translate the enemy body into a source of grisly, but metaphorically apt, memento.

Soldiers are technically not allowed to bring back war trophies from Iraq, only legally purchased souvenirs. Most types of war trophies, including body parts, weapons, ordnance, and personal items are banned by military law.[165] Souvenir photos of prisoners of war are also a violation of the Geneva Convention, which prohibits photographing detainees or mutilating or degrading dead bodies. However, despite this prohibition, extreme examples of war tro-phy collection are emerging into public awareness. At a Citizens' Hearing on the Legality of U.S. Actions in Iraq, various decorated soldiers gave accounts of incidents contravening international law they witnessed in Iraq. One of-ficer described a particularly gruesome incident: "According to Chanan Suarez-Diaz, who also received a Purple Heart for his service in Iraq, the psy-ched up emotions among the troops resulted in U.S. soldiers taking 'trophies' of brain matter from Iraqis they killed and putting such in their refrigerators on base."[166]

Despite their contravention of the Geneva Convention, this kind of trophy-taking has been largely sanitized by media and government. By refer-ring to such acts as "prisoner abuse" rather than as war crimes, they are made to seem less systemic, more the rogue activities of a few individuals acting on their own initiative, or of a few understandably stressed soldiers letting off steam by allowing "hazing" rituals to get out of hand.[167] The widespread phe-nomenon of "trophy videos" emphasizes that trophy-taking, like the abuse and degradation of detainees, is not a rare or marginalized activity. Attach-ing video cameras to their helmets during combat, many soldiers send video footage back home, documenting scenes from the comic to the appalling and horrific. Often set to a thrash metal soundtrack, hundreds of hours of such footage is now posted on a range of internet sites; one soldier compared his footage to a video game, saying that like a game "you're stepped away from reality . . . you're seeing it through the camera lens."[168] Another made the ex-plicit connection between such trophies and the trophies of the literal hunt, saying that these videos made him feel proud of his work, "like a big game hunter feels proud of his kills."[169]

The trophy videos emerging from Iraq, notes Susan Sontag, represent an important shift from previous wars, in which the photography of war was chiefly "the province of photojournalists."[170] In contrast, new technologies allow all soldiers to be photographers, capturing and circulating war images at will. These records can be swapped individually, as old war snapshots used to be, but they can also be sent digitally around the globe, viewed by other military personnel and by civilians. Collectively, these images have come to be called "War Porn" after the term coined by social theorist Jean Baudrillard in an influential 2004 essay. Baudrillard argues that the video trophies emerg-ing from Iraq, with their "garishly explicit images," crude aesthetics, and low production values, even share the look of much modern porn.[171] Like "spe-cialist" porn produced for and distributed to a niche market, Baudrillard sug-gests, the "posing of Iraqi inmates for those famous pictures in Abu Ghraib prison," which featured several female GIs in the role of dominatrixes over bound and naked prisoners, were taken with digital cameras and, like specialist porn, originally intended for private distribution.[172]

Mary Ann Tetreault echos Baudrillard's equation of video war trophies with pornography. "If," she argues, "we define pornography as a record of the violation of a subject's physical and psychic integrity," then we must understand images of torture, corpses, and brutal interrogation as similar to "stills from snuff films, statements of the utter worthlessness of the prisoners and the life-and-death power over them exercised by their captors."[173] The link between war porn and sexual porn is disturbingly solidified by an internet site claiming to "support the troops" by supplying sexual pornography in exchange for images of war porn submitted by American soldiers. The site, eventually closed in 2006, was immensely popular, reporting 150,000 registered users, of whom 45,000 were American military personnel.[174] It became a showcase for horrifically violent images, including close-ups of Iraqi insurgents and civilians with their heads shattered or blown off, or with organs spilling from gaping wounds. A popular game on the website involved guessing which indecipherably mangled body part was being displayed.[175]

Another kind of trophy can be detected in the images of men in American military uniform raping Iraqi women that have been circulating on the web for some time now. There is some dispute over whether the photos are real or posed, but they have appeared on pornography websites advertising "Iraqi babes." Given that war and occupation often result in the rape and abuse of women, the concern over the veracity of the photos is perhaps not as chilling a question as what the photos symbolize and what life is like for women living under military occupation. A report published by the Iraqi National Association for Human Rights in 2005 found numerous cases of rape and assault of female Iraqi detainees by soldiers. These violations will not end, writes Haifa Zangana, so long as Iraq is occupied by forces enjoying "immunity from prosecution under Iraqi law and as long as the occupation authorities continue to treat Iraqi citizens with racist contempt in order to feel better about plundering the nation's wealth and depriving its people of their most fundamental rights under international law and human rights conventions."[176]

The violence and contempt denounced by Zangana is neither "exceptional nor hidden," argues sociologist Sherene Razack. The trophy videos that capture and endlessly replay this violence are not solely strategic; they are not produced, Razack states, "in order to intimidate and humiliate the enemy, as the American military claimed . . . but for the use of individual soldiers themselves, to be tacked up on the fridge door or sent home as souvenirs."[177] These souvenirs memorialize acts enabled by racism in the service of conquest; they document potent narratives of power relations. Tétreault argues that the Abu Ghraib photos insist upon American global dominance by punishing the inferior Oriental enemy: "With a few exceptions, the subjects of these photos are not corpses. They are living persons in the thrall of powerful and sadistic captors. We see them terrified, abject, forced to perform humiliating acts, and subjected to physical torture. Their images are not harmless war souvenirs . . . they are evidence. They document the crimes as well as the impunity with which they were committed."[178] Like another example of the pornography of violence, lynching photographs from the Southern U.S., the Abu Ghraib pictorial trophies clearly unfold a visual narrative of power.[179]

As with much sexual pornography, it is difficult to separate issues of power from the images we find in the pornography of war. The control of the scene, its costumes and lighting, its postures and props belong to the producer of the image, who stages and choreographs the scene that the lens will capture. Paradoxically, war trophies of this sort are both artificial and authentic: they stage only a certain part of the story for the camera, but they document a very real abuse, and in that documentation, they intensify its reality. James Harkin writes in *The Guardian* that, as with pornography, the producers of war porn "heighten their sense of reality by videoing themselves in the act, while its audience does the same by ogling the videos."[180]

Sontag argues that these photo-trophies are "less objects to be saved than messages to be disseminated."[181] What, then, is at the heart of these messages? What narrative do they repeatedly circulate? For Beaudrillard, the message is one of annihilation; through trophies like the Abu Ghraib photos, "the other will be exterminated symbolically. One sees that the goal of the war is not to kill or to win, but abolish the enemy."[182] This suggests how far our need to eradicate extends: we need not only to exterminate the enemy but to immortalize and endlessly re-witness the symbolic scenes of that extermination. We need to be able to create documents that testify to the enemy's otherness and abjection, and to that end we mount spectacles, as we mount trophies, of dominance and humiliation. These spectacles tell us not simply a triumphant story of our own superiority and prowess, but more chillingly, we rely on them to tell us a consolatory story of survival. After all, these war trophies tell us a narrative that echoes the big game hunter's: a story of contact with the hunter's savage beast and survival of its menace. However uncivilized the images in the photographic war trophy, they tell an old, old story of a civilizing mission; for Razack, the Abu Ghraib photos demonstrate what, in the name of survival, "must be done to savages."[183] In this sense, these acts are performed in all our names, in the name of the entire, threatened West. It is not only that we tacitly allow such acts to continue without calling for judgment that confirms, in Tétreault's words, "we are all torturers now,"[184] but that these acts of trophy-taking symbolically express our society's need to distance itself from and annihilate the unknown, alien, threatening other. That this need plays itself out so brutally on the bodies of our captives and so devastatingly in the psyches of our soldiers is one more reason to critically examine and resist such narratives of dominance and destruction.

Notes

1. Kenneth Burke. *Language as Symbolic Action: Essays on Life, Literature and Method*. Berkeley, CA: University of California Press, 1968: 3.

2. Hans Biedermann. *Dictionary of Symbolism*. New York City: Facts on File, 1992: viii.

3. Hans Biedermann. *Dictionary of Symbolism*.

4. Arnold Whittick. *Symbols, Signs and Their Meaning*. Newton, MA: Charles T. Branford Co., 1971: 4.

5. Cited in Arnold Whittick. *Symbols, Signs and Their Meaning*.

6. Arnold Whittick. *Symbols, Signs and Their Meaning*.

7. Hans Biedermann. Dictionary of Symbolism.

8. George Lakoff. "Metaphors of War." *In these Times*. October 29, 2001. See www.inthesetimes.com/issue/25/24/lakoff2524.html (June 28, 2007).

9. *Toronto Sun*, April 18, 2003.

10. *Grand Rapid Press* (Michigan), June 9, 2005.

11. *Daily News* (New York), July 8, 2005.

12. *London Daily Telegraph*, June 15, 2002.

13. *The Star-Ledger* (Newark, New Jersey), March 27, 2003.

14. *Daily News* (New York), July 20, 2005.

15. *China Daily*, December 15, 2003.

16. *Grand Rapid Press* (Michigan), October 31, 2005.

17. *The York Dispatch* (York, PA), March 11, 2003.

18. *Deseret Morning News* (Salt Lake City), May 29, 2004.

19. *Florida Times-Union* (Jacksonville, FL), December 18, 2003.

20. *Lancaster New Era* (Lancaster, PA), April 2, 2003.

21. *Weekend Australian*, September 9, 2006.

22. *The Kansas City Star*, June 23, 2004.

23. *The Sun* (London), September 23, 2005.

24. *The Nation* (Kenya), September 15, 2006.

25. *Agence France Presse*—English, October 15, 2004.

26. David Corn. "George Won't Be Reading This: the President Prefers Spin to News." *Los Angeles Weekly*. October 23, 2003. See www.laweekly.com/news/news/george-wont-be-reading-this/2295/ (June 28, 2007).

27. *New York Post*, July 3, 2004.

28. *Deutsche Presse-Agentur*, May 13, 2007.

29. *The Sun* (England), December 30, 2006.

30. *Western Daily Press*, November 17, 2004.

31. *Daily Post* (Liverpool), April 15, 2003.

32. *Sunday Mercury*, April 6, 2003.

33. *Australian*, August 6, 2003.

34. *The Toronto Star*, May 8, 2005.

35. *Pakistan Press*, October 24, 2004.

36. *New York Times*, October 11, 2002.

37. *Daily Star* (UK), January 16, 2007.

38. *Daily Star* (UK), July 16, 2005.

39. Sunday Express (UK), February 6, 2005.

40. *Pakistan Press*, October 24, 2004.

41. *The Herald* (Glasgow), September 4, 2004.

42. *The Times* (London), July 24, 2004.

43. *Daily Telegraph* (London), April 19, 2004.

44. *Daily Telegraph* (Sydney, Australia), July 14, 2005.

45. *The New Zealand Herald*, September 12, 2002.

46. ONASA *News Agency*, November 22, 2003.

47. *NY Daily News*, July 8, 2005.

48. Hans Biedermann. *Dictionary of Symbolism*.

49. *NY Post*, May 25, 2002.

50. *Daily News* (New York), May 9, 2007.

51. *St. Petersburg Times* (Florida), December 15, 2003.

52. *The Christchurch Press*, December 16, 2003.

53. *Irish News*, June 7, 2005.

54. *Yorkshire Evening Post*, November 8, 2004.

55. *The Australian*, December 18, 2003.

56. See news.bbc.co.uk/2/hi/programmes/newsnight/3045574.stm

57. E. W. H. Huntley. "United Kingdom: Desert Rats." *allstates-flag*. December 6, 2002. See www.allstates-flag.com/fotw/flags/gb percent5Edesrt.html

58. E. W. H. Huntley. "United Kingdom: Desert Rats."

59. Hans Biedermann. *Dictionary of Symbolism*.

60. C. Douglas Lummis. "The Terrorist as a New Human Type: You Are Charged With Being Evil. Defend Yourself!" Z. January 19, 2004. See www.zmag.org/content /showarticle .cfm?ItemID=4853 (June 28, 2007).

61. *The Herald* (Scotland) April 25, 2003.

62. *The Times* (London), January 31, 2006.

63. *Skegness News*, July 11, 2006.

64. *Bath Chronicle*, February 8, 2006.

65. Jose A Carillo. "English Plain and Simple." *Manila Times*. May 27, 2003. See www.manilatimes.net/national/2003/may/27/top_stories/20030527top13.html (June 28, 2007).

66. *New York Post*, January 24, 2003.

67. *New York Post*, February 14, 2003.

68. *New York Post*, February 18, 2003.

69. *New York Post*, April 23, 2004.

70. *New York Post*, May 23, 2006.

71. *Grand Rapid Press* (Michigan), March 15, 2003.

72. *Toronto Sun*, April 4, 2003.

73. *Sunday Express* (UK), April 13, 2003.

74. Arnold Whittick. *Symbols, Signs and Their Meaning.*

75. Beryl Rowland. *Animals with Human Faces.* Knoxville, TN: University of Tennessee Press.1973.

76. *New York Post*, December 2, 2001.

77. *Financial Express*, May 18, 2002.

78. *London Daily Telegraph*, June 15, 2002.

79. *London Sunday Times*, March 23, 2003.

80. *The Weekend*, Australian, April 5, 2003.

81. *The Daily Telegraph* (Sydney, Australia), April 16, 2003.

82. *Birmingham Post*, March 13, 2003.

83. *Calgary Sun*, July 17, 2005.

84. *Your Dictionary.* "Top Ten Word Lists of 2003." December 26, 2003. See www .yourdictionary.com/about/topten2003.html (June 28, 2007).

85. Libby Copeland. "Spider hole's web of meanings." *Washington Post.* December 18, 2003.

86. Libby Copeland. "Spider hole's web of meanings."

87. *Cox News Service*, December 30, 2003.

88. *The Post and Courier* (Charleston, SC), October 9, 2003.

89. *The Advertiser*, December 15, 2003.

90. *The Independent* (London), January 24, 2004.

91. *Houston Chronicle*, December 16, 2003.

92. *Boston Herald*, December 15, 2003.

93. Terril L. Shorb & Yvette A. Schnoeker-Shorb (eds). *Least Loved Beasts of the Really Wild West.* Prescott, AZ: Native West Press, 2003.

94. *The Oregonian* (Portland, Oregon), December 29, 1998.

95. *Sudbury Star*, May 12, 2004.

96. *St. Louis Post-Dispatch* (Missouri), November 8, 2005.

97. *Tampa Tribune* (Florida), August 28, 2002.

98. *St. Louis Post-Dispatch* (Missouri), November 13, 2004.

99. *The Herald* (Glasgow), May 7, 2004,

100. *The Australian*, May 2, 2003.

101. *Washington Post*, November 13, 2004.

102. B. Raman. "Use a Cockroach to Catch a Cockroach." *South Asia Analysis Group.* September 19, 2001. See www.saag.org/papers4/paper316.html (June 28, 2007).

103. *Toronto Star*, June 22, 2003.

104. *Sudbury Star*, May 12, 2004.

105. *Toronto Star*, November 26, 2006.

106. *Times* (London), November 11, 2006.

107. *BBC Monitoring International Reports*, January 4, 2004.

108. *Turkish Daily News*, November 21, 2003.

109. *News of the World* (England), August 13, 2006.

110. *Irish Times*, October 4, 2005.

111. *National Post*, July 23, 2003.

112. *National Post*, July 23, 2003.

113. *Daily Herald*, (Portland, Maine), September 16, 2001.

114. *Australian*, October 22, 2002.

115. *UPI*, January 20, 2005.

116. *U.S. News and World Report*, April 14, 2003.

117. *Providence Journal-Bulletin* (Rhode Island), April 16, 2003.

118. *Hamilton Spectator* (Ontario, Canada), July 16, 2004.

119. *Agence France Presse*—English, April 1, 2006.

120. *New York Times*, July 16, 2004.

121. *Press Association* (Central Command, Qatar), April 2, 2003.

122. *JihadWatch*. See www.jihadwatch.org/archives/016467.php

123. Hara M. Fard. "Islam, America's Cancer." *Dhimmi Wits*. May 17, 2007. See upyourcult.blogspot.com/ (June1, 2007).

124. germaninamerica. "bomb islam." *Jihadwatch*. December 9, 2006. See www .jihadwatch.org/archives/014346.php (June 28, 2007).

125. Florian. "Islam: The Cancer of the Earth." *florians-insensitivity-training*. February 7, 2007. See florians-insensitivity-training.blogspot.com/2007/02/islam-cancer -of-earth.html (June 28, 2007).

126. Rastaman. "Muslims Show Their Love Of Children." February 27, 2007. *Islamanzi*. See islamanazi.com (June 28, 2007).

127. Subsunk. "Untitled." *An Idiot's Blog*. May 9, 2007. See kbarrett.corse.net/idiot /index.php?title=feds_wonder_if_jihadis_nuke_us_who_do_we&more=1&c=1&tb=1 &pb=1 (June 28, 2007).

128. Sultan Knish. "Whatever You Do, Don't Fight Back." *Sultanknish*. February 28, 2007. See sultanknish.blogspot.com/index.html (June 28, 2007).

129. Ronin. "Blair, Pakistan PM to open conference on Islam." *Doctor Bulldog*. May 29, 2007. See doctorbulldog.wordpress.com (June 28, 2007).

130. Sleepycat. "Britain 'is now biggest security threat to US'." *JihadWatch*. August 26, 2006. See www.jihadwatch.org/archives/012914.php (June 28, 2007).

131. Latrell Washington. "Untitled." *Realm of the Sphinx*. June 2, 2007. See realm ofthesphinx.blogspot.com/ (June 28, 2007).

132. Patrick McGuinness. "Common Sense." *Freedoms Truth*. March 27, 2007. See freedomstruth.blogspot.com/index.html (June 28, 2007).

133. Darrin Hodges. "Muslim vermin seething." *Voice of the Shire*. May 28, 2007. See voiceoftheshire.blogspot.com/ (June 28, 2007).

134. Conan. "Untitled." *Scotsman*. June 4, 2007. See www.scotsman.com/?id=869642007 (June 28, 2007).

135. Cfinstr. "End Islam." *Jihad Chat*. February 6, 2007. See www.jihadchat.com/index.php?showtopic=521&pid=2174&mode=threaded&start=—30k—(June 28, 2007).

136. Jester. "Untitled." My Pet Jawa. October 30, 2005. See mypetjawa.mu.nu/archives/129768.php (June 28, 2007).

137. Supercaffinated. "Untitled." *Storage Review*. July 7, 2005. See forums.storagereview.net/index.php?showtopic=20229 (June 28, 2007).

138. Forresloon. "London Terrorist Bombings." *This is North Scotland Bulletin*. July 10, 2005. See www.nepforums.co.uk/thisisnorthscotland/showflat.php?Cat=&Number=17594&page =&view=&sb=5&o=&fpart=all&vc=1 (June 28, 2007).

139. *The Liberty Papers*. May 18. 2007. See www.thelibertypapers.org/2007/05/18/explaining-the-reaction-to-ron-paul/ (June 28, 2007).

140. Andrew Buncombe and Justin Huggler. "*Iraq: Abuse Crisis: Abu Ghraib: inmates raped, ridden like animals.*" *Independent* (London), May 22, 2004.

141. Scott Higham and Joe Stephens. "New Details of Prison Abuse Emerge: Abu Ghraib Detainees' Statements Describe Sexual Humiliation and Savage Beatings." *Washington Post*. May 21, 2004.

142. *Amnesty International*. "Human dignity denied Torture and accountability in the 'war on terror.'" *Amnesty International*. October 27, 2004. See web.amnesty.org/library/Index/ENGAMR511452004 (June 29, 2007).

143. *Democracy Now*. "Report: U.S. Treated Elderly Woman Like a Donkey." *Democracy Now*. May 6th, 2004. See www.democracynow.org/article.pl?sid=04/05/06/149239

144. "Detention of Enemy Combatants Act." 109th CONGRESS 1st Session H. R. 1076. March 3, 2005.

145. Leonard Doyle. "'A dead Iraqi is just another dead Iraqi.' You know, so what?" *The Independent*. July 12, 2007.

146. "Detention of Enemy Combatants Act."

147. *Cageprisoners*. "Profile: Mamdouh Habib." *Cageprisoners*. January 29, 2005. See www.cageprisoners.com/articles.php?id=5011

148. *Amnesty International*. "Human dignity denied torture and accountability in the 'war on terror.'" op. cit.

149. Nigel Morris. "War on Terror: Guantánamo: I Was Tied up like a Beast and Beaten.'" *The Independent* (London). August 4, 2004.

150. Robert Verkaik. "Joy and Despair: a Tale of Two Fathers." *The Independent* (London). March 10, 2004.

151. Vikram Dodd and Tania Branigan. "US Abuse Could Be War Crime." *Guardian*. August 5, 2004.

152. Dahlia Lithwick. "The Prisoners' Dilemma." *Slate*. April 20, 2004. See www.slate.com/id/2099223/

153. Alex Danchev. "Like a Dog!" Humiliation and Shame in the War on Terror." *Alternatives: Global, Local, Political*. Volume 31, Issue 3, July 2006: 259–83.

154. Alex Danchev. "Like a Dog!"

155. Alex Danchev. "Like a Dog!"

156. Alex Danchev. "Like a Dog!"

157. Alex Danchev. "Like a Dog!"

158. Bob Wing. "The Color of Abu Ghraib." *War Times*. May 17, 2004. See www
.why-war.com/news/read.php?id=4270

159. Mary Ann Tétreault. 'The Sexual Politics of Abu Ghraib: Hegemony, Spectacle, and the Global War on Terror." *NWSA Journal* 18.3, 2006: 33–50. See muse
.jhu.edu/journals/nwsa _journal/v018/18.3tetreault.html

160. Tom Engelhardt. "War Porn." Z. June 14, 2006. See www.zmag.org/content
/showarticle.cfm?ItemID=10429

161. Matt Smith. "Soldiers put Iraq 'war trophies' on eBay." *CNN*. March 18,
2004. See www.cnn.com/2004/US/03/18/iraq.war.booty/

162. DeWayne Wickham. "Iraq war 'souvenir' stories reawaken guilt." *USA Today*. April 28, 2004. See www.usatoday.com/news/opinion/columnist/wickham/2003
-04-28-wickham_x.htm

163. Dahr Jamail. "Trophy Hunting in Iraq." *AntiWar*. December 5, 2004. See www
.antiwar.com/jamail/?articleid=4112

164. Eric Schmitt and Carolyn Marshall. "Before and After Abu Ghraib, a U.S.
Unit Abused Detainees." *New York Times*. March 19, 2006.

165. *Marine Corps News Service*. "War Trophies." *About.com*. August 20, 2003.
See usmilitary.about.com/cs/wars/a/wartrophies.htm

166. Chanan Suarez-Diaz. "Citizens' Hearing Panel Declares Iraq War Illegal."
wartribunal.org. February 2, 2007. See www.wartribunal.org/

167. Kurt Nimmo. "Torture Party: Limbaugh and the Babes of Abu Ghraib."
CounterPunch. May 8–9, 2004. See www.counterpunch.org/nimmo05082004.html

168. Chris Shaw. "Don't look now: U.S. soldiers' 'trophy videos' of Iraq make uncomfortable viewing for the American government next to TV networks' coverage."
Guardian. August 4, 2006.

169. Chris Shaw. "Don't look now."

170. Cited in Tom Engelhardt. "War Porn."

171. Jean Baudrillard. "War Porn." *International Journal of Baudrillard Studies*. Volume 2, Number 1, January 2005.

172. Jean Baudrillard. "War Porn."

173. Mary Ann Tétreault. 'The Sexual Politics of Abu Ghraib."

174. George Zornick. "The Porn of War." *The Nation*. September 22, 2005. See
www .thenation.com/docprint.mhtml?i=20051010&s=the_porn_of_war>.

175. Ibid.

176. Haifa Zangana. "All Iraq Is Abu Ghraib." *Guardian*. July 5, 2006.

177. Sherene Razack. "When Is Prisoner Abuse Racial Violence." Z. May 24,
2004. See www.zmag.org/content/showarticle.cfm?ItemID=5594

178. Mary Ann Tétreault. 'The Sexual Politics of Abu Ghraib."

179. Mary Ann Tétreault. 'The Sexual Politics of Abu Ghraib."

180. Haifa Zangana. "All Iraq Is Abu Ghraib." *Guardian*. July 5, 2006.

181. Cited in Tom Engelhardt. "War Porn."
182. Jean Baudrillard. "War Porn."
183. Sherene Razack."When Is Prisoner Abuse Racial Violence."
184. Mary Ann Tétreault. "The Sexual Politics of Abu Ghraib."

CHAPTER FIVE

Infestation and Eradication: Exterminationist Rhetoric in Political Cartoons

> Good cartoons . . . hit you primitively and emotionally. . . . A cartoon cannot say, "on the other hand" and it cannot defend itself. It is a frontal assault, a slam dunk, a cluster bomb.[1]
>
> —Doug Marlette

Popular Culture and the War on Terror

Dehumanizing metaphors do not only circulate through explicitly political texts such as government speeches and press releases or through media reporting. Just as animal metaphors tend to become more extreme when they enter less regulated spheres such as internet blog sites, so negative stereotyping appears in some of its most vicious forms in popular culture. It's important to examine these images both because they are so pervasive and because, by virtue of the modes through which they reach us, they are often absorbed without any of the filtering apparatus of critical thought that we might employ when faced with texts that are more obviously political in nature. Because these images are apparently transmitted so innocently through the vehicles of pop culture, they come to seem natural, as if they are simply reflecting the world. Far from merely showing reality, however, they actively create it through fostering a specific understanding of the world. Because they come to us through movies, television, and other forms of popular entertainment, it's easy to perceive these images as being less motivated, less interested, and less ideological than they might seem if they came to us from the mouths of pundits or politicians.

Yet the distance between the worlds of politics and pop culture is often not nearly as great as we might think. Jack Valenti, president of the Motion Picture Association of America, acknowledged this when he said "Washington and Hollywood spring from the same DNA."[2] This close genetic relationship can be most clearly detected when we consider some of the many Hollywood films that were produced in active cooperation of the U.S. Department of Defense (DoD).[3] Films such as *Death Before Dishonor*, *Black Hawk Down*, *Executive Decision*, *Patriot Games*, *Navy Seals*, *Rules of Engagement*, *Iron Eagle* and *True Lies*, all produced in partnership with the DoD and showing American armed forces personnel killing Arabs and Muslims on a huge scale, solidify Washington's connection with Hollywood. While these connections often go unrecognized and unexamined, Jack Shaheen, author of the most comprehensive analysis of Arab representations in film and television, argues that "Politics and Hollywood images are linked. They reinforce one another. Policy enforces mythical images; mythical images help enforce policy."[4] The power of film is such that "in spite of the reality, in spite of the material that we know to be true, we still embrace the mythology."[5] This mythology is one we originally inherited from European Orientalists who conjured images of the Arab as the perpetual Other; now it makes up "part of our psyches,"[6] and we regularly draw upon it in setting policies and establishing courses of action. For example, America's entrance into war with Iraq was made much easier, asserts Shaheen, because of the accumulation of images vilifying Arabs established over more than a century by huge numbers of movies (nearly one quarter, Shaheen documents, of all movies produced by Hollywood) and popular television shows like Fox's *24* or Showtime's *Sleeper Cell*.

Video games are another source of violently negative imagery. One notable example is *Left Behind: Eternal Forces*, in which players win by converting or killing non-Christians. Making its advent just in time for Christmas 2006, the game is based on a series of best-selling Christian novels, and pits players against the Anti-Christ, whose minions includes characters with Muslim-sounding names. Rev. Tim Simpson, a Presbyterian minister from Jacksonville, Florida, and president of the Christian Alliance for Progress, expressed his shock in an interview with the *San Francisco Chronicle*: "So, under the Christmas tree this year for little Johnny is this allegedly Christian video game teaching Johnny to hate and kill?"[7] Other games rewarding players for hunting down Arabs and Muslims include Microsoft's *Counter-Strike*, released in 2002 by the U.S. Army to help bolster its recruitment efforts; the game now has more than 7.5 million users.[8] Less mainstream are games produced by white supremacist groups allowing players to assume the first-person-shooter position as they hunt visible minorities in games such as *Ethnic Cleansing: The Game* in which players, dressed as Skinheads or in KKK robes, roam the streets and subways murdering "predatory sub-humans" and thereby "saving" the white world.[9]

Some of the strongest images and highest levels of violence arise from hybrid forms of pop culture. Movies based on first-person-shooter games such as *Alone in the Dark* (2005) and *House of the Dead* (2003) blend the genres of action movie and video game, escalating the death count far beyond that usually found in Hollywood action thrillers. While often in these films the enemy is literally unhuman, such as zombies or vampires, one movie hybrid is worth examination for its radical dehumanization of a human, highly racialized enemy. In Zack Snyder's *300* (2007), a film based on Frank Miller's 1998 comic book of the same name, we find a powerful embodiment of the "clash of civilizations" paradigm that pits heroic, fair-skinned Spartans against dark-skinned, marauding Persians, their indiscriminate and undifferentiated nature symbolized by the identical masks worn by their advancing hordes. Computer graphics allow individual images to be multiplied and expanded in ways that were previously impossible; however, *300* tellingly uses this technology not to individuate the dark-skinned masses, but to endlessly re-duplicate them as interchangeable; they are as indistinguishable in their long, kinky black hair and crazed, charcoal-rimmed eyes as they are in their identical masks.

In his indictment of *300*, New York artist John Powers expresses outrage over the "septic timing" of the film's release, "a brand of propaganda [he] had imagined was a thing of the past. *300* would make Leni Riefenstahl blush."[10] A film propagandistic in both message and timing, Powers argues *that 300* promotes a vision glorifying total war against an inhuman enemy, and it does so at a social moment when critical questions about the Iraq war are arising. The film answers such questions with a ringing endorsement of aggressive militancy, telling its audience unambiguously to "hate and destroy its inhuman enemy."[11] In a film in which good and evil are separated by race, Powers says, fear is stoked by racist imagery, and the annihilation of the "undifferentiated dark-skinned horde" is lavishly celebrated. The consistency of this message makes it the perfect cure for "a fearful America," and panders to young men and women of fighting age who can be reassured by and enlisted into this vision of triumphant militancy destroying the barbaric threat to civilization. In this message we find a "pornographic vision of power and perfection" that demonstrates "only contempt" for the imperfect Other, and justifies the Other's extermination.[12]

Through these kinds of representations, the transmission of the hostile image of the Middle Eastern male as rabid, barbaric, and innately violent has become so pervasive that, paradoxically, it has become invisible. Widely re-broadcast movies like *True Lies* reinforce this image and are televised so often that their catalogue of images have now become "part of our visual heritage."[13] We are so saturated in these images from childhood on that we no longer really see them; we certainly don't object to them the way we would if such a coherent body of negative stereotypes were still being created of Blacks, Jews, or Hispanics.

But, we may say in response, the images being so repeatedly transmitted though popular culture aren't unfair or accidental; they do reflect the reality that we see so often on the nightly news, in which screaming, angry Arabs appear looking just like the ones we see over and over on TV and movie screens. And yet this commonsense equation, say critics like Shaheen, Said, and Laurence Michalak[14], overlooks some important points. The first is the selectivity of the images emerging from news broadcasting; by definition, the news documents unusual and hence newsworthy events, events with enough inherent drama to catch and hold an audience. The second is the suppression of diversity in media and broadcasting; only very consistent depictions tend to be shown. We often see scenes of crowds of Muslims prostrated in prayer at a Mosque, for example, an image which obscures the fact that there are over 20 million Arab Christians in the Middle East living alongside Muslims, and that much of Arabic society is actually quite secular.[15] Third, there is a tendency to generalize from relatively small groups of people to all others who share the same race or ethnicity. Racism and Islamophobia drive us to represent the actions of the nineteen 9/11 terrorist as a reflecting the desires and actions of the 1.3 billion people who make up the Arab world, effortlessly conflating individuals with their entire race or religion. We don't do this with those who look more like us: for example, we don't claim that the actions of Ku Klux Klan members who are Christian represent all of Christianity.[16] When Timothy McVeigh bombed the Oklahoma City federal building his race, religion, and ethnicity were not highlighted by news reports of the bombing or portrayed as central to his motivations. In fact, the media and government initially attributed the bombing to Middle Eastern terrorists. CBC's Connie Chung reported that a U.S. government source "told CBS news that [the bombing] has Middle East terrorism written all over it."[17] The Department of Defense offered to provide local investigators with Arabic speakers to help in the investigation."[18] Over two hundred incidents of bias against the Muslim community followed in the next few days, including attacks on private homes and mosques.[19] The hypocrisy of such a response was clear to members of the American Islamic community. Enver Masud wrote in an on-line column that media reports rarely identify the religion of leading figures or organization in any news except when that leader is Muslim. "But when McVeigh was caught," writes Masud, "and alleged to be the bomber, there was no mention of Christianity. In the case of Muslims, guilt by association casts blame on the billion or so Muslims worldwide. In the case of Christians, the blame was narrowed, and rightly so, to McVeigh and his accomplices."[20] Such assumptions about guilt and causality intersect with and arise from the derogatory images that regularly re-circulate through our popular culture, reaching massive audiences, and continually inducting new generations into the frames of these old, enduring characterizations.

Carl Boggs and Tom Pollard have provocatively argued in *The Hollywood War Machine* that this is part of a larger, more complicated problem informing changing American political attitudes. They observe that U.S. foreign policy has been moving in the direction of an ever-broadening imperial vision of global domination, and that this vision is being supported and furthered by the messages of popular media. Quoting neo-conservative writer Robert Kaplan's assertion that America's "prize" for winning the Cold War is that "*we and nobody else will write the terms for international society,*" they comment that it "would be difficult to find a bolder contemporary reaffirmation of Manifest Destiny."[21] For Boggs and Pollard, one of the key mechanisms for endorsing this brand of American policy is found in popular culture, which acts as a kind of legitimation-machine for American dominance or hegemony. All power structures require cultural supports as well as ideological and political supports, they suggest, and the workings of popular culture tend to serve the "imperatives of empire" by making a "bloated war economy," increasing numbers of armed interventions in other countries, and increased American expansionism seem natural, routine, inevitable, and desirable.[22] Increased government, military, and corporate powers, argue Boggs and Pollard, bring with them things like more refined weapons and increased powers of surveillance, but while these things may be indispensable to the imperial project, the one thing they cannot furnish by themselves is the necessary legitimation, that is, the ability to endorse and justify this project in the public mind. That task, they suggest, is "the function of media culture."[23] In film, television, video games, political cartoons, comics and music we find both the opportunity to creatively re-examine old, familiar wartime tropes, and powerful ways to reinvest ourselves in these tropes.

The power of the image of the Arab in popular culture lies in its consistency and reiteration. The repetition of negative stereotypes over a century of Hollywood film constitutes a systematic cultural education of viewers; the narrowness and repetitiveness of Hollywood images add up, Shaheen argues, to a "systemic, pervasive, and unapologetic degradation of a people."[24] From the release of *Imar the Servitor* in 1914 to 2000's *Gladiator*, distorted stereo-types create a "synergy of images" equating "Arabs from Syria to the Sudan with quintessential evil."[25] Collectively, these stereotypes have changed sur-prisingly little over time; it is their sheer durability across popular culture that has given them such a noteworthy cumulative force. The "Screen Arab" is, says Shaheen, exactly "what he has always been"—different, threatening, the cultural Other.[26] In 1937, the American heroine of Hollywood's *The Sheik Steps Out* says that Arabs "all look alike to me," a sentiment echoed in 1968's *Commando*, in which the hero admits "All Arabs look alike to me" and again in 1986's *Hostage*, in which the U.S. ambassador concedes "I can't tell one [Arab] from another . . . they all look the same to me."[27] In Holly-wood movies, says Shaheen wryly, they certainly do. Although these repre-sentations are fictional, they require our attention because of the way Holly-wood has become, as William Greider argues, "the authoritarian creator of commonly shared attitudes."[28] The persistence of defamatory stereotypes means that such representations can be sustained across generations. As fu-ture directors grow up immersed in these stereotypes, they are unconsciously recycled into the productions of the next generation. Boggs and Pollack agree that the repetition of such images solidifies their power: "The repeti-tive fantasies, illusions, myths, images, and story lines of Hollywood movies can be expected to influence mass audiences in predictable ways."[29] These tactics enlist us into prescribed discourses of a narrowly defined patriotism in subtle, effective, often unconscious ways.

Pop Culture and Dissent

While some forms of pop culture, such as folk music, documentary, or alter-native film have associations with traditions of dissent and provocation, in times of war tremendous pressures can be brought to bear to limit, control, or marginalize that dissent. The possibilities for different kinds of patriotism are often narrowed or eliminated. While there may be more than one way to be a good citizen, only certain versions of citizenship are endorsed. In wartime, these representations tend to be dichotomized as simple, binary oppositions: one is either *Alladin*'s Jafar or Rambo, terrorist or patriot, weasel or hawk. This binarism is exemplified in the "Deck of Weasels" produced by NewsMax.com, a deck of playing cards "depicting the 59 worst leaders and celebrities who opposed America and were key members of the 'The United Nations of Weasels.'"[30] The deck is based on the popular "Deck of Death" playing cards given by the Pentagon to U.S. soldiers, featuring the faces of "Iraqi's Most Wanted" enemies; it shows the faces of critics or questioners of the war, labeled "enemies of America," wearing "the beret of Saddam Hussein's Republican Guard"—now dubbed "Saddam's Weasel Brigade."[31] The conservative website that sells the cards promises that we'll "laugh out loud looking at the faces of the world's greatest weasels" and that the deck is both "relevant and useful."[32]

The "Deck of Weasels" is particularly relevant and useful in illustrating how even those exercising democratic rights of expression can be attacked with dehumanizing animal metaphors if they are seen as too closely associated with the enemy Other. It's as if our humanity is such a fragile or contested thing that it must constantly be protected by distancing itself from those we brand as other. If we believed our own humanity to be unassailable, why would we be so quick to diminish that of the people who pose uncomfortable questions about the wisdom or morality of our actions? The "Deck of Weasels" shows how readily our contempt for the enemy Other can be broadened and generalized, narrowing ever further those we allow into our human camp.

Contempt joins with commerce in the selling of pop culture artifacts. In America, argues Heather Havrilesky, we both attack and grieve "by buying stuff"; we fuel our search for "revenge and healing through retail."[33] Commodified contempt has a durable shelf life: in the first Gulf War anti-Arab merchandise proliferated, including bumper stickers, T-shirts, pins and posters. A popular poster depicted a Bedouin on a camel in the cross-hairs of a rifle, atop the slogan "I'd fly 10,000 miles to smoke a camel."[34] Currently available is Osama toilet paper ("Help wipe out terrorism!"), Osama "Pin" Laden voodoo dolls, and Osama bin Laden golf balls.[35] Websites offer a range of T-shirts and giftware showing all-American boy Calvin, from the comic strip *Calvin and Hobbes*, peeing on the word "terrorists," on a map of Iraq and on the Islamic insignia of the star and crescent.[36]

One of the most popular and chilling lines of merchandise plays on the idea of nuclear annihilation, turning it into a visual joke suitable for T-shirts, housewares, and postcards. The joke celebrates the possibility of replacing an entire nation of human beings with an annihilated landscape. The central image is a map of Iraq or Afghanistan, its recognizable outline all that remains; the nation itself has been utterly excised. One such image shows a parking grid marked on the site of where Afghanistan used to be, with the tag line "Future site of the 'world's largest parking lot.'" Another shows a picture of a huge mushroom cloud with the caption "CNN live over Afghanistan." Variants show depictions of "Lake Afghanistan" and "Lake Iraq,"[37] with the country's outline on the map blanked out with ominous black. Another Lake Iraq cartoon features the tag line "Bush's final solution." For those who didn't get the joke, a blogger spelled out the message: "I saw a bumper sticker a while back that said "Say Yes to Lake Afghanistan." I'll say yes to Lake Afghanistan and Lake Iraq. Just drop a couple of those small nuclear bombs they tested earlier this week and the war is over. No need to get American troops killed."[38] Apparel and household products featuring Lake Iraq emblazoned on them are readily available for sale online: shirts come in six styles from raglan-sleeves to hooded sweatshirts; there are two styles of coffee mugs plus a beer stein; also available are kitchen aprons, baseball caps, magnets, stickers, postcards and journals ranging in price from $3 to $30.[39]

Political Cartoons and the War on Terror

Editorial cartoons offer one of the most interesting examples of the way negative images permeate our consciousness. These cartoons are intriguingly situated at the intersection of popular and political culture, speaking irrevocably of both, and comprising a hybrid of the two. Timely and topical, they are meant to elaborate and comment upon current events, and usually articulate a specific political message from an ideological perspective. At the same time, they are allied to other graphic forms, like newspaper comics or "funny pages," and they draw upon some of the same visual codes and shorthand techniques. Like satire and stand-up comedy, they often bring together the strange bedfellows of humor and outrage. Like newspaper headlines, they also reach a wider audience than full-text news articles do; they are the most widely read feature of the editorial section.[40]

Lucy Shelton Caswell observes that editorial cartoons have a complex function; they both reflect and mould the opinions of their readers. While good cartoonists may be "driven by a sense of moral duty" to support what they believe to be right or oppose what they believe to be wrong, they must also not irrevocably alienate newspaper management or readers.[41] In this way, although North American journalistic tradition treats editorial cartoons not as mere illustrations but as persuasive communications with the rhetorical force of editorials or op-ed columns, they are also the product of the "seemingly incongruous partnership of capitalism and freedom of expression."[42] Editorial cartoons are, therefore, complex in their workings and effects. Michael DeSousa and Martin J. Medhunt suggest that the cartoon has a tri-partite role as a "culture-creating, culture-maintaining, culture-identifying artifact."[43] While the cartoonist traditionally has a certain license to forcefully articulate his or her political views, views which, as Virginia Bouvier observes, "reflect and contribute to" the formation of political attitudes,[44] the effectiveness of the cartoon is limited by readers' knowledge of the issues and contexts. This means that the cartoonist "must gauge the community's familiarity with the topic of the day and choose images to express her or his opinion succinctly and appropriately."[45] The economy of the cartoon form ensures that the artist has a limited space in which to make his or her point; while, as several scholars have noted, this intensifies the immediate impact of the cartoon,[46] it also limits the cartoonists' control of the message, since it is the reader who must decode the cartoon's visual metaphors within an economical, sometimes cryptic, frame. Elizabeth El Refaie points out that, for both readers and scholars of cartoons, their "metaphors must always be studied within their socio-political context."[47] While a cartoon's visual metaphors are perhaps its most powerful strategies,[48] they are also its most volatile. Although early theorists of cognitive metaphor like Lakoff and Johnston postulated that metaphors are influenced by our physical experience as infants and are therefore universal to all humans, others building on their work have since argued for a greater specificity of interpretation. Metaphor's connection to thought, suggest recent scholars, cannot be considered as entirely universal but must be examined within specific socio-political contexts, which means that readers are likely to bring "their own experiences and assumptions" to the process of interpreting visual metaphors."[49] This individuality of interpretation, however, must be balanced with the recognition that there are dominant tropes which are broadly shared across a given community. While an idiosyncratic interpretation of an image may still exist, or be facilitated by a cartoonist (such as the snake being represented as benign, as it might be for botanists or owners of pet reptiles), shared, long-standing, communal associations of the snake as something evil, deceptive and deadly will inevitably dominate any reading of the metaphor.

Perhaps it is the complexities of these broader questions of interpretation, added to the complexities concerning the balance of responsibility with traditions of provocation in editorializing, that have led to one of the most heated public debates to emerge during the war on terror.

Cartoons and Crisis

In 2005, a controversy costing the lives of at least fifty people[50] occurred when the Danish newspaper *Jyllands-Posten* published "The Face of Mohammed," twelve cartoons representing Allah and his prophet Muhammed, along with an explanatory text from the newspaper's culture editor. The text stated that special consideration for Muslims' religious feelings is incompatible with contemporary democracy: in which anyone should "be ready to put up with insults, mockery and ridicule."[51] These cartoons offended against the Islamic tradition explicitly prohibiting depictions of Allah or Muhammad;

one drew Mohammed as a saber-wielding terrorist accompanied by women in burqas, another showed him with a lit bomb bearing the Islamic creed in his turban.

Reaction from Danish Muslim organizations was immediate. Many Muslim organizations and Imams expressed outrage and demanded an apology, while *Jyllands-Posten* defended its right to freedom of speech. An organization of ambassadors from Muslim countries attempted to meet with Danish Prime Minister Anders Fogh Rasmussen but was refused.[52] The prime minister, head of a center-Right minority coalition dependent for its survival on support from an anti-foreigner party, called the cartoons a "necessary provocation."[53] Protests exploded across the Middle East and Asia as the cartoons were reprinted around the world. In Lebanon, a demonstrator was killed after jumping from a third-floor window of the Danish embassy after it was set on fire. Hundreds of Muslims burned Danish flags, and strikes were called from Gaza to Indonesia to Nigeria. When Italian Reforms Minister Roberto Calderoli wore a T-shirt displaying one of the controversial cartoons on state TV, protests erupted in the streets.[54] Protesters organized boycotts of Danish products that may have reduced exports by 15.5 percent, costing about 134 million euros or 180 million U.S. dollars.[55] European countries evacuated the staffs of embassies and non-governmental organizations while Muslim countries withdrew ambassadors. In Turkey, an Italian priest was gunned down by a high school student who was enraged by the cartoons. According to *The Independent*, 150 people were killed in five days of violence between Nigerian Christians and Muslims, sparked by protests over the Danish cartoons.[56]

Jyllands-Posten culture editor Flemming Rose apologized for the offense caused by the cartoons, but not for his decision to publish them.[57] The cartoonist who drew the "bomb in turban" picture of Mohammed insisted that the popular Muslim interpretation of the cartoon is incorrect; he claimed that

> The general impression among Muslims is that it is about Islam as a whole. It is not. It is about certain fundamentalist aspects that of course are not shared by everyone. But the fuel for the terrorists' acts stem from interpretations of Islam . . . if part of a religion develops in a totalitarian and aggressive direction, then I think you have to protest. We did so under the other 'isms.[58]

The cartoon incident became the centerpiece of a debate on censorship and freedom of speech. Muslim scholars situate the cartoon controversy within the current climate of ethnic and religious tension in Europe, underlying such events as the murder of film director Theo van Gogh and the 2005 Paris riots. Cartoonist Khalil Bendib states,

It is generally accepted, as taught in Journalism 101, that the concept of freedom of expression in a democratic society must always be balanced by the no-less-important notion of social responsibility. Even in the name of free speech, yelling "fire" in a crowded theater is considered reprehensible, as should be yelling contempt in a crowded mosque.[59]

The central question articulated by scholar Reza Aslan concerns the usefulness of publishing the cartoons and the justification of free speech if the image is deliberately meant to be provocative:

> In the minds of many Muslims in Europe, the cartoons were intentionally inflammatory, published to further humiliate an ethnic and religious minority that has been socially and economically repressed for decades. Indeed, it seems as though the cartoons were deliberately meant to provoke precisely the reaction they did.[60]

Aslan goes on to point out that while the press is free to satirize, some of the *Jyllands-Posten* cartoons deliberately advance noxious stereotypes of Muslims as terrorists. Freedom must be balanced with civic responsibility, especially when extremists on both sides employ dangerous rhetoric based on the "clash of civilizations" paradigm. Many governments in the Middle East, observes Aslan, are eager to demonstrate the hostility of the West to the East in order to procure support from their own people. Unfortunately, the violent protests surrounding the cartoons risk confirming these dichotomies and offering more fodder to those who wish Muslims to be seen as incompatible with "European values and culture."[61] Examining the marginalization experienced by European Muslim communities, which feeds the destructive behavior and isolationism that in turn reinforces European attitudes about Islam, Aslan indicts European xenophobia as the starting point of this dangerous cycle:

> And that is why as a Muslim American I am enraged by the publication of these cartoons. Not because they offend my prophet or my religion, but because they fly in the face of the tireless efforts of so many civic and religious leaders both Muslim and non-Muslim to promote unity and assimilation rather than hatred and discord; because they play into the hands of those who preach extremism; because they are fodder for the clash-of-civilizations mentality that pits East against West. For all of that I blame *Jyllands-Posten*. We in the West want Muslim leaders to condemn the racial and religious prejudices that are so widespread in the Muslim world.[62]

Bendib points out that while violent Muslim reaction to the cartoons works to reconfirm crude stereotypes, the xenophobic European press adds fuel to the fire. The occupations of Afghanistan, Iraq, and Palestine, coupled with the imagery found in the cartoons confirms both Muslim fears that the West is contemptuous of their beliefs and their suspicion that denigration and humiliation are still standard features of Western imperialism. Bendib accuses Western media and governments of having double standards when it comes to offending Christian and Jewish versus Islamic sensibilities:

> Take, for example, the impressive strides made in Europe to protect against anti-Semitism, to the point that it is now against the law in some European countries to publish or publicly express any denial or downplay the horrors of the holocaust. Why should the same high standards of sensitivity and respect not apply to Muslims, who are at least equally represented as Jews in Europe? When you study the offensive Danish cartoons, it's almost as if old Third Reich-era anti-Semitic cartoons have been simply dusted off and recycled, using a Muslim name instead of Jewish ones.[63]

As'ad Abu Khalil maintains that the Danish cartoons are primarily offensive in their linking of Islam to terrorism. He does not believe that the cartoonists were ignorant of what they were doing.[64] Tariq Ali similarly claims that the *Jyllands-Posten* cartoons were meant to provoke rather than engage in quality debate, and points to the newspaper's earlier decision in 2003 not to print a cartoon caricature of Jesus.[65] Ali calls the cartoon depicting Mohammed with a bomb in his turban a "crude racist stereotype. The implication is that every Muslim is a potential terrorist. This is the sort of nonsense that leads to Islamophobia."[66] These kinds of "crude racist stereotypes" find a familiar expression in the animal metaphors that are frequent features of editorial cartoons.

Just as there is a persuasive body of work analyzing the dangerous effects of the dehumanizing imagery employed in wars in the first half of the twentieth century, scholarly analysis demonstrates that these images have been frequently mobilized in the Gulf conflicts. In 1996, Artz and Pollack examined how Saddam Hussein was depicted in political cartoons in the period leading up to the 1991 Gulf War. Grouping the cartoons into two clear categories, Hussein as a danger and Hussein as marginalized and barbaric, they argued that "the laughter, sarcasm and anger directed at Hussein through these cartoons "helped mobilize an American public to tolerate the killing of over 100,000 people in Iraq" and that, in conjunction with the media's "video game" portrayal of the war, these "images helped dehumanize the enemy."[67] In 1998, J. L. Conners argued that portrayals of Hussein as dehumanized, criminal, or aggressor reflected and furthered "Bush administration rhetoric labeling him as a threat that the United States needed to control."[68]

These images intensified in the aftermath of 9/11. Examining editorial cartoons between September 11, 2001, and October 8, 2001 (shortly before the invasion of Afghanistan), William Hart and Fran Hassencahl found that 91 percent used Keen's categories of dehumanization to portray the enemy as animal and as aggressor. Echoing Murray Edelman's caution that metaphors may dangerously over-simplify complicated issues, Hart and Hassencahl argue that in order to better "understand the motives and future actions of Osama bin Laden and the al Qaeda, we may find value in not accepting too quickly over-simplifying metaphor."[69]

Cartoons and Animal Metaphors

The extent of our symbolic coding is evident in oppositional pairings such as the eagle and the vulture. Each of these birds is so closely identified with their respective qualities of nobility, fierceness, and protectiveness on the one hand and with rapacity, sinister appetite, and sly, scavenging greed on the other that it is hard to recall that these characteristics are not natural but assigned. An eagle looks after its young no more assiduously than a vulture does, while a vulture is no more greedy in tearing at its food than an eagle is. While both birds act naturally, their behavior is interpreted culturally. The eagle becomes so much a symbol of qualities like courage and integrity that, when the U.S. is pictured as an eagle in a political cartoon, it is hard to divorce the symbol from its associations, even if the cartoon is intended to be critical of some aspect of American policy or activity. As Stanley Fish points out, while we may interpret certain aspects of a text individually, the scope of that interpretation always occurs within an "interpretive community" that establishes the parameters for interpretation. This explains why, within a community made up of many individual readers, certain interpretations will dominate.[70] Depending on the interpretive community an individual reader belongs to, then, the understanding of a political cartoon might vary greatly: a cartoon questioning some aspect of the war might be read as supporting it, or vice versa. Almost inevitably, within the American interpretive community the eagle will connote strong, positive qualities, and these qualities will structurally reinforce their perceived opposites when the enemy is pictured as an eagle's symbolic inferior. There is a powerful and immediate emotional impact created by such juxtapositions, as we see in a cartoon by Jeff Parker showing a proud eagle, clad in a stars-and-stripes breast plate, swiftly descending, with powerful wings outspread, towards the shifty, hunched vulture labeled "Terrorism."[71] The complications of interpretation can be seen in another cartoon by Steve Breen and from the *San Diego Union Tribune*,[72] which shows a large, imposing-looking eagle seated upon a stool; the stool's relative size reinforces the bird's impressiveness largeness. With furrowed brow and intent expression, the eagle sharpens its talons with a giant file; motion-lines drawn around the filed talons visually confirm the deadly sharpness of their glinting points. Isolated from surrounding text or clues as to the cartoonist's own political views, this image could be interpreted as endorsing or criticizing American use of deadly force; the potent symbolic qualities metaphorically associated with the eagle, however, make a critical reading of the cartoon far less likely to dominate.

A similar question of iconography and interpretation circulates around the enemy-as-snake metaphor. In one popular variant of this metaphor, the single snake appears as progenitor of a horde of serpentine spawn. In Cox and Forkum's 2006 cartoon, for example, a rearing cobra labeled "*Islamic Republic of Iran*" assures us, through fanged and forked-tongued mouth, "Don't worry. My babies will be harmless," while curled protectively around a pile of eggs marked with the symbol of radioactivity.[73] In Deng Coy Miel's 2005 cartoon entitled "Terrorism as a Snake-Hydra,"[74] (see figure 5.1) a dead, decap-

Figure 5.1. Deng Coy Miel. "Terrorism as a Snake-hydra." *The Straits Times* (Singapore). November 27, 2005.

itated snake labeled "Terrorism" gives posthumous birth to a grotesque brood of vipers that stream from the neck of its gaping, headless body. The same spawn trope is critically called up in Mike Lester's cartoon "Spawn,"[75] in which a clearly very dead terrorist lies on the ground, while an intelligence officer in a suit labeled "National Intelligence Estimate" brandishes a report saying "Killing Terrorists Spawns More Terrorists." He warns the armed U.S. soldier standing over the corpse, "STAND BACK!! He's about to spawn." Lester's cartoon is overtly satiric: the corpse is so clearly, like Monty Python's famous parrot, an ex-enemy that the notion of its spawning is ludicrous. Intention, however, does not always govern interpretation. Even here, the word "spawn" works in complex ways, calling up deeply entrenched symbolisms of the monstrous and reptilian; while the cartoon sets out to debunk such charged language, it is also part of the larger discursive universe of cartoons in which such language works immediately and potently on the level of anxiety and paranoia. As viewers, we may become entangled in familiar symbolism to the extent that we cannot completely distance ourselves from it. Dennis Mumby and Carole Spitzack call this "metaphoric entrapment." In metaphoric entrapment, a concept is understood so thoroughly and consistently in terms of a particular metaphor that it doesn't appear to make sense in any other terms. Our thinking about something (the war, the enemy) "becomes so tied up with a particular metaphoric structure that alternative ways of viewing the concept are obscured, or appear to make less sense."[76]

This is evident in cartoons depicting Arab news outlet Al Jazeera as a snake (see figure 5.2).[77] In Sandy Huffaker's cartoon, Al Jazeera is drawn as a hypnotic cobra, lightning-bolts streaming from its demonic-looking eyes and a snake-charmer's pipe in its mouth, as a bearded Muslim, eyes glazed, stares blankly ahead murmuring "yes, master." This image is a particularly useful example of metaphoric entanglement: although the station has gained a reputation among media analysts for its high quality journalism and for its unusually independent voice in a region where many news media are government-controlled, it is caricatured as a serpent hypnotizing its hapless viewer into submission. Because, within this metaphoric entanglement, we can only understand Al Jazeera as dangerous and reptilian, we can only see it as negative, a predisposition evident in the fact that a recent poll found that 53 percent of Americans opposed the launch of the channel and two-thirds of Americans thought the U.S. government should not allow it entry to the U.S. market.[78] The extent of this distrust is evident in the fact that its offices in Afghanistan and Iraq were bombed in the early days of the war, and reports have suggested that President Bush considered bombing Al Jazeera's headquarters in Doha, stopped only by the dissent voiced by Britain's Tony Blair.[79] The consequences of such metaphoric entanglement,

Figure 5.2. Sandy Huffaker. "Al Jazeera." *Cagle Cartoons.* **March 27, 2003.**

then, can clearly be serious, echoing Murray Edelman's caution that we must be careful of our metaphors because they often permit us to confidently inhabit over-simplified worlds in which "the causes are simple and neat and the remedies are apparent."[80]

Like the Al Jazeera cartoon, many editorial cartoons echo the animal, hunt, and disease metaphors found in other media, and often work towards similar results of ridicule, diminishment, or dehumanization. The *Indianapolis Star* ran a cartoon by Gary Varvel in May 2004 showing an image of a Saddam-headed rat trapped in a box, huddled out of the beam of an infantryman's flashlight.[81] Jeff Parker's "Foxy Saddam"[82] shows British Prime Minister Tony Blair considering a solution to the controversy over a fox hunting ban by showing a picture of Saddam's head on a fox's body. Daryl Cagle's "Saddam Skin Rug" shows George Bush posed in a big-game hunter's pith helmet on a bearskin rug; the head of the bear is the head of Saddam Hussein (see figure 5.3)[83] This human-animal fusion, a common feature of the visual shorthand of cartoons, is sometimes called homospatiality, in which two distinct visual images are merged into a single image within which separate components can still be detected.[84] In "Saddam Skin Rug" then, Saddam's head is still clearly discernable as a human head, while the attached body is still clearly an animal. Technically, the clear presence

Figure 5.3. Daryl Cagle. "Saddam Skin Rug." *MSNBC.com.* **December 29, 2006.**

of both visual elements in the fused form makes it difficult to misunderstand or misidentify the cartoon's figures. Visually, however, it solidifies and confirms the mutated otherness of the monstrous figure, to the extent that we may feel no recognition of its debased humanity even in its death and defeat. Its very visual monstrosity suggests that it is right and natural that it be the hunter's prey. As with any system of metaphors that collaborate to supply a consistent visual vocabulary, one of the key effects here is that such metaphors come, in themselves, to be considered "relatively 'natural' and unremarkable."[85]

Another example of the hunt metaphor in action is found in Mark Streeter's depiction of a giant, plumed, heroic-looking eagle descending with talons spread to grasp a tiny creature labeled Saddam popping his head out of the earth; the caption reads "Eagle Captures Chicken in Rat Hole."[86] The diminution of the enemy into inhuman insignificance is a thread that can be identified in several cartoons: in the *Los Angeles Times*, Michael Ramirez's cartoon shows a huge hand in a sleeve decorated with American stars clutching a tiny, be-whiskered rat labeled "Saddam" over the caption "Gotcha!"[87] In Rod Emmerson's "A Weapon of Mass Humiliation,"[88] a rat with the face of Saddam sighs in resignation as Uncle's Sam's arm, with its identifying stars-and-stripes sleeve, reaches out a gloved hand to fastidiously pluck up the annoying vermin by the tail. In Allen Lauzon Falcon's "Saddam Rat Caught" (see figure 5.4),[89] we find yet another depiction of Uncle Sam's gloved hand, in the familiar stars-and-stripes sleeve, holding between thumb and forefinger a bedraggled-looking "Saddam Rat," pictured with a scaly tail snaking out from beneath a patched, filthy robe. The enemy as a slightly ridiculous, trivialized pest is also present in Jeff Parker's 2005 cartoon[90] showing an imperious but irritated British lion, draped in the Union Jack, directing an annoyed glance at a black rat labeled "terrorism" that is chomping on the lion's tail. In the "America's hand" cartoons, however, we see something not present in the English cartoon, that is, the significant suggestion of precision, cleanliness, and fastidiousness. The aim of America's giant hand is excellent; it holds in its grasp only the singular enemy. Like the paterfamilias whose job is to protect wife and children by plucking up and disposing of the rodent, the symbolic American hand does not turn away from the dirty job that must be done but performs it, with neatness and precision, on our behalf. In these images the task is portrayed as necessary and almost surgical. In fact, in Emmerson's and Lauzon's cartoons, the rolled wrists of Uncle Sam's white gloves visually suggest a doctor's gloves, donned for serious tasks and disposed of later for reasons of hygiene. In each of the "America's hand" cartoons, we see no messiness, no blood, no civilian deaths, only the singular and easily identified enemy dangling mid-air; the scale, scope, and damage of

caglecartoons.com/espanol

Figure 5.4. Allen Lauzon Falcon. *"Saddam Rat Caught." Caglecartoons.com* December 14, 2003.

the war are completely unrepresented in this image of paternal protection. The paternal hand metaphor, in suggesting a surgical precision to the act of stopping the enemy, does something similar to what Lakoff observes at work in the "Nation as a Person" metaphor, in which a country's leader represents and stands in for all its people. Lakoff notes that this metaphor hides the fact that "the 3000 bombs to be dropped in the first two days [of the war on Iraq] will not be dropped on that one person. They will kill many thousands of the people hidden by the metaphor, people that according to the metaphor we are not going to war against."[91]

Hiding a nation's citizens behind a metaphor that obscures their individuality is also a key function of insect and, especially, swarm metaphors. Metaphors associating the enemy with the indiscriminate (they attack blindly because of their inherently destructive nature) and with the interchangeable (they are identical in nature, motivation and intent) appear in editorial cartoons as in other forms of media. In Cameron Cardow's 2006 cartoon from the *Ottawa Citizen* (see figure 5.5),[92] terrorists are drawn as realistic-looking cockroaches crawling over the surface of the Canadian flag, with a caption that reads "Terrorists.

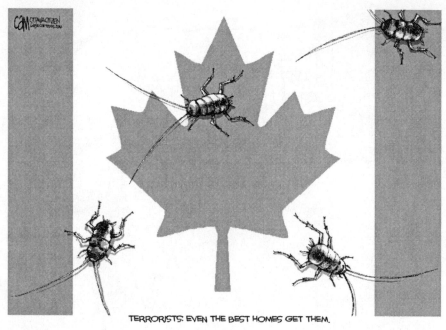

TERRORISTS: EVEN THE BEST HOMES GET THEM.

Figure 5.5. Cameron Cardow. "Canada Buggy Flag." *Ottawa Citizen.* June 11, 2006.

Even the best homes get them." This message generates anxiety in Canadians who may have felt safe in their presumption that terrorism is something that happens elsewhere; it delivers a jarring message of vulnerability: your home, too, is prey to these inhuman incursions. On an intellectual level, the cartoon plays with the idea of the domestic and the political: on an emotional level, however, it strikes viscerally. By verbally and visually conflating "nation" with "home" in the cartoon's juxtaposition of the flag with its reference to "the best homes," alarm is elevated to paranoia: the word *home* calls up all that is closest to us, and makes the threat appear not political but deeply personal. In this way, the cartoon's internal logic is not far from historical propaganda images of the enemy as invader and defiler. The insects crawling over the flag recall images from *The Eternal Jew* of Jews as rats crawling across a map of Europe. Enemies come at us, these images imply, through our families and our homes. The enemy is portrayed as corrupter, entering and despoiling the sacred space of home, bringing filth, disease, and spoilage in its wake. In Cardow's cartoon the elaborate visual detail of the roaches evokes a shudder; their flat bodies and sweeping antenna seem to desecrate the flag they crawl upon. The grotesqueries of the depiction seem to demand a response of extermination; as Keen reminds us, the "lower down in the animal phyla" enemy metaphors descend, "the greater sanction is given to the soldier to become a mere exterminator."[93] This is reflected in Daryl Cagle's

2001 cartoon "Dead or Alive" (see figure 5.6)[94] George Bush, dressed in cowboy costume complete with sheriff's star, fires his six-shooters repeatedly into a teeming swarm of cockroaches, under a "WANTED: Dead or Alive" poster of a single, huge roach. There is a significant visual tension in the cartoon between the single "criminal" roach shown in the poster and the massed, teeming swarm into which Sheriff Bush is firing. It is clearly impossible for either Bush or the viewer to identify the individual "wanted" cockroach among the horde; they all merge into a single, inseparable identity. While Bush's use of pistols to kill cockroaches is offered as a kind of comic overkill, viewers may find themselves identifying with Bush's stance, since we, like him, cannot be expected to differentiate between individual bugs in the advancing tide. Within this conceptual frame, there are no "innocent" insects, a frame that extends to encompass the human enemy so frequently, through the lens of Orientalism, de-individualized.

In R. J. Matson's "Iraq Hornets,"[95] a frantic Uncle Sam, covered with swollen bug bites, swings a baseball bat at the swarm of insects emerging from a smashed hornet's nest labeled "Iraq." In the background, George Bush pokes at stick at an apparently empty hornet's nest labeled "Iran," saying "I'm guessing most of these bad boys are coming from here." Matson's cartoon seems critical of the hornet's nest that Bush has embroiled Uncle Sam in while he stands at a safe distance. The metaphoric entrapment of the insect

Figure 5.6.   Daryl Cagle. "Dead or Alive." *MSNBC.Com*. September 20, 2001.

metaphor is still at work, however, reduplicating the conceptual structures through which we see the enemy.

Within the persuasive or rhetorical text even of a cartoon intending critique, then, metaphors may still, as Hart and Hassencahl observe, "oversimplify a complex situation" or "hide important facts."[96] In capturing a complex situation through its compressed graphics, a cartoon may employ visual codes that confirm an understanding of the enemy that the overt message of the cartoon would refute. In this way, what Gamson and Stuart call the "condensing symbols" of a political cartoon may "suggest the core frame" of the issue[97] and that conceptual frame may, in subtle ways, work against the cartoon's dominant meaning, and confirm a construction of the enemy that the cartoonist might never choose consciously to advocate.

In Monte Wolverton's "Insurg-ants,"[98] streams of ants descend on a picnic of "U.S. Corporate Interests in Iraq." The cartoon is clearly intended to be critical of Bush's policies: stamping madly on the insurgent ants, the President is portrayed as a demented-looking hillbilly with flapping ears and goofy scowl; motion lines around feet, elbows and knees suggest the comically frantic speed of his desperate jig. The business-suited picnickers labeled "US Corporate Interests" are represented as grinning stupidly or scowling slyly, toasting themselves with champagne against the backdrop of a war-torn desert landscape. The streaming "insurg-ants" in the foreground, however, are still apt to provide a stronger visceral shudder than the human businessmen in the background: while it takes a few minutes to decode their depiction of corporate greed, interest, and self-satisfaction, the message of the massing bugs is much more immediate. For a reader predisposed to look for a confirmation of his or her existing metaphors of the enemy, the cartoon's vision of the tide of insects provides just such a corroboration.

There are a few examples of political cartoons that overtly take on not only government policy in the war on terror but also the conceptual framework through which those policies are articulated. In a 2003 cartoon by Mike Lester[99] (see figure 5.7), for example, we see in the foreground Uncle Sam wearing a uniform labeled "Sam's Pest Control" and holding a canister of poison. In the other hand, he proudly holds up a dangling rat. Around him is an utterly destroyed house. Furniture is overturned amid piles of rubble, and there are only a few walls left standing; behind one broken wall we see a glimpse of a tank, and through a ragged hole in the roof we see the tower of a mosque. In the middle of this wreckage stands an Arabic family. Mother and son gaze in blank shock at the ruin of their home; the father, a pained smile on his face, stammers, as Sam proudly proffers the rat, "Thanks . . . I

Figure 5.7. Mike Lester. "Sam's Pest Control." *The Rome News-Tribune* **(Georgia). April 4, 2003.**

think." This cartoon is remarkable for the way it turns the pest metaphor back on itself, clearly implying that the wanton degree of destruction caused by the hunt for a single enemy rat is dangerously disproportionate. Equally remarkably, the cartoon paints both the result of the hunt and the Arab family in pointedly human terms: the humanity of the pictured Iraqis is emphasized by their domestic setting and family grouping, an image radically different from the undifferentiated swarms through which they are often represented. The human costs of the war in Iraq are thus poignantly evoked, as symbolized in the small but central image of a family photograph, knocked carelessly aside by the exterminator's violence.

Exterminating Enemies

Metaphors, far from being merely descriptive, affect the way that we think and act. By defining the challenging task of addressing terrorism as a "war," we define our response as a militaristic one. We undermine our ability to conceive of and win support for the alternative solutions that could be called up by a different set of metaphors. When we describe our enemies and people who look like them through sub-human metaphors, we foster human rights violations and war crimes. When we define people as pests it becomes more legitimate, imaginatively and politically, to consider exterminating them. What happens, then, when the actual weapons of war are designed for literal extermination? Edmund Russell's book *War and Nature: Fighting Humans and Insects with Chemicals from World War I to Silent Spring* documents the development of chemical warfare against human and insect enemies by the American military and the chemical industry in the last century. Russell chronicles how corporations developing insecticides applied their skills to the invention of chemical weapons such as poison gas, incendiary bombs, and antimalarial DDT spraying for use in tropical war zones, leading to the use of chemical defoliants as weapons. The use of chemical warfare against both humans and insects was facilitated by the economic and institutional interrelationship developed between military, government, industrial and educational institutions. Russell argues that chemical poisoning as a way to eradicate both human and insect enemies reflects a particular fear and hatred of enemies who transgress boundaries. As the use of chemical warfare and insecticides increased, humans and insects were metaphorically figured as trespassers. Although most insects were present in North America long before human farmers, fences and walls offered a sense of ownership to landholders, who spoke of the insects in the field as "invaders."[100] Similarly, national borders confirmed the distinction between insiders and outsiders, emphasizing the necessity of protecting citizens by "exterminating" enemies or driving them beyond the civic boundary. Propaganda in official and unofficial forms reinforced the equation of pests and enemies; in an advertisement for insecticide, for example, the Rohm and Haas Company "paired a drawing of a soldier shooting a Japanese soldier (in the back) with a drawing of another person shooting a fly with a [poison spraying] Flitgun. 'Whether Japs or flies,' the text read, 'it's fast action that counts.'"[101] This symbolic conflation of insect and enemy was echoed by Chief William N. Porter of the Chemical Warfare Service in 1944 when he wrote that "We wish, at the moment, to poison insects because they threaten the health of our troops. Coincidentally the Chemical Warfare Service . . . is actively at work in an attempt to improve our methods for poisoning Germans and Japanese. . . . The fundamental biological principles of poisoning Japanese, insects, rats, bacteria, and cancer are essentially the same.[102]

While Porter's words speak to the practical similarities between "poisoning Japanese, insects, rats, bacteria, and cancer,"[103] the ideological similarities linking enemy, disease, and insect were already well established. A year after Chief Porter spoke of the same "fundamental biological principles" involved in killing human and inhuman pests, a cartoon published in the U.S. Marine magazine *Leatherneck*, illustrated the linking of the two, a rhetorical and metaphorical linkage that continued to support the pragmatic efforts of developing and applying chemical tools of annihilation. The *Leatherneck* cartoon depicts the "*Louseous Japanicas*,"[104] a hairy, multi-legged, pincered louse with huge protruding fangs, slanted eyes, and devil horns; examined closely, its spatulate tail reveals the Japanese rising sun military insignia. The artist, Sargent Fred Laswell, noted in the cartoon's caption that the Marine Corps was "especially trained" in fighting "this lice epidemic," and was thus assigned "the gigantic task of extermination." Before a "complete cure" of "the plague" may be affected, the caption continues, "the insects' breeding grounds around the Tokyo area . . . must be completely annihilated."[105] While, Russell observes, the intent of the cartoon was surely meant as "humorous and hyperbolic," it expressed a very real, very serious shift in the technologies of warfare; by the end of WWII, the annihilation of human enemies had become a realistic possibility, thanks to the production of ever more effective chemical weapons; while the cartoon's personifications may have been exaggerated, the threat they represented was not.

While Russell acknowledges the difficulty in quantifying the impact that ideas about insects and nature had on the war's policies and conduct,[106] the fact that American military propaganda, soldiers in the field, and journalism at home all employed similar language about the insect-enemy is suggestive. U.S. government posters such as *Enemies Both*[107] (see figure 5.8) illustrate this: it shows a gun-toting Uncle Sam clutching an oversized, fanged mosquito labeled "Malaria" in one hand and a bucktoothed Japanese soldier in the other. To reinforce their visual equivalence, both bug and human dangle in exactly the same posture, limbs identically splayed. The poster's caption confirms their equivalence, labeling insect and human "ENEMIES BOTH!" and reminding soldiers "It's your job to help eliminate them."[108] Soldiers readily absorbed this message: in his book *God Is My Co-Pilot*, pilot Robert L. Scott Jr. said that every time he killed a "Jap" he felt as though "he had stepped on another blackwidow spider or scorpion," a stance echoed in his naming of his airplane "Old Exterminator."[109] Journalism echoed this language; in a 1945 article called "Rodent Exterminators," *Time* Magazine called America's victory in Iwo Jima the completion of "the Pacific's nastiest exterminating job."[110]

Predictably, this language spread to civilian discourse; Russell cites a letter written in 1945 to the editor of the *Milwaukee Journal* by Leonie M. Cole complaining that America had stopped short of its aims by accepting Japanese surrender. "Japan," says Cole, is a "terrible evil," and should be "wiped away completely, once and for all." Making the link with insect annihilation explicit, she continues: "When one sets out to destroy vermin, does one try to leave a few alive in the nest? Most certainly not!"[111]

Figure 5.8. "Enemies Both." U.S. Government poster, 1944.

This language of extermination and eradication is not exclusive to the twentieth century; history tells us it has been a long-standing feature of warfare and enemy construction. Since so much of Western thought has rested on the notion that to subdue the natural world and its creatures is a moral duty, part of the great civic endeavor of civilization, linking the enemy to the sub-human world has often been used to provide an answer to those debating the morality of war.[112] What changed in the twentieth century was our ability, through new technologies, to act on extermination fantasies on a scale previously unimagined, and our ability to disseminate on an unforseen scale a metaphorical vocabulary that ideologically and imaginatively supports that enactment. This merging of technology and ideology calls us, more urgently than ever, to hold ourselves to account for the form taken by our public discourse as we face a new century in which the relation of the worlds of culture and nature are ever more central and ever more urgent.

We tend to look back in horror at the dehumanizing depictions of the enemy that emerged in the wars of the early twentieth century. As enlightened citizens, we want to distance ourselves from their blatant hatefulness, their cultivated anxiety, their vicious rhetorical extremities; we want to point instead to the progress we have made away from propaganda, paranoia, and the kinds of genocidal slaughter made infamous by regimes such as Nazi Germany. How is it, then, that we find ourselves facing in our current media echoes of those earlier metaphors? How is 1944's cartoon "Louseus Japanicus" substantively different from 2006's "Forked Tongue," with its fanged and slant-eyed snake labeled "Iran"? How is Chief Porter's assertion of the similarities in the principles of poisoning Japanese people and cancer different from the sentiment expressed in Cox and Forkum's 2007 cartoon "Metastasis,"[113] in which the X-ray of a cancerous patient reveals a brain tumor labeled "Islamism," suggesting that not terrorism but an entire religion is, as the doctor somberly tells the patient, "Malignant"? The fact that we treat such images merely as jokes, like the "Lake Iraq" merchandise that offers humourous reference to nuclear annihilation, might obscure the somber second half of the equation of enemies with insects. If such images suggest that we are already imaginatively half-way to a deadly endpoint of dehumanization, do we really want to complete the equation and go the rest of the distance to nuclear war? If we can find nothing to smile about in the memorials for the nuclear bombing of Nagasaki and Hiroshima, then perhaps we need to begin publically questioning our production of images that memorialize projected fantasies of death, resisting the urge to hide hatred beyond the obscuring, if sickly, smile.

Notes

1. Doug Marlette. "Journalism's Wild Man." *American Journalism Review*. January/February 1992. See www.ajr.org/Article.asp?id=1444 (July 3, 2007).

2. Jack Valenti. "Speech before the Los Angeles World Affairs Council." October 1, 1998. posted on *Los Angeles World Affairs Council* web site. See www.lawac.org/speech/pre percent20sept percent2004 percent20speeches/valenti.html (July 3, 2007).

3. David Robb. *Operation Hollywood: How the Pentagon Shapes and Censors the Movies*. New York: Prometheus Books, 2004.

4. Jack Shaheen. Interviewed in *Reel Bad Arabs*. [videorecording]. Media Education Foundation, 2006.

5. Jack Shaheen. Interviewed in *Reel Bad Arabs*. [videorecording].

6. Jack Shaheen. Interviewed in *Reel Bad Arabs*. [videorecording].

7. Ilene Lelchuk. "'Convert or die' game divides Christians: Some ask Wal-Mart to drop Left Behind." San Francisco Chronicle. December 12, 2006. See sfgate.com/cgi-bin/article.cgi?file=/c/a/2006/12/12/MNG8TMU1KQ1.DTL&type=printable (July 3, 2007).

8. Jose Antonio Vargas. "Way Radical, Dude: Video Games with an Islamist Twist." *Washington Post*. October 9, 2006.

9. *Anti-Defamation League*. "Racist Groups Using Computer Gaming to Promote Violence against Blacks, Latinos and Jews."*Anti-Defamation League*. February 12, 2002. See www.adl.org/videogames/default.asp (July 3, 2007).

10. John Powers. "300: Racist War Propaganda with Septic Timing." *Art Threat Political Art Magazine*. March 2007. See www.artthreat.net/2007/03/95 (July 1, 2007).

11. John Powers. "300: Racist War Propaganda with Septic Timing."

12. John Powers. "300: Racist War Propaganda with Septic Timing."

13. Jack Shaheen. Interviewed in *Reel Bad Arabs*. [videorecording]. Media Education Foundation, 2006.

14. Laurence Michalak. "Arab in American Cinema." *Social Studies Review*. Fall 2002, 42(1), 11–17.

15. Jack Shaheen. Iinterviewed in *Reel Bad Arabs*.

16. Jack Shaheen. Iinterviewed in *Reel Bad Arabs*.

17. Sam Smith. "The semiotics of a terrorist bombing." *Insight on the News*, June 5, 1995. See findarticles.com/p/articles/mi_m1571/is_n22_v11/ai_16936757 (July 3, 2007).

18. Kenneth H. Bacon. "DoD News Briefing." *U.S. Department of Defense*. April 24, 1995. See www.defenselink.mil/transcripts/transcript.aspx?transcriptid=123 (July 3, 2007).

19. Human Rights Watch. "We Are Not the Enemy: Hate Crimes against Arabs, Muslims, and Those Perceived to be Arab or Muslim after September 11." Human Rights Watch, November 2002, Vol. 14: 12.

20. *The Wisdom Fund*. "The 'Who' In American Media." *The Wisdom Fund*. August 9, 1995. See www.twf.org/News/Y1997/Who.html (July 3, 2007).

21. Carl Boggs and Tom Pollard. *The Hollywood War Machine*. Paradigm Publishers, 2006: 9.

22. Carl Boggs and Tom Pollard. *The Hollywood War Machine*.

23. Carl Boggs and Tom Pollard. *The Hollywood War Machine*.

24. Jack Shaheen. *Reel Bad Arabs: How Hollywood Vilifies a People*. Interlink Publishing Group, 2001.

25. Jack Shaheen. *Reel Bad Arabs: How Hollywood Vilifies a People*.

26. Jack Shaheen. *Reel Bad Arabs: How Hollywood Vilifies a People*.

27. Jack Shaheen. *Reel Bad Arabs: How Hollywood Vilifies a People*.

28. Jack Shaheen. *Reel Bad Arabs: How Hollywood Vilifies a People*.

29. Carl Boggs and Tom Pollard. *The Hollywood War Machine.*

30. Matthew Rothschild. "'Deck of Weasels' Lists 54 'Anti-American, Pro-Saddam' Leaders and Celebs." *The Progressive.* May 14, 2003. See www.progressive.org/mag _mcweasel (July 1, 2007).

31. Matthew Rothschild. "'Deck of Weasels' Lists 54 'Anti-American, Pro-Saddam' Leaders and Celebs."

32. Matthew Rothschild. . "'Deck of Weasels' Lists 54 'Anti-American, Pro-Saddam' Leaders and Celebs."

33. Heather Havrilesky. "The selling of 9/11." *Salon.* September 7, 2002. See dir.salon.com/story/mwt/feature/2002/09/07/purchase_power/index.html? pn=2 (July 1, 2007).

34. Nabeel Abraham. "The Gulf Crisis and Anti-Arab Racism in America." In *Collateral Damage: The New World Order at Home and Abroad.* Cynthia Peters (ed). Boston: South End Press, 1991: 259.

35. Heather Havrilesky. op. cit.

36. See www.therightthings.com

37. See www.almostaproverb.com

38. Pat. "Untitled." *patshideout.* March 14, 2002. See www.patshideout.com/the attic.htm (July 3, 2007).

39. See www.cafepress.com

40. Lucy Shelton Caswell. "Drawing Swords: War in American Editorial Cartoons." *American Journalism.* 21(2), 2004:13–45.

41. Lucy Shelton Caswell. "Drawing Swords."

42. Lucy Shelton Caswell. "Drawing Swords."

43. Michael DeSousa and Martin Medhurst. "Political cartoons and American Culture: Significant Symbols of campaign 1980," *Studies in Visual Communication.* 8:1, Winter 1982.

44. Virginia Bouvier. "Imaging a Nation: U.S. political cartoons and the war of 1898." In *Whose War; the War of 1898 and the Battles to Define the Nation.* Virginia Marie Bouvier (ed). Westport, CT: Praeger, 2001: 91.

45. Lucy Shelton Caswell. "Drawing Swords."

46. Lucy Shelton Caswell. "Drawing Swords."

47. Elizabeth El Refaie. "Understanding Visual Metaphor: the example of newspaper cartoons." *Visual Communication.* 2 (1), 2003: 75–95.

48. E. H. Gombrich cited in Elizabeth El Refaie. "Understanding Visual Metaphor: the example of newspaper cartoons." *Visual Communication.* 2 (1), 2003: 75–95.

49. Elizabeth El Refaie. "Understanding Visual Metaphor."

50. Gelu Sulugiuc. "Danish paper cleared in Muslim libel lawsuit: Muhammad cartoons." *National Post.* Oct 27, 2006: 12.

51. Shanti Kumar. "Religious Tolerance versus Tolerance of Religion: A Critique of the Cartoon Controversy in Jyllands-Posten." *FlowTV.* March 10, 2006. See flowtv .org/?p=150 (July 3, 2007).

52. Pernille Ammitzbøll and Lorenzo Vidino. "After the Danish Cartoon Controversy." *Middle East Quarterly*. Winter 2007. See www.meforum.org/article/1437#_ftn14 (July 3, 2007).

53. *Warriors for Truth*. See www.warriorsfortruth.com/mohammedpercent20cartoons .html (July 3, 2007).

54. *CNN*. "In Libya, 11 reportedly die in cartoon protests." February 18, 2006. See edition.cnn.com/2006/WORLD/africa/02/17/libya.cartoons/index.html

55. *BBC*. "Cartoons row hits Danish exports." *BBC News*. September 9, 2006. See news.bbc.co.uk/2/hi/europe/5329642.stm (July 3, 2007).

56. Christian Allen Purefoy. "Five days of violence by Nigerian Christians and Muslims kill 150." *The Independent*. February 24, 2006. See news.independent.co.uk /world/Africa/article347374.ece (July 3, 2007).

57. Flemming Rose. "Why I Published Those Cartoons." *Washington Post*. February 19, 2006. See www.washingtonpost.com/wpdyn/content/article/2006/02/17 /AR2006021702499.html (July 3, 2007).

58. Flemming Rose. "Muhammeds ansigt." *Jyllands-Posten*. September 30, 2005.

59. Khalil Bendib. "Your Islamophobic Fist Must Stop At My Muslim Nose." *altmuslim.com*. February 17, 2006. See www.altmuslim.com/perm.php?id=1658_0_25 _0_C42 (July 3, 2007).

60. Reza Aslan. "Depicting Mohammed: Why I'm offended by the Danish cartoons of the prophet." *Slate*. February 8, 2006. See www.slate.com/id/2135661/ (July 3, 2007).

61. Reza Aslan. "Depicting Mohammed."

62. Reza Aslan. "Depicting Mohammed."

63. Khalil Bendib. "Your Islamophobic Fist Must Stop At My Muslim Nose."

64. As'ad. "Danish Cartoons (not pastries)." *Angry Arab*. February 4, 2006. See angryarab.blogspot.com/2006/02/danish-cartoons-not-pastries.html (July 3, 2007).

65. Tariq Ali. "This is the real outrage." *The Guardian*. February 13, 2006. See www .guardian .co.uk/cartoonprotests/story/0,,1708319,00.html (July 3, 2007).

66. Tariq Ali. "This is the real outrage."

67. Artz and Mark A Pollock. "Limiting the Options: AntiArab Images in U.S. Media Coverage of the Persian Gulf Crisis." in *The U.S. Media and the Middle East: Images and Perception*. Kamalipour, Yahya R (Ed). Westport, CT: Greenwood Press, 1995.

68. J. L. Conners. "Hussein as enemy: The Persian Gulf War in political cartoons." *Harvard International Journal of Press/Politics*. 3 (3), 96–114. 1998.

69. William Hart and Fran Hassencahl. "Dehumanizing the enemy in editorial cartoons." in B. S. Greeberge (ed). *Communication and Terrorism: Public and Media Responses to 9/11*. Cresskill, NJ: Hampton Press, 2002: 137–51.

70. Stanley Fish. *Is There a Text in This Class? The Authority of Interpretive Communities*. Cambridge, MA: Harvard University Press, 1980.

71. Jeff Parker. "9 11 Terror Eagle." *Florida Today*. September 7, 2002.

72. Steve Breen. "Untitled." *San Diego Union-Tribune*. September 13, 2001.

73. John Cox and Allen Forkum. "Forked Tongue." *Cox and Forkum.com*. June 18, 2006. See www.coxandforkum.com/archives/000868.html (July 3, 2007).

74. Deng Coy Miel. "Terrorism as a Snake-hydra." *The Straits Times* (Singapore). November 27, 2005.

75. Mike Lester "Spawn." The Rome News-Tribune (Georgia). September 25, 2006.

76. D.K. Mumby and C. Spitzack. "Ideology and Television News: a Metaphoric Analysis of Political Stories." *Central States Speech Journal*. Vol. 34, 1983 162–71.

77. Sandy Huffaker. "Al Jazeera." *Cagle Cartoons*. March 27, 2003.

78. BBC. "Al-Jazeera English TV date set." *BBC*. November 1, 2006. See news .bbc.co.uk/2/hi/middle_east/6105952.stm (July 3, 2007).

79. Jeremy Scahill. "Did Bush Really Want to Bomb Al Jazeera?" *The Nation*. November 23, 2005. See www.thenation.com/doc/20051212/scahill (July 3, 2007).

80. Murray Edelman. *Politics as Symbolic Action: Mass Arousal and Quiescence*. Chicago: Markham,1971.

81. Gary Varvel. "We Got Him." *The Indianapolis Star News*. May 2004.

82. Jeff Parker. "Foxy Saddam." *Florida Today*. September 24, 2002.

83. Daryl Cagle. "Saddam Skin Rug." *MSNBC.com*. December 29, 2006.

84. Cited in Elizabeth El Refaie. "Understanding Visual Metaphor."

85. Elizabeth El Refaie. "Understanding Visual Metaphor."

86. Mark Streeter. "Untitled." *The Savannah Morning News*. May 14, 2004.

87. Michael Ramirez. "Gotcha." *Los Angeles Times*. December 15, 2003.

88. Rod Emmerson. "Untitled." *The New Zealand Herald*. April 23, 2004.

89. Allen Lauzon Falcon. "Saddam Rat Caught." *Caglecartoons.com* December 14, 2003.

90. Jeff Parker. "London Bombings." *Florida Today*. July 7, 2005.

91. George Lakoff. " Metaphor and War, Again." *AlterNet*. March 18, 2003. See www .alternet.org/story/15414/ (July 3, 2007).

92. Cameron Cardow. "Canada Buggy Flag." *Ottawa Citizen*. June 11, 2006.

93. Sam Keen. *Faces of the Enemy: Reflections of the Hostile Imagination*. New York: Harper Collins; Reprint edition. September 1991.

94. Daryl Cagle. "Dead or Alive." *MSNBC.com*. September 20, 2001.

95. R.J. Matson. "Iraq Hornets." *St. Louis Post Dispatch*. March 24, 2006.

96. William Hart and Fran Hassencahl. op. cit.

97. William Gamson and D. Stuart. "Media Discourse as a Symbolic Contest: the Bomb in Political Cartoons." *Sociological Forum*. Vol. 7, No. 1, 1992: 55–86.

98. Monte Wolverton. "Insurg-ants." *Cagle Cartoons*. February 20, 2005.

99. Mike Lester. "Sam's Pest Control." *The Rome News-Tribune* (Georgia). April 4, 2003.

100. Edmund Russell. *War and Nature*. London: Cambridge University Press, 2002.

101. Edmund Russell. *War and Nature*.

102. Edmund Russell. *War and Nature*.

103. Edmund Russell. *War and Nature.*

104. Fred Laswell. "Louseous Japanicas: Bugs every marine should know." *Leatherneck* 28 March 1945: 35–27.

105. Edmund Russell. *War and Nature.*

106. Fred Laswell. "Louseous Japanicas."

107. Frank Mack 23rd Bomb. "Enemies Both." *U.S. government poster.* 1944. USGPO 44PA 720. Still Pictures Branch, U.S. National Archives and Records Administration.

108. Edmund Russell. *War and Nature.*

109. Edmund Russell. *War and Nature.*

110. Edmund Russell. *War and Nature.*

111. Edmund Russell. *War and Nature.*

112. Edmund Russell. *War and Nature.*

113. John Cox and Allen Forkum. "Metastasis" *Cox and Forkum.com.* July 2, 2007. See www.coxandforkum.com/archives/000868/html (July 3, 2007).

CHAPTER SIX

HateSpeak: Discourses of Dehumanization in Talk Radio

In the end, we will remember not the words of our enemies, but the silence of our friends.

—Martin Luther King, Jr.

Talking about Talk Radio

In recent years, without a great deal of resistance or commentary, hate speech has been institutionalized as part of contemporary mainstream media. It now can be found on radio and television stations across the U.S., addressing audiences numbering in the millions. Popular right-wing talk show hosts broadcast inflammatory rhetoric daily, abusing and demonizing minorities, environmentalists, liberal politicians and government social programs. These furious communications are not, as Sidney Blumenthal observes, an "underground phenomenon" circulating surreptitiously, but are "available daily in any city or town on the radio dial, or on TV, or in the pages of conservative publications."[1] The vitriolic extremity of the views expressed by so-called shock-jock talk radio hosts and their callers have led them to be frequently disregarded or marginalized as merely "fringe" voices, oddities of the far-right that need not be taken seriously or given credence by offering them attention. The popularity and sheer pervasiveness of these particular voices, however, suggest that attention must be paid: through their programs, columns, and best-selling books, such extreme views have entered, if only through the size of the audience they regularly reach, the media mainstream, with all the power that implies. Since 9/11, their prime target has been Muslims, particularly Arab Muslims. Yigal Carmon of the Middle East Media Research Institute noted at the 2004 Stockholm International Forum on Genocide Prevention that genocide does not occur without dehumanization, and the media, especially when it purveys hatred, is a key vehicle for accomplishing this.[2]

Hate speech is more than an onslaught of insults; it attacks on a variety of levels, sometimes overt, sometimes subtle. It may be direct or indirect; it may involve open threats or it may not. It may focus upon a single person or a group, disparaging through sweeping attacks on race, sex, religion, sexual orientation, or national origin. Hate speech may fester within our social consciousness and prompt violent action. Since race-based hate speech can call up and even replicate a history of violent acts, such as lynchings or the American Indian wars, it is often more potent than other insults based on individual characteristics: insults alluding to a person's clumsiness, size, or plainness may be hurtful without carrying the potent ideological freight found in racist insults that evoke generations of violence or oppression.[3] Just as the rise of reality television suggests a renewed relish in watching individual humiliation played out on a public stage, the rise of hate speech suggests that collectively we share an uncomfortable pleasure in acting as its audience and witness.

Violent inflammatory speech has become a staple of several talk radio shows that have risen to prominence over the last decade. The hosts of these programs are profoundly influential in shaping opinion among the documented 100 million Americans who listen regularly. Their messages are widely broadcast on more than 1200 radio stations and are available on the Internet, satellite radio, and television. Some, like Bill O'Reilly, have programs on both television and radio stations. Commentaries by big-name hosts draw big ratings and, for the station's corporate owners, translate to big money from advertisers and profits for shareholders. Such success creates local and regional imitators who echo the unrestrained style and vocabulary of the originals. Programs hosted by Michael Savage, Rush Limbaugh and Bill O'Reilly have become big business.

A new era in talk radio began in 1987 with the Federal Communications Commission's repeal of the Fairness Doctrine. The Fairness Doctrine was intended to prohibit stations from airing only programs with a single perspective. Stations were obligated to provide some opportunity for alternative views to be heard; while equal time for divergent views was not required, at least some portion of the broadcasting schedule had to represent diverse opinions or perspectives. Since the repeal of the Fairness Doctrine, says Todd Gitlin, radio networks have been governed by their "capacity to collect eardrums without any regard for veracity let alone civility."[4] As a result, an imbalance of opinion and representation has developed: according to the Senate Democratic Policy Committee, the top five radio station owners in the U.S. with stations of 50,000 watts or more broadcast only five hours of alternative opinion relative to 310 hours of right-wing talk.[5] One of the first radio personalities to benefit from this new freedom was Rush Limbaugh. His vigorous denunciations of Democrats, liberals, feminists and the left wing functioned less as news than entertainment, and listeners couldn't get enough of his uninhibited, provocative style. When ratings soared, stations across the country rushed to sign his syndicated show. Steve Rendall, author of *The Way Things Aren't: Rush Limbaugh's Reign of Error*, notes that talk radio "was born in the backlash of a bunch of white guys on the right railing against the Civil Rights Movement, the women's movement and the peace movement. Forty years later," Rendall continues, "little has changed."[6]

Talk radio's audience increased dramatically over the last two decades of the twentieth century. Between 1980 and 1998, the number of programs increased from 75 to 1,350. The better sound quality provided by FM stations left AM stations unable to compete in a music format; they found an unfilled niche by switching to talk radio. A shift in population demographics also played a role, since as people age, studies show, they begin to prefer talk to music programming.[7] Technological advances also contributed; inexpensive 800 numbers, cell phones, and satellite communications made the call-in format more accessible, while nationwide syndication provided stations with relatively low-cost programming. The audience for talk radio is still growing: the Pew Research Center for People and the Press found that the number of adults in the US who are regular listeners increased from 17 percent in 2004 to 20 percent in just two years.[8] Nearly one-third of Americans listen to the syndicated programs of Rush Limbaugh, Bill O'Reilly and Michael Savage. Surprisingly, a report by the Center for American Progress and the Free Press discovered that only 43 percent of the audience of right-wing talk shows described themselves as conservative. Of the rest, 23 percent identified themselves as liberal and 30 percent as moderates. While fewer than half of their listeners are conservatives, network owners provide programming in which nine out of ten hours of talk radio is right-wing and conservative. Therefore, argues the Center, it appears to be corporate ownership of the media rather than the political or social bent of the audience that is shaping programming.[9]

Talk Icons

Rush Limbaugh

Rush Limbaugh, whose career began in 1984, is the pre-eminent American radio talk show host, boasting 13.5 million listeners across more than five hundred stations.[10] His books have topped the bestseller lists: the record-breaking *The Way Things Ought to Be* was a bestseller for over a year and ranked #1 on the *New York Times* bestseller list for over twenty-five weeks. Rush's second book, *See, I Told You So*, sold so well it broke sales records.[11]

Limbaugh was the 1992, 1995, 2000 and 2005 recipient of the Marconi Radio Award for Syndicated Radio Personality of the Year given by the National Association of Broadcasters. In 1993, he was inducted into the Radio Hall of Fame. In 2002, the industry's *Talkers Magazine* ranked him as the greatest radio talk show host of all time.[12] Currently, Limbaugh is the highest paid radio syndicator,[13] earning approximately $30 million a year.[14] In 2007, Limbaugh was awarded the inaugural William F. Buckley, Jr. Award for Media Excellence by the Media Research Center, a conservative media analysis group.[15] Clearly, then, Limbaugh's is not a marginalized voice but one that is popular, influential, and broadly disseminated.

The dominance of Limbaugh's voice in radio is echoed and reinforced through the format of his three-hour daily program. Episodes feature extended monologues presented in Limbaugh's characteristically confident and fervent tones. While the information he presents is often, critics say, far from factual, his definitive manner and rapid-fire delivery appear to be compelling, expert, and authoritative. Limbaugh's voice dominates the show, which has few guests, although high-profile Republicans such as Vice President Dick Cheney provide legitimacy to the program through occasional guest appearances. Few of the show's pre-screened callers disagree with the host; in fact, a popular caller shorthand is to say "ditto" as a quick way of signaling agreement with Limbaugh's opinions. The word suggests the extent of his influence: in 1994, Limbaugh was widely credited with helping Republicans regain control of Congress, and several newly elected Congressman openly acknowledged this by calling themselves "the Dittohead caucus."[16] In recognition for his role in promoting the Republican ticket, Limbaugh was invited to Washington, where he was made an honorary member of the 104th Congress.

Not everyone is as enthusiastic about Limbaugh as his Dittohead fans. In 2003, he was forced to resign as a football commentator at ESPN amid allegations of racism, after he remarked on-air that Philadelphia Eagles quarterback Donovan McNabb was given "extra credit" because the league and the media wanted a black quarterback to be successful. He once told a black caller to "take that bone out of your nose and call me back"; on another occasion he asked, "Have you ever noticed how all newspaper composite pictures of wanted criminals resemble Jesse Jackson?"[17] When denounced for such remarks by his critics, Limbaugh seems to relish the additional notoriety; certainly such criticisms have yet to diminish his number of listeners.

Controversy fuels his popularity, and Limbaugh embraces it. While most media voices were raised in shock or outrage at the scenes of abuse documented in the Abu Ghraib photos, for example, Limbaugh trivialized them, likening them to a "hazing" or "fraternity prank," something no more serious than a college initiation.[18] His rage was reserved for the torture victims and those decrying the abuse. He called the Iraqi prisoners, shown terrorized by guard dogs, beaten and sexually humiliated, "sick" and "perverted"; he told his listeners, "They are the ones who are dangerous. They are the ones who are subhuman. They are the ones who are human debris, not the United States of America and not our soldiers and not our prison guards."[19] Limbaugh also railed against those demanding accountability for the abuses of Abu Ghraib, lamenting that "we're going to ruin people's lives over it and we're going to hamper our military effort, and then we are going to really hammer them because they had a good time."[20] Limbaugh linked the outrage over Abu Ghraib to a general softening of American rigor that is part of his larger complaint about feminism; weak Americans couldn't stomach the humiliation of the Iraqis, he claimed, because "a lot of the American culture is being feminized. I think the reaction to the stupid torture is an example of the feminization of this country."[21]

In 2004, *Media Matters for America* launched an online petition to have Limbaugh bounced from tax-payer funded American Forces Radio and Television Services in response to Limbaugh's "condoning and trivializing the abuse, torture, rape and possible murder of Iraqi prisoners."[22] *Media Matters* founder David Brock said "It is abhorrent that the American taxpayer is paying to broadcast what is in effect pro-torture propaganda to American troops." The effort to withdraw the program was unsuccessful and it continues to be broadcast to military personnel.[23]

Bill O'Reilly

Bill O'Reilly, host of Fox News' highest-rated show "The O'Reilly Factor," which attracts 3 to 3.5 million viewers daily, is another influential media voice. O'Reilly's "Radio Factor" is heard on more than four hundred stations in the nation's top markets. He also writes a syndicated newspaper column that appears in hundreds of newspapers.[24] O'Reilly's six best-selling books have spent multiple weeks on *The New York Times* best-sellers list. There are over four million copies of his books in print, including a children's book entitled *The O'Reilly Factor for Kids: A Survival Guide for America's Families*, which was 2005's best-selling nonfiction children's book.

A two-time Emmy Award winner for excellence in reporting, O'Reilly served as national correspondent for ABC News and as anchor of the nationally syndicated news magazine program *Inside Edition*.[25] He has been the subject of profiles in GQ, Newsweek, People, The New York Times, The Washington Post, The Wall Street Journal, New York, New York Observer, Newsday and the New York Post. The magazine Brill's Content named him one of the top fifty journalists in the country. According to Forbes magazine, O'Reilly charges a reported $50,000 per speaking engagement and earns $9 million a year. [26]

O'Reilly is known for his abrasive treatment of guests who oppose him, regularly shouting at them to "shut up." A profile in Salon magazine stated that "His style is neither to engage the logic of an opposing point of view nor to acknowledge an inconvenient fact."[27] While this style might make for lively television, it does not reflect the highest standards of journalism or debate. Researchers at the Indiana University School of Journalism analyzed O'Reilly's "Talking Points Memo" editorials using propaganda analysis techniques and found that O'Reilly's rhetoric included many of the techniques and devices of propaganda, including frequent name-calling and the use of fear.[28]

One of the threats O'Reilly regularly alludes to is Iraq. He describes Iraqis as "primitive" and "prehistoric" and has compared the Muslim holy book, the Koran, to Hitler's Mein Kampf. He suggests that the only apt intervention in the Muslim world is destruction: "What we can do is bomb the living daylights out of them."[29] O'Reilly advocates the destruction of troublesome countries, questioning why the U.S. military did not simply level Fallujah or "bomb the Afghan infrastructure to rubble."[30] Just as Limbaugh blamed the victims of Abu Ghraib for their abuse, O'Reilly blames Afghan civilians for the hardships they experience because they are collectively "responsible for the Taliban."[31] America should not "target civilians," he says, "but if they don't rise up against this criminal government, they starve, period."[32] For O'Reilly, human life in certain countries seems inherently less valuable than human life in America; he notes, for example, that since life expectancy in Afghanistan is so short, "killing someone there is not like killing people here."[33]

When he says these things, advocating what critic Thomas Wheeler has called Bill O'Reilly's Final Solution: Bomb the Living Daylights out of Them,[34] O'Reilly may consider he is only engaging in the hyperbolic rhetoric that has become a convention in some kinds of media. His exhortations need to be examined, however, in light of the strictures established in the Geneva Convention. It defines the destruction of infrastructure such as water treatment facilities and power plants as a war crime since it puts the survival of the civilian population at risk and thus violates international law. Deliberate starvation of civilians as a method of warfare is also prohibited by the Geneva Convention.

O'Reilly's open advocacy of these strategies should not, then, be taken lightly, since they could involve the U.S. in activities which are defined as war crimes.

Michael Savage

Michael Savage hosts *The Savage Nation*, a nationally syndicated radio show broadcast by more than three hundred stations to an audience of 8.25 million listeners. His program is characterized by caustic comments aimed at his favorite targets, including homosexuals, feminists, and pacifists. His brief foray into television ended after five months when he was fired by MSNBC for telling a caller to "Get AIDS and die, you pig."[35] According to *Salon*'s Sidney Blumenthal, "[Savage] had just gone an insult too far for a mainstream network that had hired him in the first place on his reputation for slurs that it hoped would attract an audience share from Fox."[36] Despite this reputation, or because of it, in June 2007, Michael Savage was given *Talkers* magazine's Freedom of Speech Award.[37]

Not only does Savage have an outlet for his opinions on radio but his book *The Savage Nation* was on the *New York Times* bestseller list for over twenty weeks. In it he labels opponents of the Iraq war "traitors" and "America's most dangerous enemy." In this he echoes O'Reilly, who advised listeners that once "the war against Saddam Hussein begins, we expect every American to support our military, and if you can't do that, just shut up. Americans, and indeed our foreign allies who actively work against our military once the war is underway, will be considered enemies of the state by me."[38]

Savage furiously attacked Americans who commented publicly on the massacre in Haditha, in which U.S. Marines were accused of deliberately shooting twenty-four Iraqi civilians, including unarmed women and children.[39] Savage claimed that *Time* magazine reporter Tim McGirk, CNN host Wolf Blitzer, and U.S. Congressman Jack Murtha, who have all commented on the massacre, belong in "shackles."[40] Like O'Reilly, Savage has advocated extreme tactics, warning that Israel would lose in Lebanon unless "nothing is left living in southern Lebanon."[41] He has declared that "there shall be no mercy shown to these sub-humans. I believe that a thousand of them should be killed tomorrow. I think a thousand of them held in the Iraqi prison should be given 24 hours [for a] trial and executed."[42] He has even suggested a method for such executions: "They should put dynamite in their behinds and drop them from 35,000 feet, the whole pack of scum out of that jail."[43]

In such comments, Savage reflects the two overlapping metaphorical frames of the indistinguishability of the sub-human enemy and their spreading verminous nature. This double-frame justifies and in fact calls for massive, sweeping retaliation, in which the death of any of the enemy-Other is justified. We see this in Savage's recommendation that the U.S. flatten the U.N. building in New York with a "bunker-buster bomb" when Iranian president Mahmoud Ahmadinejad spoke to the General Assembly: after warning "our friends," Savage argued, the United States should "just take him out with everyone in there."[44] He's called Iraqi civilians "vermin" and called U.S. Marines held in American custody in connection with the slaughter at Haditha "prisoners of war."[45] In May 2004, Savage commended the abuse of prisoners at Abu Ghraib, repeatedly referring to it as "Grab-an-Arab" prison. He argued that their treatment by U.S. guards was not torture but merely humiliation and "we need more of the humiliation tactics, not less": "These people don't fear death, they fear humiliation. The only way to humiliate them is take their deepest fear, the pig, the dog, the woman with the leash, and use it on them to break them!"[46]

Ann Coulter

Not having a radio or television program of her own has not kept controversial pundit Ann Coulter out of the media spotlight. A conservative political commentator whose fame initially derived from a variety of print media, she has parlayed her celebrity status into invitations to appear on other conservative radio and television talk programs, on which the extremity of her opinions and language drew startled attention from fans and critics alike. Coulter's most notorious comment concerning the war on terror was published in her column in the *National Review* immediately after 9/11, in which she suggested that the U.S. invade Muslim countries, kill their leaders and convert them to Christianity. Three years later, Coulter wrote: "I am often asked if I still think we should invade their countries, kill their leaders, and convert them to Christianity. The answer is: Now more than ever!"[47] This has proved to be an influential remark; Savage alludes to it and applauds its sentiments when he says, "In fact, Christianity has been one of the great salvations on planet Earth. It's what's necessary in the Middle East. Others have written about it, I think these people need to be forcibly converted to Christianity."[48] Continuing, Savage explicitly links what he perceives as the Middle East's non-human status to its not being Christian; forcible conversion, he says, is "the only thing that can probably turn them into human beings."[49]

If Muslims don't have human status, they neither require nor deserve human rights. Perhaps this is why Coulter feels free to denigrate them, writing that collectively they have a "predilection for violence" and that "Islam is a car-burning cult."[50] She urges deportation for Arabs and Muslims, suggesting that "Congress could pass a law requiring that all aliens from Arabic countries leave . . . Congress could certainly pass a law requiring all aliens to get approval from the INS before boarding an airplane in the United States."[51] Muslims who want to avoid deportation, she says, could prove their loyalty by spying on their fellow citizens.[52] These appeals are neither veiled, euphemistic nor encoded; indeed, her language is deliberately provocative. Far from marginalizing her, this seems to further her popularity: her column for the Universal Press Syndicate appears in more than one hundred newspapers across the U.S., and she is a legal affairs correspondent for the conservative newspaper *Human Events* as well as a frequent guest on many TV shows, including *Hannity and Colmes*, *Wolf Blitzer Reports*, *At Large With Geraldo Rivera*, *Scarborough Country*, HBO's *Real Time with Bill Maher*, *The O'Reilly Factor*, and *Good Morning America*. She has been profiled in numerous publications, including *TV Guide*, the *Guardian* (UK), the *New York Observer*, *National Journal*, *Harper's Bazaar*, and *Elle* magazine, among others. In 2001, she was named one of the top 100 Public Intellectuals by federal judge Richard Posner. Coulter's five books have all appeared on the *New York Times* bestseller list and have sold more than a million copies in hardcover sales.[53] "Every single book she has done has become an instant best-seller," says Bob Wietrak, a vice-president for merchandising at Barnes and Noble: "Her fan base is phenomenal and she is in the media constantly. When she is in the media, it creates more media coverage. And every single day, the book sells more."[54] This notoriety is profitable: Coulter is listed with the Premiere Speakers Bureau as available for conferences with a speaking fee of $25,000 per appearance.

While Coulter is vilified by her critics and, in recent years, several newspapers have stopped publishing her column, she still has enormous support. The media watchdog organization *Media Matters For America* found that while many newspapers received thousands of letters and emails protesting her column, those supporting her won the day. The *Clarion-Ledger* of Jackson, Mississippi, stated that it would continue to run Coulter's column despite receiving about 3,000 negative e-mails. Clark Walworth, editor of the Casper *Star-Tribune*, said that his newspaper would continue to run Coulter's column despite "dozens" of messages urging him to drop it; Walworth wrote that "lots of Wyoming conservatives relish" Coulter's diatribes. The managing editor of the Elko *Daily Free Press* in Nevada stated "As of this morning we had received nearly 60 phone calls or faxes, and about nine out of 10 wanted us to keep running Ann Coulter."[55] She has also received awards for her work: in 2000 the Media Research Center presented Coulter with its "Conservative Journalist of the Year" award; the Clare Boothe Luce Policy Institute bestowed upon her its annual conservative leadership award "for her unfailing dedication to truth, freedom and conservative values and for being an exemplar, in word and deed, of what a true leader is."[56]

It is not only right-wing associations that have offered Coulter a platform. Mainstream news programs, including MSNBC and USA Today, have hired and eventually fired her, but have continued to provide her space on the airwaves. Hosts on CNN describe her as "downright hateful" while advertising their upcoming interviews with her, rewarding her for her notoriety and cashing in on her controversiality.[57] Her public persona seems well crafted for the cultivation of continued controversy; David Carr wrote in the New York Times that "seeing hate speech pop out of a blonde who knows her way around a black cocktail dress makes for compelling viewing. . . . You can accuse her of cynicism all you want, but the fact that she is one of the leading political writers of our age says something about the rest of us."[58]

Consequences

Millions of Americans and, thanks to streaming audio, people around the world, tune in for a daily diet of right-wing talk radio that is overwhelmingly racist, homophobic, and anti-immigrant. What does the popularity of such shows say about us? How are our attitudes and social policies affected by these influential platforms? "Talk radio can be one of the most divisive mediums in the nation," says Fairness and Accuracy in Reporting's (FAIR) Steve Rendall. "Some of these shows, to a greater or lesser degree, engage in kinds of bigotry by saying things like, 'These peaceniks are traitors' [or] 'These black people are undermining our society,' and they are bound to find some resonance with some listeners."[59] A report from the University of Pennsylvania's Annenberg Public Policy Center confirmed, after a year of studying political call-in radio, that many journalists identify conservative talk radio as "a discordant perhaps dangerous discourse that is intolerant and histrionic, unmindful of evidence, [and] classically propagandistic," and that it dangerously spread the kind of hate and divisiveness that led to the bombing of the Federal Building in Oklahoma City."[60]

Part of their influence can be found in the appeal of their confident, vehement and straight-forward message. As our lives become more complex, we may search for reassuring simplicity in the messages from our media. As our lives become more hurried, we may look for news that is presented quickly and in a way that demands less of our own interpretive skills. Limbaugh, O'Reilly, Savage and Coulter all offer us a clear framework through which we can understand events, and talk radio that does not distinguish between news and opinion pre-interprets events for us so we don't have to. A broad range of ideas can be re-framed through these interpretations: there is one "patriotic" way to think; the rest are traitors. Inflammatory rhetoric seems to encourage us to loathe others' ideas rather than disagree with them, and hate speech encourages us to loathe not just ideas but the people who hold them.

One reason that this transference of hatred from ideas to people deserves careful attention is that it can be linked to real action. Especially in times of threat or hardship, hate speech can mobilize action. One example occurred in Kalispell, Montana, where a local talk show host on KGEZ began a tirade against environmentalists and conservationists, blaming them for the loss of forestry and aluminum industry jobs in the community. Verbally linking them to al-Qaeda, he read out their names and addresses on air, calling them "Green Nazis" and blaming them for the town's economic downturn. The people whose names were broadcast found their cars vandalized and received harassing phone calls. When some concerned residents spoke out against the attack by the radio host they, too, were named on-air and became in turn targets of abuse. Law enforcement officials were contacted and urged to look at the harassment in a broader context. A direct link was found between the harassment and the broadcasts. Each incident alone could seem insignificant but, for the community being targeted, there was a cumulative effect. Ken Toole, program director of the Human Rights Network, noted that "we believe [the incidents] point to a pattern of escalating tension which may result in more serious criminal activity."[61]

The situation in Montana prompted the Human Rights Network to document the impact of talk radio and its ability to elicit violence. One effect of the dominance of hate-filled talk on-air is that listeners tend to be confirmed in their existing opinions, and may generalize these opinions beyond their own experience. The "ugly rhetoric may change," observes journalist Ken Olsen, reflecting "anti-Hispanic bias in the Southwest, anti-gay slurs in the Northeast, anti-Arab bias in the Midwest," but "the fact remains: There are a phenomenal number of no-holds-barred hosts pounding their bullying pulpits on talk radio."[62] The public broadcasting of hate speech, especially when it is not balanced by dissenting opinion, gives it a patina of legitimacy and respectability. University of Washington communications professor David Domke asks, "Does talk radio reinforce stereotypes and prejudice? That's the million-dollar question. My take on that is yes."[63]

Prosecuting Media Hate Speech

The balance between freedom of speech and moral or legal responsibility is the source of on-going debate. In the twentieth century there have been movements towards a greater democratization of media than ever before; at the same time, media voices also have been publicly held to account for their role in fomenting hatred. The most famous of these international account-ings were the Nuremberg Trials following World War II, in which judges from Allied countries tried twenty-two Nazi leaders on charges of conspiracy for crimes against peace, planning wars of aggression, war crimes, and crimes against humanity. One of those prosecuted was Julius Streicher, founder and editor of the anti-Jewish publication *Der Stuermer* and publisher of anti-Jew-ish children's books. Founded in 1923, *Der Stuermer*'s editorials blamed the Jews for Germany's economic depression, unemployment, and inflation. It was Streicher's active role as editor that brought him before prosecutors at Nuremberg. In convicting him, judges considered Streicher's role in advo-cating genocide against the Jews, including his admonition, published in May 1939, that "A punitive expedition must come against the Jews in Rus-sia. A punitive expedition which will provide the same fate for them that every murderer and criminal must expect. Death sentence and execution. The Jews in Russia must be killed . . . exterminated root and branch."[64] While Streicher did not physically participate in killing Jews, he repeatedly encouraged their annihilation; based on this, the court found him guilty of crimes against humanity and he was executed in 1946. Streicher's case ex-emplifies the limits of free speech and the legal culpability that may be in in-volved in inciting violence. The Nuremberg Trials made it clear that indi-viduals can be held liable in an international court if their country is charged with war crimes. Provocative parallels might be drawn between Streicher and modern-day political pundits who profit by encouraging attacks on Is-lam. If, as studies have shown, such messages can influence people's attitudes and may invoke violence against a demonized group, then should not the his-torical precedents of the Nuremberg Trials create a sense of caution in those who think that extermination may be urged with impunity?

A more recent example of prosecution connected to hate speech and in-citement to violence can be found at the 1994 International Criminal Tri-bunal for Rwanda that brought to trial the leaders of the one-hundred-day frenzy of violence that resulted in the deaths of nearly one million Rwan-dans. Prior to colonization the Hutu and Tutsi, the two main ethnic groups of Rwanda, lived peaceably together. Under Belgian colonial rule, local gov-erning powers were granted to the Tutsis based on findings from the then-popular eugenics movement in Europe: scientists deemed Tutsis superior based on larger skull size and a lighter skin color compared to the shorter, darker Hutus, features which hinted at superior Caucasian ancestry. Under Belgian colonial rule, each citizen was issued an identification card defining citizens as legally Hutu or Tutsi. This emphasis on racial division helped lay the groundwork for the conflicts between Hutu and Tutsis that erupted in the latter years of the twentieth century, triggered by the assassination of the country's Hutu president on April 6, 1994. Believing Tutsis to be responsible, Hutu extremists began to systematically murder Tutsi and moderate Hutu in retaliation. They whipped up genocidal sentiments against the Tutsi, encouraging other Hutus to join in the slaughter. According to Philip Gourevitch, "The dead of Rwanda accumulated at nearly three times the rate of Jewish dead during the Holocaust."[65] In one hundred days, approximately 800,000 people were killed, although some estimates are as high as one million. The United Nations' International Criminal Tribunal for Rwanda (ICTR) was created in 1994 to prosecute those responsible.

Among those brought to trial were three Rwandan journalists: Hassan Ngeze, editor-in-chief of *Kangura*, and Ferdinand Nahimana and Jean-Bosco Barayagwiza, founders of Radio-Television Libre des Milles Collines (RTLM). Prior to the genocide, both the radio station and newspaper carried virulent propaganda, repeatedly referring to Tutsis as serpents and cockroaches. The November 1991 issue of *Kangura* contained the ominous message, "What arms shall we use to conquer the *Inyenzi* (cockroaches) once and for all?" "Let whatever is smoldering erupt," Ngeze urged in his paper days before the genocide began, adding "a lot of blood will be poured."[66] Once the massacre began in the spring of 1994, the RTLM not only broadcast direct calls to violence but included the names and addresses of Tutsi targets to facilitate their murders.

The trial provided a further example of the media's liability for the violence it incited through the spread of hate. It judged inciting media voices as guilty of crimes against humanity as those wielding the machetes. Ngeze, Nahimana, and Barayagwiza were all found guilty and sentenced to life imprisonment. Head prosecutor Hassan Bubacar Jallow observed that "This tribunal has set an important precedent that says if the media in this day and age uses their power to attack an ethnic group or racial group, they will have to face justice."[67]

Freedom and Responsibility

The Nuremberg Trials and the International Criminal Tribunal for Rwanda clearly regarded certain media voices as participants in war crimes. Their hate speech was seen as complicit in the violent acts they urged on in others. When contemporary right-wing commentators make statements suggesting that all Arabs and Muslims should be killed when Arabs and Muslims are, indeed, being massacred by U.S. and Allied forces, could they be at risk of being charged with war crimes if America were indicted for its illegal occupation of Iraq? Would parent companies, newspaper editors, and radio stations be held accountable for distributing, producing, and publishing suspect content? Would Disney, owner of the American Broadcasting Network whose radio stations carry Limbaugh's and Savage's programs, find its family-friendly image jeopardized by a charge of crimes against humanity?

Under current legal definitions, the utterances of Coulter, Limbaugh, Savage and their colleagues fall short of the requirements for prosecution under the UN's Genocide convention. Other international legal agreements and UN conventions, however, contain articles applicable to inciting hatred, especially in times of war. Article 19 of the United Nations' International Covenant on Civil and Political Rights (ICCPR) stipulates that everyone shall have the right to freedom of expression but that this freedom is subject to restrictions pertaining to the rights or reputations of others, national security, and public health or morals. Article 20 prohibits any propagandistic advocacy of national, racial or religious hatred that incites discrimination, hostility or violence. While the UN provides guidelines and urges compliance, the articles are not legally binding and enforcement is voluntary for states signing the Covenant. The U.S. is one of the signatories to the ICCPR but added a formal exemption stating that its constitutionally protected right to freedom of speech and association override the provisions of the Covenant. Making the issue more difficult, the existing ICCPR definitions for war and propaganda are so vague that they could describe a wide range of comments. Doug Cassel, Director of the Center for International Human Rights, argues that the ICCPR's definition of propaganda as "factual exaggeration" and "overly-simplistic value judgements" could be applicable to the utterances of many politicians, American and otherwise, and would make them guilty of disseminating propaganda. The better option, says Cassel, is not to criminalize hate speech and violence-inciting language, but to publically and collectively denounce them.

In June 2006, the United Nations Human Rights Commission issued a report sharply critical of the U.S. government's failure to enforce the protections provided under the Covenant. The *Report on Failure of Compliance with Article 20 Prohibiting Propaganda for War* expresses concern over American violations, noting that "The U.S. government has sought to justify its actions and policies on the basis of the 'war on terror' and the exigencies of its illegal war in Iraq" but does not acknowledge the role of public propaganda campaigns in stoking fear and xenophobia and supporting the resulting illegal war. The UN Report argued that propaganda and hate campaigns contributed to violations of many other rights protected by the Covenant.[68]

The U.S. has insisted it will take no action contrary to its constitutional provisions for freedom of speech and association. It is worth noting, however, that the First Amendment protects the rights of citizens rather than countries; since governments are the signatories to the Covenant, they are the ones responsible for enforcement of Article 20. The UN *Report* contains arguments refuting U.S. claims that First Amendment rights supersede the Covenant. Freedom of speech, it states, is not absolute: federal courts, for example, have ruled that incitement is exempt from First Amendment protection. Not only did Bush's administration actively propagate unsubstantiated claims (such as Saddam Hussein's putative involvement in the 9/11 attacks and the existence of infamous, still undiscovered weapons of mass destruction) to justify its attack on Iraq, but many officials made these claims knowing they were not substantiated. Dissenting views within government and intelligence communities were ignored, sanctioned, or punished by an administration which continues to use propaganda to justify future pre-emptive attacks on other countries, such as Iran. As a result, the UN considers the U.S. to be in contravention of the ICCPR. There appears to be a potent gap between the U.S. government's belief in the sanctity of free speech and association and the international covenant that prohibits war propaganda. Through its allegiance to free speech, the government protects itself from culpability before international courts by invoking the Constitution. Freedom of speech, however, does not belong only to the loudest or most vocal speaker; it is also the right of those most actively silenced by hate speech and propaganda. As Cees Hamelink, of the University of Amsterdam, puts it, "You have to choose between two evils—the evil of limiting freedom of speech on the one hand, and allowing incitement of violence on the other hand. Persons who propagate hate speech take away their victim's right of free speech."[69]

International Hate Speech Laws

Several countries have devised hate speech laws more restrictive than those of the United States. The Criminal Code of Canada, for example, prohibits the expression of hatred or the advocacy of genocide based on color, race, religion, ethnic origin, or sexual orientation. Individuals can be arrested for public comments so hateful they are likely to provoke violence against others, even if no violence occurs. In 2002, Sweden, motivated by the hate speech of a neo-Nazi group, passed a bill criminalizing hate speech. Britain's *Serious Organised Crime and Police Bill* includes protection from racial hate speech. Like Sweden, Australia bans certain types of hate speech with no exemption for religious speech.

In 2001, the Australian state of Victoria passed a bill, the *Racial and Religious Tolerance Act*, making it illegal to incite hatred based on religion or race. In contrast to such laws in other countries, as the U.S. government engages in war propaganda in violation of international treaties, using the First Amendment as its justification, it can hardly restrict American media from making similar, if greatly exaggerated, statements regarding enemies of the state. While the Fairness Doctrine at least maintained a greater diversity of viewpoints on the public airwaves, its demise has allowed for a hyperbolic right-wing frenzy ensuring a perpetual open season on minorities and liberals, groups bearing the brunt of much of the hate speech generated in by right-wing conservative commentators. When Kathryn Ruud analyzes the metaphors and language used by talk-radio hosts to describe liberals, she finds it disturbingly similar to "the language of Hitler's genocidal machine," an extremity of speech used to confirm and denigrate difference.[70]

The issue of free speech is a contentious one, as York University professor Evelyn Kallen demonstrates. There are, she notes, two groups dominating the debate: those who argue that freedom of speech is without check or limit, and those who argue that freedom of speech does not protect the right to vilify others.[71] The latter group argues that the threat posed by hate speech is urgent enough to require limits on free speech.

Re-Framing the Debate: From Freedom of Speech to the Voices of Our Friends

One way out of the polarities of the free speech versus hate speech debate is to reject state-mandated limitations to speech and to call instead for heightened and mobilized public resistance to the rise of hate. Its prevalence on our public airwaves has conspired to make it appear, by virtue of its endless recirculation, somehow less shocking. Those who can't bear to hear it turn the channel; those who listen are often so blunted by its vehemence that they tune out its most pernicious expressions. Instead, we need to challenge the erroneous, irresponsible assumptions of hate speakers as fervently as they are disseminated. While we defend freedom of speech, we must rally our creative energies to find solutions other than the blunt one of censorship. We must be as ingenious as the teenagers of Palatine, Illinois, who, when the local Ku Klux Klan announced its plan to register for the state's Adopt-a-Highway program, showed up in a flood at City Hall and filled in so many applications for the program that the Klan chapter's application was pushed onto a waiting list. We must be as bold as the town of Pulaski, Tennessee, which in 1989 closed its doors to white supremacists when members of the

KKK and Aryan Nation attempted to rally there. When they arrived, the town was closed: there were no open stores, restaurants, bathrooms, or public areas available. Instead, the Klan found the town draped in orange banners, the international color of brotherhood.[72] Such united community responses fight hatred with empathy and bigotry with compassion. The need to combat hatred—whether directed at those of other races, religious beliefs, or sexual orientation—brings people together in creative ways. In contrast, conservative talk radio appears to succeed only in uniting like-minded people who view difference as a threat and are not outraged by calls for the annihilation of a country's population. If the hosts of these programs used their medium's impressive ability to mobilize public sentiment towards creating a more harmonious society, instead of an increasingly divisive, fearful, and intolerant one, there would be even more examples like these. "Somehow," says the University of Washington's Margaret Gordon, "we have to reawaken the American public and have them be more demanding about the information coming their way."[73] Part of this re-awakening involves holding both ourselves and our media to higher standards: we must demand nuance over simplicity, contexts over slogans. We must challenge misinformation and deception, reveal narrowness of thought, expose distortion. If speakers like Coulter offer us, as author Jane Smiley insists, a constant "test of our humanity,"[74] we fail that test when we do not say no to speech that offers only the morbidly fascinating lure of its rage and bitterness. Instead, we might exercise a different brand of freedom, and freely choose to stop buying the books, stop listening to the programs, and vocally repudiate our role as hatred's complicit witness.

Notes

1. Sidney Blumenthal. "The right wing's summer of hate." *Salon*. August 15, 2003. See dir.salon.com/story/opinion/feature/2003/08/15/hate/index.html (July 3, 2007).

2. Yigal Carmon. "Option Paper: Creating Awareness: Education, Media and Memory." *Stockholm International Forum*. January 26–28, 2004. See www.manskligara ttigheter.gov.se/stockholmforum/2004/page1589.html (July 3, 2007).

3. Richard Delgado and Jean Stefancic. *Understanding Words That Wound*. Boulder, CO: Westview Press, 2004: 16.

4. Todd Gitlin quoted in Brad Kava. "Experts predict move to civility on talk radio after Imus firing." *San Jose Mercury News*. April 13, 2007.

5. Sidney Blumenthal. "The right wing's summer of hate."

6. Ken Olsen. "Does Talk Radio Incite Hate?" *Tolerance.org*. April 25, 2003. See www.tolerance.org/news/article_tol.jsp?id=752 (July 3, 2007).

7. Richard Delgado and Jean Stefancic. *Understanding Words That Wound*.

8. PEW study cited in *Project for Excellence in Journalism*. "The State of the News Media." 2007. *Project for Excellence in Journalism*. See www.stateofthenewsmedia.org /2007/narrative_radio_talk_radio.asp (July 3, 2007).

9. Joshua Holland. "The Structural Imbalance of Political Talk Radio." *alternet .org*. June 29, 2007. See alternet.org/mediaculture/55269/?comments=view&cID= 686257&pID=686181 (July 3, 2007).

10. *Talkers Magazine*. "Top Talk Personalities." *Talkers Magazine*. June 2007. See www.talkers.com/main/index.php?option=com_content&task=view&id=17&Itemid= 34 (July 3, 2007).

11. Ted Gregory. "Right and wrong; Rush Limbaugh critics want to set the facts straight, but it's not easy." *Chicago Tribune*. August 18, 1995.

12. *Talkers Magazine*. "The 25 Greatest Radio Talk Show Hosts of All Time." September 2002.

13. Dan Weil. "Limbaugh's New Radio Contract Worth $285 Million." *The Palm Beach Post*. July 20, 2001.

14. Lea Goldman. "The Celebrity 100." *Forbes*. July 3, 2006.

15. *Media Research Center*. "Rush Limbaugh to accept media excellence award at MRC 20th anniversary gala."*Media Research Center*. March 20, 2007. See www.media research.org/press/2007/press20070320.asp (July 30, 2007).

16. Margaret Carlson. "Public Eye." *Time*. Jan. 23, 1995.

17. Jeff Cohen and Steve Rendall. "Can a Man Who Has a Problem with People of Color Be a Color Commentator On 'Monday Night Football'?" *Los Angeles Times*. June 7, 2000.

18. Paul de Rooij. "Glossary of the Iraqi Occupation." *Dissident Voice*. April 29, 2004. See www.dissidentvoice.org/April2004/DeRooij0429.htm (July 3, 2007).

19. Paul de Rooij. "Glossary of the Iraqi Occupation."

20. Kurt Nimmo. "Limbaugh and the Babes of Abu Ghraib." *Counterpunch*. May 8–9, 2004. See www.counterpunch.org/nimmo05082004.html (July 3, 2007).

21. Kurt Nimmo. "Limbaugh and the Babes of Abu Ghraib."

22. Bryon York. "A New Attack on Rush." *The National Review on line*. May 28 2004. See www.nationalreview.com/york/york200405280844.asp (July 3, 2007).

23. Bryon York. "A New Attack on Rush."

24. Bill O'Reilly. "Newspaper Column List." *BillOReilly.com*. January 8, 2007. See www.billoreilly.com/pg/jsp/general/newspapercolumn.jsp (July 3, 2007).

25. *Random House*. "Author profile: Bill O'Reilly." See www.randomhouse.com /author/results.pperl?authorid=22596 (July 3, 2007).

26. Lea Goldman. "The Celebrity 100."

27. Sidney Blumenthal. "The right wing's summer of hate."

28. Mike Conway and Maria Grabe. "Content analysis of O'Reilly's rhetoric finds spin to be a 'factor'." *Indiana University Press Release*. (May 2, 2007). See newsinfo .iu.edu/news/page/normal/5535.html (July 3, 2007).

29. O'Reilly: Iraqi people are "primitive," "prehistoric group." Fri, Jun 18, 2004 at 4:44 P.M. EST. See mediamatters.org/items/200406180005

30. *Fairness and Accuracy in Reporting.* "Media Pundits Advocate Civilian Targets." *FAIR.* September 21, 2001. See www.fair.org/index.php?page=1675 (July 10, 2007).

31. *FAIR.* "Media Pundits Advocate Civilian Targets."

32. Thomas Wheeler. "O'Reilly's Final Solution." *Z.* June 22, 2004. See www.zmag .org/content/showarticle.cfm?ItemID=5753 (July 10, 2007).

33. Rayan El-Amine. "The Making of the Arab Menace." *Left Turn.* May 1, 2005. See www.leftturn.org/?q=node/345 (July 3, 2007).

34. Thomas Wheeler. "O'Reilly's Final Solution."

35. *Fairness and Accuracy in Reporting.* "Savage Homophobia on MSNBC." July 7, 2003. See www.fair.org/index.php?page=1621 (July 10, 2007).

36. Sidney Blumenthal. "The right wing's summer of hate."

37. John Lillpop. "Michael Savage Honored With Prestigious Freedom of Speech Award!" *Canada Free Press.* March 28, 2007. See www.canadafreepress.com/2007 /lillpop032807.htm (July 3, 2007).

38. *Fairness and Accuracy in Reporting.* "Iraq and the Media." March 19, 2007. See www.fair.org/index.php?page=3062 (July 10, 2007).

39. *Associated Press.* "Evidence suggests Haditha killings deliberate: Pentagon source." August 2, 2006.

40. *Media Matters for America.* "Savage called Iraqi witnesses of alleged Haditha massacre 'vermin' and 'scum,' proclaimed detained Marines are American 'POWs'." June 9, 2006. See mediamatters.org/items/200606090010 (July 3, 2007).

41. *Media Matters for America.* "Savage: Israel must ensure 'nothing is left living in Southern Lebanon' and must 'free itself of the men . . . act[ing] like Holocaust Jews hiding in the sewer'." Jul 31, 2006. See mediamatters.org/items/200607310004 (July 3, 2007).

42. *Media Matters for America.* "Savage Nation: It's not just Rush; Talk radio host Michael Savage: 'I commend' prisoner abuse; 'we need more'." May 13, 2004. See mediamatters.org/items/200405130004 (July 3, 2007).

43. *Media Matters for America.* "Savage Nation: It's not just Rush."

44. *Media Matters for America.* "Savage: 'Use a bunker-buster bomb on the U.N.'" July 24, 2006. See mediamatters.org/items/200607240007 (July 3, 2007).

45. *Media Matters for America.* "Savage called Iraqi witnesses of alleged Haditha massacre."

46. *Media Matters for America.* "Savage Nation: It's not just Rush; Talk radio host Michael Savage: 'I commend' prisoner abuse; 'we need more'." May 13, 2004. See mediamatters.org/items/200405130004 (July 3, 2007).

47. Ann Coulter. *How to Talk to a Liberal (If You Must).* New York City: Crown Publishing Group, 2004.

48. *Media Matters for America.* "Savage: Arabs are 'non-humans' and 'racist, fascist bigots'." May 14, 2004. See mediamatters.org/items/200405140003 (July 3, 2007).

49. *Media Matters for America.* "Savage: Arabs are 'non-humans'"

50. *Media Matters for America.* "Islam is 'a car-burning cult.'" February 10, 2006. See mediamatters.org/items/200602100003 (July 3, 2007).

51. *Washington Monthly.* "The Wisdom of Ann Coulter." October 2001. See www
.washingtonmonthly.com/features/2001/0111.coulterwisdom.html (July 10, 2007).

52. *Washington Monthly.* "The Wisdom of Ann Coulter."

53. David Carr. "Deadly Intent: Ann Coulter, Word Warrior." *New York Times.*
June 12, 2006.

54. David Carr. "Deadly Intent."

55. *Media Matters for America.* "Citing reader support, several papers will keep
publishing Coulter." March 12, 2007. See mediamatters.org/items/200703120010
(July 4, 2007).

56. *Washington Monthly.* "The Wisdom of Ann Coulter." October 2001. See www
.washingtonmonthly.com/features/2001/0111.coulterwisdom.html (July 10, 2007).

57. *Media Matters for America.* "Coulter's reward for her 'downright hateful' comments: another appearance on CNN!" March 5, 2007. See mediamatters.org/items
/200703050003 (July 4, 2007).

58. David Carr. "Deadly Intent."

59. Ken Olsen. "Does Talk Radio Incite Hate?" *Tolerance.org.* April 25, 2003. See
www.tolerance.org/news/article_tol.jsp?id=752 (July 3, 2007).

60. Joseph Cappella, Joseph Turow, and Kathleen Hall Jamieson. "Call-In Political Talk Radio: Background, Content, Audiences, Portrayal in Mainstream Media."
University of Pennsylvania Annenberg Public Policy Center. July 22, 1996.

61. Ken Olsen. "Does Talk Radio Incite Hate?"

62. Ken Olsen. "Does Talk Radio Incite Hate?"

63. Ken Olsen. "Does Talk Radio Incite Hate?"

64. *Trial Watch.* "Julius Streicher."See www.trial-ch.org/en/trial-watch/profile/db
/facts/julius_streicher_22.html; and, motlc.wiesenthal.com/site/pp.asp?c=gvKVLc
MVIuG&b =395155 (July 4, 2007).

65. Philip Gourevitch. *We wish to inform you that tomorrow we will be killed with our
families: Stories from Rwanda.* New York City: Picador, 1998.

66. Charity Kagwi-Ndungu. "The challenges in prosecuting print media for incitement to genocide." *International Development Research Centre.* See www.idrc.ca/fr
/ev-108292-201-1-DO _TOPIC.html (July 10, 2007). Document(s) 34 de 37.

67. Emily Wax. "Journalists Sentenced In Rwanda Genocide. Prosecutor Said
'Hate Media' Urged Killings." *Washington Post Foreign Service.* December 4, 2003.

68. *Media Matters for America.* "Help Stop Conservative Hate Speech on Public Airwaves." August 24, 2005. See mediamatters.org/items/200508240007 (July 4, 2007).

69. Ernst-Jan Pfauth. "When Hate Speech Turns Deadly, Who Can Stop It?" *Inter-
Press Service News Agency (IPS).* Apr 13, 2007. See ipsnews.net/news.asp?idnews=
37345 (July 4, 2007).

70. Kathryn Ruud. "Liberal parasites and other creepers: Rush Limbaugh, Ken
Hamblin, and the discursive construction of group identities." In *At War With Words.*
Mirjana Dedaic and Daniel Nelson (Eds). Berlin: Mouton de Gruyter, 2003: 27–62.

71. Evelyn Kallen. "Hate on the Net: A Question of Rights/A Question of Power."
Electronic Journal of Sociology. 1998. See www.sociology.org/content/vol003.002/kallen
.html (July 4, 2007).

72. Joseph Cappella and Joseph Turow, Kathleen Hall. "Call-In Political Talk Radio: Background, Content, Audiences, Portrayal in Mainstream Media. *University of Pennsylvania Annenberg Public Policy Center*. July 22, 1996.

73. Ken Olsen. "Does Talk Radio Incite Hate?"

74. Jane Smiley. "All-American Hate Speech." *The Huffington Post*. June 7, 2006. See www.huffingtonpost.com/jane-smiley/allamerican-hate-speech_b_22463.html (July 4, 2007).

PART THREE

DANGEROUS DISCOURSES

CHAPTER SEVEN

Media March to War:
Understanding News Filters

If you're not careful, the newspapers will have you hating the people who are being oppressed, and loving the people who are doing the oppressing.

—Malcolm X

Media Propaganda and Dehumanization

Since 9/11, mainstream media have consistently used metaphor to present terrorists, those suspected of terrorism, and even civilians linked through religion, culture, or ethnicity to countries associated with terrorism, as inhuman, non-human, or sub-human. Metaphoric language has called, openly or subtly, for indiscriminate violence and extermination. In the way that it serves and reproduces government interests, this propaganda is a far cry from the principles of responsible investigative reporting. As *New York Times* columnist Anthony Lewis memorably phrased it, "Journalism's high purpose is not to get close to power but to speak truth to power."[1] In order to understand the media's role in constructing and reproducing racist propaganda about the war on terror and its willingness to uncritically apply largely unexamined metaphoric frames, it is necessary to understand the context of contemporary monopoly media in which powerful political and economic forces significantly shape the content of the daily news. Understanding the monopoly culture in which media operates is crucial, given the complex interplay between media producers, sponsors, and viewers. As Norman Fairclough observes, media is socially significant because of its cumulative effect, as are the controls and contexts of media production. While the influence of what Fairclough calls "power-holders" on a single text can be negligible, the "effects of media power are cumulative, working through particular ways of handling causality and agency" and "particular ways of positioning the reader." Because of this repetitive, cumulative effect, "media discourse is able to exercise a pervasive and powerful influence in social reproduction."[2] Understanding the sources and operations of what cultural critic bell hooks calls media's "motivated representation"[3] allows us to discern the links between media contexts and real-world consequences, consequences that are critical to national, even global safety.

When studying media effects, it is tempting to emphasize the audience's passivity and impressionability. Media are often portrayed as a top-down structure with audience opinion and understanding directly shaped by the selection of stories offered, the amount of coverage provided, and over-reliance on the media's objectivity and professional distance. Far from being passive, however, viewers and listeners are active participants in media's creation of symbols and meanings. This is particularly evident in media coverage of the developing world and disadvantaged groups, all of which are linked to stories about the war on terror.

While media content and audience response are inextricably linked phenomena, media portrayals are undeniably influential, especially when they are seen as neutral and unbiased. Greg Philo suggests that providing news coverage without any related or contextualizing discussion distinctly shapes audience understanding of a story.[4] In the war on terror, for example, neocolonial assumptions regularly skew the underlying interpretation of stories. Neo-colonialism, in which economic and political means are used by a major power to maintain or extend its influence on underdeveloped nations, shapes news stories from the Global South, for instance, which is overwhelmingly presented as primitive or backward, populated by people portrayed as savage, mindless, or violent. The audience consuming this information comes to regard conflicts in the developing world as disconnected from their own social, political, and commercial lives. Events in the developing world are seen as stemming from corrupt leaders and a primitive citizenry, resulting in a perspective that assumes "It's their own fault." Since problems are portrayed as relating to the essential inferiority of the country and its inhabitants, conflicts are seen as hopeless and inevitable. The treatment of the Other in news media supports Ruth Wodak's observation that racism "as both social practice and ideology" tends to "manifest itself discursively." [5] In particular, many media voices perpetuate neo-colonial portrayals of the Middle East in general and Iraq in particular as culturally primitive. When an audience brings its own stereotypes to the media's broader misperceptions, biases are continually reinforced and re-circulated. Together, then, media, speech writers and journalists share many of these assumptions with their audience, assumptions reinforced by coverage that is overwhelmingly negative. Further, the media assume the audience has knowledge of the context and background of news events; when a story is presented it often fails to provide sufficient historical, political, or cultural background and audiences are left with an unclear understanding of the details or nuances of a story.

Philo's findings on the potential dangers of media distortion on audience understanding have a new-found significance when examining public comprehension of the war on terror. A 2003 study by the University of Maryland's Program on International Policy shows that a majority of Americans have "significant misperceptions" about the Iraq war; the frequency of these misconceptions varied significantly according to the individual's primary source of news. People who mostly watched Fox News, for example, were more likely to have misperceptions than those who primarily turned to NPR or PBS for coverage.[6] Steven Kull, director of PIPA, comments, "While we cannot assert that these misperceptions created the support for going to war with Iraq, it does appear likely that support for the war would be substantially lower if fewer members of the public had these misperceptions."[7]

Journalism can, if it chooses, mitigate these misperceptions. One web posting discusses the work of journalists like *The Washington Post's* Anthony Shadid and author Asne Seierstad's *The Bookseller of Kabul*. The blogger says their work "can be seen as attempts to humanize the other by telling you how similar they are to us. More pointedly, they 'humanize' the 'other' by endowing them with cultural values that we value and admire—like reading books or going to theater. . . . The sad fact is," the writer continues, "it is inconceivable for a lot of Americans to imagine people living in [a] shanty town among mounds of garbage, with tattered clothes and emaciated bodies, to have a fully formed emotional life with their own frustrations and aspirations. It is almost as if these masses are a lower form of life—whose lives are as inconsequential as their deaths are immaterial."[8]

This rare journalistic humanizing effect is remarkable for its near-absence in contemporary media. In the midst of this absence, it is easier to take the step of dehumanizing and demonizing the Other. Abetting this mind-set, according to media analyst Howard Zinn, is "an even bigger lie: the arrogant idea that this country is the center of the universe, exceptionally virtuous, admirable, superior." Zinn argues, "If our starting point for evaluating the world around us is the firm belief that this nation is somehow endowed by Providence with unique qualities that make it morally superior to every other nation on Earth," then "we are not likely to question the President when he says we are sending our troops here or there, or bombing this or that, in order to spread our values—democracy, liberty, and let's not forget free enterprise—to some God-forsaken (literally) place in the world."[9]

Framing and Representation

"The most effective propaganda," says political analyst Michael Parenti, "relies on framing rather than on falsehood."[10] Parenti examines methods by which media maintain the appearance of objectivity while actually packaging information in a way that creates a desired impression; Parenti calls this "bending the truth rather than breaking it."[11] These techniques include the amount of time the story is covered, where the story is situated in a broadcast, and the story's tone, headlines, photographs and accompanying visuals. Furthermore, Parenti points out, "Many things are reported in the news but few are explained."[12] Ideologically and politically, a story's deeper aspects are rarely articulated: "Little is said about how the social order is organized and for what purposes. Instead we are left to see the world as do mainstream pundits, as a scatter of events and personalities propelled by happenstance, circumstance, confused intentions, bungled operations, and individual ambition—rarely by powerful class interests."[13] The media's portrayal of news as a "scatter of events and personalities" is enmeshed not only in frames of ideology, interest, and economics, but in the larger, enduring frame of race. Karim H. Karim indicts Anglo-American reporting for its stereotyped, dichotomized discourse, which relies on polarizing representations suggesting "we're" good and "they're" bad. Karim also notes the frequency, throughout western journalism, of loaded language; generalizations of diverse Islamic states; erroneous interpretations of cultural phenomena; loaded language; historical and contextual omissions; dehumanizing portrayals and dangerous analogies.[14]

These problematic frames are significant because the media provide the primary lens through which most people view a conflict. Journalists' choices of images to focus on, questions to pursue and facts to report or ignore can have a significant effect on audience comprehension. The news should not be seen, therefore, as a series of facts or a mirror of external reality but as a cultural product. Its accounts of the world are produced from within specific interpretive frameworks. A media frame tells viewers what kind of conflict they are observing, which sources of information are relevant, what questions to ask, and how to interpret the answers. Mainstream media set the agenda through their selection of topics, distribution of concerns, emphasis and framing of issues, filtering of information, and presentation of the debate. As Noam Chomsky explains, "They determine, they select, they shape, they control, they restrict," all in order to "serve the interests of dominant, elite groups in the society."[15]

With emotions running high after 9/11, the media cooperated with government interests by failing to demand answers from the President and the Secretary of Defense, and by zealously reproducing, often verbatim, government and military directives. Fundamental journalistic principles of objectivity, investigation, and asking tough, probing questions were abandoned. Gary Kamiya argued that "the real failing was not in any one area; it was across the board. Bush administration lies and distortions went unchallenged, or were actively promoted," while "problematic assumptions about terrorism and the war on terror were rarely debated or even discussed. Vital historical context was almost never provided." This wasn't just, says Kamiya, a failure of analysis. With "some honorable exceptions, good old-fashioned reporting was also absent."[16]

Media critics point to the lack of historical contexts included in media coverage of terrorist attacks, and its resistance to offering insight, analysis or reflection on what might compel a terrorist group to attack for fear of being accused of justifying, rationalizing, or sympathizing with terrorists. David Edwards states that

> The media has consistently denied the public access to authoritative voices that predicted, and could help explain, the causes of bitter opposition to Western policies in the Middle East. By suppressing these insights, the media is denying the public access to credible alternatives for ridding the world of terrorism that do not involve the slaughter of untold numbers of people in Afghanistan and Iraq.[17]

One example of the media's neglect of context is the dearth of media coverage of the U.S.-imposed sanctions in Iraq between the first Gulf War and the current war in Iraq. Many in the Arab world have grievances against the U.S. because of its policy towards Iraq: by the UN's admission, the sanctions regime contributed to the deaths by illness and starvation of 500,000 Iraqi children. Denis Halliday, former UN Assistant Secretary-General, says that the sanctions were "a deliberate policy to destroy the people of Iraq."[18] But, as Edwards contends, there is little in the media to link the sanctions to the rise of terrorism or Arab-Muslim anger. One reason, therefore, to seek understanding of the historical contexts of terrorism is not to rationalize or justify it, but to understand rationally its root causes in the hope that, by addressing them, we can prevent further terrorism.[19]

We expect that citizens who keep abreast of the news will be educated and informed with information relevant to understanding critical issues. This cannot happen when media employs more propaganda than insight, and fosters discourses of hatred that make our world less safe by cementing, through its coverage, difference and dehumanization.

The Media's Coverage of the War

Kenneth Payne asserts that contemporary media are "indisputably an instrument of war," helping governments win "domestic and international public opinion," a task as essential to winning modern wars as "defeating the enemy on the battlefield."[20] Media's role as an instrument of war, argues Payne is "true regardless of the aspirations of many journalists to give an impartial and balanced assessment of conflict."[21] Kamiya and Payne are not alone in their critical analysis of the media's dereliction of duty: a study of British news conducted by the University of Manchester found the media most likely to report good news about the coalition forces. Study leader Dr. Piers Robinson stated that the news media tends to report the official word from coalition leaders, offering a positive spin on events. "Coverage of the war was narrated largely through the voice of the coalition with much less attention given to other actors," said Robinson. "This suggests that factors such as reliance upon elite sources, patriotism and news values rooted in episodic coverage continue to be important in shaping war-time coverage."[22]

Lies and propaganda, known to journalists and critical observers at the time, were presented in the press as factual. Amy Goodman, of the American radio and television news program *Democracy Now*, commented that U.S. media reached an "all-time low" in failing to reflect mainstream opinion and Americans' desire for trusted information, instead acting as a "cheerleader" for war.[23]

One way to implicitly support the war is to suppress publication of civilian death statistics, a topic Western media rarely broaches. While American and NATO soldiers killed are counted and named, the totals of Iraqis and Afghans killed by invading forces, insurgent attacks, starvation, displacement, or unexploded ordnance is unreckoned. News media rely on Pentagon figures for civilian death tolls, but the job of tracking numbers of Iraqi or Afghan deaths has fallen to independent organizations, who rarely receive media attention. The British medical journal *The Lancet* estimated that in the first year of the Iraq war, 100 000 Iraqis might have died.[24] Why does the

Western news media have such an aversion to publicizing civilian death tolls that do not come from the Pentagon, which is loath to report civilian casualties in the first place? Journalist Judith Coburn argues that civilian death tolls are innately political and that if the media turned its attention to the scale of human suffering involved in the wars in Afghanistan and Iraq, support for the war would wane.[25] CNN has directed journalists to stress that U.S. forces do everything in their power to avoid civilian casualties,[26] and a memo circulated at a Florida newspaper warned editors not to print photos of civilian casualties from Afghanistan or run stories that lead with civilian deaths on the front page.[27] Dave Markland has chronicled the lengths to which Canadian print media go to portray Canadian military involvement in Afghanistan positively. When a NATO attack killed scores of villagers, the *Toronto Star* and the *Globe & Mail* both reported the incident and used the NATO death toll of eleven civilians killed. When it was later discovered that 31 civilians had been killed by NATO forces, only the *Globe & Mail* printed a small correction. When *Human Rights Watch* and *Amnesty International* issued pointed criticisms of NATO conduct in Afghanistan and the preponderance of civilian casualties, both newspapers neglected to report their criticisms.[28]

The reality of war is rarely portrayed by mainstream media, and thus fails to reach a broad audience. These suppressions create distrust: according to a 2005 Gallup poll, only 54 percent of Americans feel the military keeps them properly informed, and only 61 percent feel the same about the media. More than 75 percent of respondents said that the military provides false or inaccurate information to the media.[29] This indicates a high level of public distrust; given the under-reporting of important issues that run counter to the interests of the U.S. government and military, perhaps such skepticism is not surprising.

The peace movement is also subject to media under-reporting. Since September 2001, universities, trade unions, faith groups, NGOs and peace groups have mobilized against the war in Afghanistan and Iraq, forming the biggest anti-war movement in history.[30] An international day of protest on the eve of the invasion of Iraq drew as many as 30 million protestors in approximately 800 cities around the world.[31] Yet, Amy Goodman notes the media's coverage of the peace movement failed to reflect this; because of the lack of coverage, the peace movement appeared to be only a fringe movement: "In the lead-up to war, the majority of people were actually against war and for more inspections and diplomacy," she said. "In fact, I would say those opposed to war were not a fringe minority, not even a silent majority, but the silenced majority, silenced by the corporate media."[32]

Media Filters

Contrary to popular thought, the media is not a window on the world. Media scholars challenge this metaphor as providing a false sense of how news production really works. While contemporary journalism claims that modern news media produce an objective, truthful, balanced, neutral account of events, social scientists identify the prevalence of subjectivity in the media.

Media scholars use the phrase the "manufacture of news" to communicate its constructed nature; the news business involves a myriad of deliberate decisions about the ordering and placement of stories, selection of sources, use of language, and tone of headlines. In addition, journalists must contend with external factors affecting the presentation of the news. "Money and power," say Noam Chomsky and Edward Herman in *Manufacturing Consent*, can "filter the news, marginalizing dissent and allowing the government and dominant private interests to get their message across to the public."[33] They argue that the production of news is affected by a powerful gate-keeping process which filters out certain issues and opinions. Governments, media owners, advertisers, key sources, flak, and ideology all shape the news we consume. As a result, mainstream for-profit news media frequently distort information: instead of a well-researched, balanced account addressing multiple perspectives in neutral language, we often find superficial or one-sided accounts that are closer to propaganda than to journalism.

Governments

There is a surprising degree of government influence on news media. It is commonly believed that a free press is a cornerstone of democracy and that only totalitarian governments actively control their national news media. This is not the case. For example, it was not long after the invasion of Iraq that the first American casualties occurred. Their bodies were transported on military planes to the mortuary at Dover Air Force Base. Images of the bodies arriving, however, were censored by a Pentagon ban forbidding publication of photos showing the unloading of military caskets. The ban was first issued in 1991, following a public-relations disaster for then-President George H. W. Bush, who was shown on a split screen in a news broadcast laughing and joking about the swift victory in the U.S. attack on Panama while, on the other screen, an Air Force transport plane unloaded caskets bearing the remains of U.S. soldiers killed in the invasion. The visual juxtaposition of the two contrasting images evoked strong public reaction, and then-Defense Secretary Dick Cheney attempted to ensure there would be no future repetitions. Although news outlets sued the government to lift the

ban, in 1996 the U.S. Court of Appeals supported it, citing the need to protect the privacy of grieving families. The ban was reissued by the Pentagon
in 2003 during the U.S. invasion of Iraq, prohibiting all photographs of "de-
ceased military personnel returning to or departing" from air bases.

For more than two years, Americans were prevented from seeing photos of
coffins arriving. The government did not want a daily visual montage of the
dead reminding the public of the grim reality of the war and putting generic
death statistics into a more immediate human context. The suppression of
the images was successful until 2004 when Tami Silico, an American cargo
worker for Maytag Aircraft in Kuwait, emailed friends and family back home
and attached a digital photo of flag-draped coffins of American casualties being loaded on a 747. On April 18, 2004, the photo and story appeared on the
front page of the *Seattle Times*. In the interviews that followed, Silico insisted
she had only intended to show the "dignity, care, and respect" given war casualties in preparation for the final trip back to the U.S; the flood of front-
page photos of military coffins that appeared in dozens of newspapers in the
days following was, she said, an unintended consequence.[34] Initially, Silico
was cautioned by her employer not to repeat this action. A few days later,
however, in response to Pentagon communications the company fired both
Silico and her estranged husband who also worked for Maytag Aircraft.

In October 2004, Ralph Begleiter, a University of Delaware journalism
professor and former CNN correspondent, sued the Department of Defense
under the Freedom of Information Act for the release of photographs and
videos of coffins arriving at the air force base.[35] The Pentagon maintained it
was simply enforcing the policy implemented in 1991 but six months after
the suit was launched, in April 2005, the Pentagon released more than 700
previously suppressed images of returning American casualties from both the
Iraq and Afghanistan conflicts. This action pre-empted a ruling in the lawsuit and confirmed that images of flag-draped coffins are rightfully part of the
public record.

In Canada, in April 2006 the newly elected Conservative government followed American policy and banned media from covering the return of bodies of soldiers killed in the Canadian mission in Afghanistan. Where previously Canadians had seen broadcast images of the solemn repatriation of its
soldiers killed in Afghanistan, occasions attended by prime ministers, cabinet ministers, generals and the Governor-General, Canadian Prime Minister
Stephen Harper imposed restrictions in order, he said, to respect the privacy
of the soldiers and their families. Military families in Canada and the U.S.,
however, have spoken out forcefully against this. Sean Bruyea, retired Canadian veteran of the 1991 Persian Gulf War, said "The cost of the war should

always be shown front and center, so we can make informed decisions. We rely a lot on public support. I would hope Canadians would step up to the plate to defend us."[36] American Jane Bright, whose son Evan Ashcraft, age twenty-four, was killed in Iraq on July 24, 2003, told a peace group that

> We must put aside the secrecy and the lies and let the American public view the coffins when they return. How else will America feel the pain that the families such as mine are feeling. Our president may be a war president, but I don't believe the American people want an open-ended war based on lies, secrecy and deceit. Let the media, and the rest of America see the coffins when they return to U.S. soil. It's the least we can do. Our children did not live in secrecy, they should not be shrouded in secrecy upon their passing.[37]

There is more at stake in government suppression of news coverage than control of images. Journalists in the field are also affected. Most notably, instead of reporting independently and interviewing their own subjects, correspondents covering the war in Iraq are required by the Pentagon to travel within military units. This is not entirely new; throughout the twentieth century, official war correspondents have been employed to cover major military conflicts, including such notables as Ernest Hemingway, Stephen Crane, and Rudyard Kipling. The "embedding" scheme implemented for the wars on Iraq and Afghanistan, however, is something unique. In this case, hand-picked reporters receive military training in order to become conditioned to identify with their assigned units. Unlike war correspondents in the past, these journalists live and travel with troops; rather than examining events from the outside, embedded journalists share the life of the soldiers, which, according to journalistic ethics instructor Aly Colon, "challenges the journalistic tradition that exhorts reporters to remain detached from those they cover."[38]

During and since the 1991 Gulf War, the White House and the Pentagon have intensified their media censorship. Journalists were permitted to travel only in pools escorted by military escorts, and since they were not allowed to use their own transport, they forfeited their autonomy in being able to track down and investigate their own stories; instead, they see only what they encounter as part of their officially limited mobility. Many military activities in Iraq and Afghanistan are off-limits to journalists altogether, and the Defense Department censors all photos, video footage, and battlefield dispatches. The Pentagon insists on pre-screening and approving any report involving normally restricted material, and its refusal to approve releases makes newsworthy material off-limits to the journalist. "Off the record" communication between military personnel and journalists was forbidden; the Pentagon insisted that all interviews be on the record, discouraging soldiers from registering criticism or divulging damaging information. This relationship allowed war crimes committed by the United States and allied forces to be systematically covered up. For example, every mainstream media outlet repeatedly reported that U.S. smart bombs had inflicted devastating damage on Iraqi military targets, while sparing civilian lives. Later it was revealed that the vast majority of the bombs were unguided missiles and that thousands of innocent Iraqi men, women and children were killed.[39]

Prior to launching the invasion in 2003, conscious of a deepening public opposition, war planners and media chiefs cooperated in a sweeping system of media control, claiming this would provide greater access to frontline war reporters. Five hundred hand-picked journalists from selected western media agencies were embedded into U.S. military operations. As the White House was issuing statements saying it hoped war could be avoided, reporters, photographers, and camera crews were being assigned to military units. In a February 18, 2003 interview, Bryan Whitman, deputy assistant Secretary of Defense for media operations, disclosed some of the motivation behind the Pentagon's new system, noting that it allowed them to "protect" information: "we want to be able to protect that information that is going to determine the success of an operation, and we don't want any reporting that's going to unnecessarily jeopardize those individuals that are executing that mission. . . . I also have never met a journalist, particularly one that's traveling with that unit, that would have any interest in compromising the mission of the unit."[40]

Critics of this practice, even among other journalists, ask who, in such situations, sets the agenda for the news. The media, however, have generally buried negative comments. Former CNN correspondent Bernard Shaw says, "The idea of journalists allowing themselves to be taken under the wing of the United States military to me is very dangerous. I think journalists who agree to go with combat units effectively become hostages of the military, which can control the movements of the journalists and, more importantly, control their ability when they file their stories."[41] Journalists' neutrality is compromised because the military sees them not as non-partisan reporters but as "force multipliers" selling the war story from the military point of view. Their close association with the military decreases distance between observer and observed, interfering with access and openness. While the majority of the embedded journalists saw themselves as performing a valuable role in the conflict, critics argued that this came at the expense of their independence. *Army Times* staff writer Gina Cavallaro, however, has said that embedded journalism is not necessarily a "bad thing": journalists are "relying more on the military to get them where they want to go, and as a result, the military is getting smarter about getting its own story told."[42] Kenneth Payne, however, argues that not only does embedding allow the military "a high degree of control over which part of the battlefield will receive media coverage," but more subtly, it identifies the reporters far too intimately with the people on whom they're reporting. There is already, claims Payne, a disposition among many American journalists to back American soldiers, and "embedding enhances this tendency, by bringing reporters closer to the soldiers of one side than the other, perhaps to the extent of prompting a subconscious bias in reporting, the product of shared hardships and camaraderie."[43] This journalistic "Stockholm Syndrome," argues Payne, "is evident even among reporters who aim for the most scrupulous objectivity."[44]

Just as the U.S. media was strongly influenced by government officials trying to shape the news, the same administration officials also had issues with the way the war on terror was covered elsewhere. In 2003, it was revealed that the U.S. military staff was paying Iraqi newspapers to publish positive, upbeat stories about the supposedly improving conditions in Iraq. Although intended to counter the propaganda presented by Al Jazeera coverage, even some members of the military opposed having stories "planted" in this manner.[45] The stories were penned by U.S. military "psyops" and placed in the Iraqi newspapers with the help of the Lincoln Group, a civilian defense contractor. Iraqi subcontractors of the Lincoln Group posed as freelance journalists or advertising executives in order to deliver stories to Iraqi media outlets. Pentagon and military officials contend that such "information operations" are standard practice during wartime, especially when insurgents and terrorists use the same tactics. However, critics of the psyops campaign did not see it as so benign. Veteran journalist John J. Schulz, dean of Boston University's College of Communications, said that

> In the very process of preventing misinformation from another side, they are creating misinformation through a process that disguises the source for information that is going out. You can't be creating a model for democracy while subverting one of its core principles, a free independent press.[46]

Similar practices occurred in the UK where, we now know, the BBC and other British media were used by MI-6, the secret intelligence service. In what they called Operation Mass Appeal, MI-6 agents planted stories about Saddam's weapons of mass destruction, purportedly hidden in his palaces and secret underground bunkers.[47]

The media are dependent upon their official contacts within government for information and reliable access to those in power. Offending these sources with unfavorable news stories could jeopardize this necessary relationship. In the UK, according to Dave Edwards, "the BBC faithfully echoed government propaganda in the lead up to the war, and even more so during the war itself."[48] But after receiving complaints from the public, the national broadcaster began to present government actions in Iraq in a more critical light. Edwards observes, "Because it is so unusual, this improved performance may have helped attract a disproportionate level of hostility from government media minders who, given their experience during the assaults on Serbia and Afghanistan, understandably took media support for granted."[49] Angered, the Blair government accused the BBC of trying to undermine the British government by giving undue prominence to opponents of the war. Edwards argued that its main motive for attacking the network was to recast widespread scepticism of the government as much more limited and based on the public broadcaster's bias. "The rewards for subservience and punishment for dissent," said Edwards, are "very real and keenly felt."[50]

Many governments reward media outlets who support them and punish those who critique them, by determining who is awarded radio and television frequencies, government advertising, and access to important military information. Jebediah Reed notes that several of the American media people who regurgitated the Bush administration's case for war have been rewarded with more prominent positions in the media while those who voiced opposition to the agenda have found their careers in sharp decline.[51] Bush's presidential aides have effectively silenced serious questioners, like veteran journalist Helen Thomas, by refusing to have the President call on reporters who challenge them. They have established a hierarchy for journalists seeking interviews with administration officials, favoring networks that give the White House favorable coverage. This is another factor that causes ambitious career journalists to practice self-censorship.

The Bush administration and U.S. military have been accused of planting fake news stories, both in Iraq and at home, that have the appearance of reliable journalism but are, in fact, attempts to influence public opinion and further their own interests. Video News Releases, or VNRs, are often used domestically to shape opinion. Mimicking news broadcast format, and presented by people who look like reporters, the slick, professional, pre-produced slots appear to the untrained eye indistinguishable from the news features produced by the station, when in fact they are funded, created, and distributed by various branches of the government or by private corporations. Frank Rich, writing in the *New York Times* in 2004, termed VNR segments "infoganda."[52] These releases are often used by local news outlets strapped for cash and time, and feature "reporters" discussing domestic policy issues surrounding health, social security, or education reform.[53]

VNRs are doubly dangerous: either viewers accept them as real news and are not impartially informed or they assume they can never trust the news because it could be created by those with vested interests. Despite being decried by many public advocacy, watchdog, and government oversight groups, VNRs continue to air on news broadcasts without acknowledgment of their source because of pressure from government, corporate lobbies and the economic imperatives of television stations.

Media Owners

Those who own and operate the mainstream media in the United States often have connections to corporate or military power that can result in conflicting interests. Perpetuating the interests of the military and large corporations can be extremely profitable, especially during wartime. One of the most obvious examples of this is the ownership of NBC by General Electric, a company that manufactures parts to many U.S. weapons systems. Whenever NBC features graphics of U.S. military hardware, the news anchor might unknowingly be participating in an unpaid advertisement for General Electric. Norman Solomon believes this has consequences for mainstream coverage of contemporary U.S. military conflicts. He argues that

> Given the extent of shared sensibilities and financial synergies within what amounts to a huge military-industrial-media complex, it shouldn't be surprising that whether in the prelude to the Gulf War of 1991 or the Iraq invasion of 2003, the U.S.'s biggest media institutions did little to illuminate how Washington and business interests had combined to strengthen and arm Saddam Hussein during many of his worst crimes? In corporate medialand, history could be supremely relevant when it focused on Hussein's torture and genocide, but the historic assistance he got from the U.S. government and American firms was apt to be off the subject and beside the point.[54]

Administration officials and retired military officers made up 76 percent of total sources used in U.S. media during the coverage leading up to the war in Iraq, according to FAIR.[55] This close relationship between the media and official power has an empowering effect on the military-industrial-media complex, and squelches critical views of U.S. policy. Chris Hedges notes that the media were willing participants in the war effort: "The notion that the press was used in the war is incorrect. The press wanted to be used. It saw itself as part of the war effort. Such docility on the part of the press made it easier to do what governments do in wartime, indeed what governments do much of the time, and that is lie."[56]

Media ownership often exercises control over the form and content of media broadcasts from its subsidiaries. When ABC's "Nightline" showed pictures of the 721 U.S. soldiers killed in Iraq, the Sinclair Broadcast Group, which owns ABC affiliates, refused to air the program, saying that showing the pictures amounted to a statement against the war. The Walt Disney company blocked its Miramax division from distributing Michael Moore's film "Fahrenheit 9/11," which criticized the Bush Administration and the war in Iraq. According to Moore's agent, Disney's chief executive, Michael Eisner, was worried that a film so critical of the Bush administration would endanger the tax breaks Disney receives for its theme parks from the Florida state government, headed by the President's brother Governor Jeb Bush. Disney denies the charges, stating that it simply had no interest in being part of a highly partisan political battle.[57]

Norman Solomon decries how the media have let military, corporate, and political officials define acceptable coverage: "countless journalists—whether they're flag-wavers at Fox News or liberal sophisticates at NPR News—keep letting authorities define the bounds of appropriate empathy and moral concern." He continues, "I know of very few mainstream American journalists who have pointed out that President Bush has the blood of many Iraqi children on his hands after launching an aggressive war in violation of the U.N. Charter and the Nuremberg principles established more than half a century ago."[58]

In at least one instance, the U.S. government has offered advice on how major newspapers and television networks should cover important, sensitive material. In the aftermath of 9/11, then-national security adviser Condoleeza Rice offered network executives from several prominent news networks, including CNN and Fox News, guiding advice concerning coverage of bin Laden's and Al'Qaeda's taped statements. Rice urged that segments of the tapes shown be shortened to avoid giving bin Laden or Al'Qaeda a platform to air their views or pass along coded messages. The networks complied, raising concern from media watch groups. FAIR observed that government "advice" could have a chilling effect on any coverage of bin Laden: "it is inappropriate for the government to dictate to journalists how to report the news. In the context of recent heavy-handedness on the part of the administration (including White House spokesman Ari Fleischer's ominous remark that Americans 'need to watch what they say'), Rice's request suggests that the White House is actually asking for something other than simple journalistic judgement." In contrast, other media executives were unconcerned: Rupert Murdoch said that Fox News would "do whatever is our patriotic duty," and Walter Isaacson of CNN said that "after hearing Dr. Rice, we're not going to step on the land mines she was talking about."[59]

Media ownership structures are often intertwined with corporate and foreign policy power. Members of a media company's board of directors often sit on other corporate boards. Douglas McCorkindale, CEO of the Gannett News Company, which has publishing interests with *USA Today* and various television and internet outlets, also serves on the board of Lockheed-Martin, a company that produces missiles. Other board members have ties to political power: Viet Dinh, a Georgetown Law professor who sits on News Corp's board, is a former Assistant Attorney General and foreign policy adviser for President Bush. William Kennard, board member at the *New York Times*, is a former FCC Chairman and sits on the board of the Carlyle Group, a military defense contractor. *Time-Warner* board member Carla Hills is a trustee at the Center for Strategic and International Studies and Vice-Chair at the Council on Foreign Relations, both establishment think tanks. Hills also sits on the board of the oil company Chevron. These are only a few examples of ties between owners of the mainstream media and military, corporations, and government.[60]

Large media corporations have benefitted from the deregulation advocated by bodies like the Federal Communications Commission (FCC). With few limits on how many media outlets a corporation can own, media corporations and government have entered into a mutually beneficial relationship. Large media companies whose outlets already rely heavily on government press releases and information from government or military sources are rewarded with the ability to buy more and more outlets. In turn, the government benefits from the reduced diversity of opinion and from ownership of virtually all major media outlets by companies that stick to the official script. Since 1983, the number of companies who own a large segment of the mainstream media has been strikingly reduced from fifty to five.[61]

Who are these powerful owners of multiple media venues? Journalist Robert Parry notes that "News organizations are hierarchical institutions often run by strong-willed men who insist that their editorial vision be dominant within their news companies." While some concessions, says Parry, are made to principles of objectivity and fairness, media owners have historically "enforced their political views and other preferences by installing senior editors whose careers depend on delivering a news product that fits with the owner's prejudices."[62] Rupert Murdoch, chief executive of News Corporation, the world's largest global media empire, exemplifies this; publishing more than 175 titles, he dominates the newspaper markets in Britain, Australia, and New Zealand. He also has substantial television holdings, including Fox News, but it is through his newspapers that Murdoch is known for promoting his own particular perspective. Murdoch is not reticent about publicly airing his views, whether in interviews or through the media he owns. Speaking of Murdoch's "unerring ability to choose editors that think just like him," *The Guardian*'s Roy Greenslade asks, "How else can we explain the extraordinary unity of thought in his newspaper empire about the need to make war on Iraq? After an exhaustive survey of News Corp's highest-selling and most influential papers across the world, Greenslade observes that "it is clear that all are singing from the same hymn sheet. . . . Their master's voice has never been questioned."[63]

Murdoch has been criticized on a number of fronts. Many of the concerns arise from the sheer size of his media ownership in particular markets. *Business Week* states

> His satellites deliver TV programs in five continents, all but dominating Britain, Italy, and wide swaths of Asia and the Middle East. He publishes 175 newspapers, including the *New York Post* and *The Times of London*. In the U.S., he owns the Twentieth Century Fox Studio, Fox Network, and 35 TV stations that reach more than 40 percent of the country. . . . His cable channels include fast-growing Fox News, and 19 regional sports channels. In all, as many as one in five American homes at any given time will be tuned in to a show News Corp. either produced or delivered.[64]

Murdoch claims to avoid partisan politics, but according to *The New Yorker*, that hasn't stopped him from using his media outlets to advance his own political and business interests. His support for Bush and the war on terror has been unwavering, sometimes at the expense of accuracy. For example, according to the *Sydney Morning Herald*, Murdoch's *The Daily Telegraph* reported that British troops in Iraq had uncovered a site containing the remains of hundreds of Saddam's "torture victims."[65] It was later reported on CNN and in the *New York Times* that the site actually housed the remains of Iraqi and Iranian soldiers killed in the Iraq-Iran war. The *Sydney Morning Herald* noted that Murdoch's "vast newspaper empire has waged a relentless pro-war propaganda war before and since the war began without even the pretense, in many cases, that even the facade of journalism—a genuine attempt to get the facts in the time available and to present what is known at the time of going to press, appropriately attributed—is being preserved. It just so happens that Murdoch wants U.S. government approval to take over DirecTV and further extend his grip on pay TV."[66] In exchange for his support, the government consented to Murdoch extending his media acquisition still further.

One of the most obvious outlets of Murdoch's brand of propaganda is Fox News. Its extent is made obvious by the resignation of producer Serene Sabbagh, who decided to leave because of Fox News' "bias and racism" in covering the Israeli invasion of Lebanon. She describes watching "the raw images of children being pulled out of the rubble," then switching to Fox News to "hear some of their anchors claiming that these little kids that were killed, these innocent victims that were killed, were human shields used by Hezbollah. And one of the anchors went as far as saying they were planted there by Hezbollah to win support in this war. And it was unbelievable. For me, that was the breaking point."[67]

David Brock, of *Media Matters for America*, disputes Fox News's claim that it is "fair and balanced" in its coverage. Brock illustrates his claim by citing *Media Matters'* many studies, demonstrating Fox News' consistent pro-conservative bias. Conservative commentators far outnumber liberal ones, and pro-Republican sentiment is often injected into coverage of "hard news" rather than being confined to editorials. Coverage of events is micromanaged at Fox, as memos from Senior Vice President John Moody to employees makes clear; Moody said that Bush's "political courage and tactical cunning" are worth "noting in our reporting through the day," and urged reporters covering on the 9/11 Commission findings not to "turn this into Watergate."[68]

Because of his media empire's extensive reach, Murdoch's use of his outlets to pursue his own agenda and interests is significant. As his media conglomerate continues to grow, the range and diversity of voices in media will shrink. As the Fox News memo scandal suggests, Murdoch outlets are strictly content-controlled; this is not lost on politicians who know that positive coverage in News Corp. outlets will help their public image. Murdoch is, therefore, a figure of enormous influence and power.

If objective journalism has suffered from too much individual control, it has also suffered from economic pressures. The decline of newspapers, the rise of infotainment, and media owners' insistence on delivering high returns to shareholders have diminished resources and led to a bottom-line fixation inconducive to aggressive reporting. The meteoric success of right-wing media outlets like Fox News and controversial commentators like Limbaugh and Coulter has not encouraged media owners to pursue critical journalism.[69]

Advertisers

In *Manufacturing Consent*, Chomsky and Herman observe that the media face pressures to show a series of programs that will encourage "audience flow," keeping an audience watching from program to program so as to sustain advertising revenues. In general, advertisers want "to avoid programs with serious complexities and disturbing controversies that interfere with the 'buying mood.'"[70] Since media owners want to keep operations highly profitable and since advertisers are the main source of revenue, it is essential not to alienate the corporations that spend millions on commercials. In its 2003 "Fear & Favor" report, media watchdog *FAIR* examines the the pressures exerted by advertisers on programming; *FAIR's* Janine Jackson told the American Free Press that 60 percent of the journalists it surveyed said advertisers "try to change stories."[71]

Advertisers are extremely influential; the media's primary goal is not to attract and keep viewers but, through their viewers, to attract and keep advertisers. Advertisers pay well for access to an audience. During the lead-up to the U.S. invasion of Iraq, broadcasters, publishers, and advertising executives were concerned revenue would drop as companies pulled ads from wartime news broadcasts, worried that they would appear in an "unfavorable editorial environment," the content of serious war coverage clashing with ads for cars, cell phones, and property insurance. Advertisers behaved similarly immediately after 9/11, pulling ads from news networks, newspapers, and radio broadcasts. For broadcasters and publishers interested in covering critical aspects of the war as well as maintaining ad revenue, the advertising pullout presented a challenge. If advertisers do not want ads to appear amid war coverage, news outlets might avoid airing controversial stories or editorials. Public reaction to advertising during wartime is also an issue, according to ad executive Ben Weiner, who observed that "Nobody wants to be the advertiser who gets beaten up for being remotely unpatriotic."[72] It is not hard to imagine, then, that advertisers might lean more towards news outlets that appear less critical of the war effort, or air less controversial editorial content, in order to disassociate their products from unpatriotic views. Such worries are not unwarranted: Deborah Johns and Michelle Souza of California Marine Moms & Military Families called for the boycott of a Sacramento radio station after it replaced a conservative talk show host with a liberal host who opposed the war in Iraq. The boycott includes any businesses that advertise during the liberal host's program.[73]

Not all advertisers can purchase time in the media, however, even when they have the money. Because of the overall lack of diversity of opinion in mainstream media, many non-profit or non-governmental organizations raise funds to buy advertising time to get their message out. While advertising is the life-blood of the media, in some instances corporate ownership is selective about the messages it broadcasts. MTV, CNN and other networks refused to air anti-war ads produced by organizations like Not in Our Name and Win Without War, citing "company policy;" these networks do, however, air recruiting ads from the armed forces.[74] "It is irresponsible for news organizations not to accept ads that are controversial on serious issues, assuming they are not scurrilous or in bad taste," says Alex Jones of the Joan Shorenstein Center on the Press, Politics and Public Policy at Harvard. "In the world we live in, with the kind of media concentration we have, the only way that unpopular beliefs can be aired sometimes is if the monopoly vehicle agrees to accept an ad."[75]

Media Sources

When a newspaper is taken over by a large monopoly, the new owners regularly start by firing 30 percent of the staff, raising the number of stories expected by the remaining writers from 40 to 80 a month, and adding new responsibilities.[76] Overburdened reporters lack the time to thoroughly fact-check material or seek out alternative viewpoints. Thus, the information obtained from "official" or "reliable"sources can often be accepted without question as truth. According to FAIR, the trend within mainstream media is to lend more space, prominence, and credence to official sources, usually current or former government representatives or spokespersons, both civilian and military.[77] Selectivity of sources leads to significant imbalances in representation: in media coverage of the 2003 invasion of Iraq, Steve Rendall and Tara Broughel note that 64 percent of news sources were pro-war, as were 71 percent of the guest commentators. Anti-war voices made up only 10 percent of all media sources, suggesting that viewers were more than six times as likely to see a pro-war as an anti-war source. Looking only at guest commentators, the ratio increases to 25 to 1. Of quoted officials, military voices outnumbered civilian sources by a two-to-one margin, providing 68 percent of U.S. official sources and nearly half (47 percent) of total sources.[78] Media scholar Robert McChesney observes that news agencies tend to regard "anything done by official sources, e.g. government officials and prominent public figures, as the basis for legitimate news. This gave those in political office (and, to a lesser extent, business) considerable power to set the news agenda by what they spoke about and what they kept quiet about."[79] It is not the pro-war nature of the sources that is dangerous, but the lack of balance in sources; FAIR observes that exaggeration occurs regardless of the political viewpoint and on both ends of the political spectrum.[80]

This imbalance is reflected in the fact that right-wing think tanks are cited in the media three times as often as center or left policy organizations.[81] By dominating public policy debates through aggressive strategies to influence the way media covers political and economic issues, argues Trudy Lieberman, they are essentially shaping the public's thinking.[82] Sound bites and citing of "reputable sources," named or unnamed, give credibility and authority to what is presented. Dependence on official sources from government or business, explains Chomsky and Herman, tends to make high-profile people automatically viewed as reputable and therefore exempted from real questioning. In contrast, when a foreign government makes similar statements, it is easier to recognize propaganda or to look for other sources to provide verification.[83]

Many forms of bias can be detected in media coverage: a 2001 *FAIR* study of the newscasts of the three major television networks found that 92 percent of all U.S. sources interviewed were white, 85 percent were male and, where party affiliation was identifiable, 75 percent were Republican.[84] More than one in four interviewees were politicians, while only three percent represented non-governmental advocacy groups. While this study focuses only on major networks, it does demonstrate heavy reliance on political sources in important mainstream outlets. *FAIR* also reports in a year-long study of CNN's Reliable Sources program that not only was the range of sources narrow but a bias was detected which "strongly favored mainstream media insiders and right-leaning pundits. In addition, female critics were significantly under-represented, ethnic minority voices were almost non-existent and progressive voices were far outnumbered by their conservative counterparts."[85]

Over-reliance on official sources allowed less space for independent or critical voices. Not only were anti-war representatives rarely seen, but not a single program in the entire study featured an in-depth, sit-down interview with a person who was against the war; instead, anti-war voices were relegated to one-sentence sound bites, often by demonstrators or "unofficial" people on the street. In a study during a two-week period prior to the Iraq war, NBC, CBS, ABC and PBS recorded 393 interviews on the conflict, of which only three reported the anti-war movement. This "does not represent mainstream opinion in the US,"Amy Goodman told the audience at a 2006 al-Jazeera sponsored media conference in Qatar.[86]

Mainstream news media are also affected by the influential public relations industry which, through VNRs, paid experts, engineered citizens' groups, press releases and canned news events, shapes the news to suit the interests of its clients. Alex Carey, pioneering scholar of PR, observed that the role of PR is to so muddle the public sphere as to "take the risk out of democracy" for the wealthy and corporations. PR is welcomed by media owners, as it effectively subsidizes programs by providing content at no cost. Surveys show that PR accounts for anywhere from 40 percent to an astonishing 70 percent of what is broadcast as news.[87]

Flak

Another influence on media, working through both external and internal mechanisms, is flak, or organized campaigns aimed at influencing media content through letters, phone calls, petitions, lawsuits and legislation. Flak can come from a number of sources, civic, corporate, or religious; whatever the source, it tends to have a conservatizing effect, as programmers internally shape future broadcast to avoid it. Chomsky and Herman point out how various right-wing media watch groups and think tanks were set up in the 1980s to heavily criticize anything in the media that appeared to have a liberal or left wing bias or be overtly anti-business. Combined with increasing monopoly ownership, this had a profound impact. Ben Bagdikian notes that "Corporations have multimillion-dollar budgets to dissect and attack news reports they dislike. But with each passing year they have yet another power: They are not only hostile to independent journalists. They are their employers.[88]

One example of this hostile climate can be detected in MSNBC's cancellation of the Phil Donahue Show in March 2003 amidst rumors that Donahue's show was viewed as too liberal by some at the network The cancellation was accompanied by the decision to add conservatives Dick Armey, Joe Scarborough, and Michael Savage to the network's contributors and hosts. Media analyst Rick Ellis proposes that Donahue's show was cancelled precisely because the network wanted to avoid flak from viewers; it commissioned a study that claimed Donahue presented a "difficult public face for NBC in a time of war" and expressed concern that the show might become "a home for the liberal antiwar agenda at the same time that our competitors are waving the flag at every opportunity."[89]

After an experiment with a balanced assortment of guests and a more moderate approach did not result in high ratings, the network allowed Donahue to steer the show in his own direction. Although this resulted in healthy ratings, the network nevertheless canceled the program. Donahue maintains his show was cancelled not because of ratings, but because MSNBC was wary of presenting a strong antiwar voice in a milieu where doing so could be publically construed as unpatriotic: "Well, we were the only antiwar voice that had a show, and that, I think, made them very nervous. I mean, from the top down, they were just terrified."[90]

Self-Censorship

The mainstream media is now admitting the extent to which they failed in their coverage of the war on terror. As early as 2002, veteran broadcaster Dan Rather told BBC Television that fear of being labeled unpatriotic had caused American journalists to engage in "a form of self-censorship."[91] By 2005, the harsh realities of the war with its loss of lives and astronomical expense had begun to quell the fevered emotions roused by 9/11. Mainstream media began to pick up rumblings of discontent among increasing segments of the American public and alternative media.

Yet self-censorship continues, according to a survey of nearly 300 journalists and news executives by the Pew Research Center and the *Columbia Journalism Review*. About one-quarter of local and national journalists acknowledge purposely avoiding newsworthy stories, while nearly as many say they have softened the tone of stories to benefit the interests of their news organizations.[92] Viewers have begun to recognize the effects of these pressures; in 2005 a McCormick Tribune Foundation/Gallup Poll found more than half of Americans did not believe they received enough information to make informed decisions about the war on Iraq. A majority of Americans, the poll notes, give low ratings to both government and the media for news for coverage of reasons for going to war, with 68 percent and 61 percent of Americans respectively giving "only fair" or "poor" ratings."[93]

A polarization of viewpoints limits the presentation of information; within a narrowly defined range of discussion, the coverage of the war on terror was detailed but far from impartial. There is a widespread expectation that news media will be free of bias or distortion but today's media are predominantly corporate-owned, their controls in the hands of a powerful few. Concentration of ownership and a corporate mentality combine to create an atmosphere in which external flak and internal pressures have pushed news coverage firmly, although perhaps not irrevocably, to the right.

Ideology

The movement of media to the right is sometimes deliberate, as when it responds to advertisers, and sometimes unintentional and unconscious, through subtle media frames and filters. Herman and Chomsky note that these filters occur so naturally that media news people, often operating with complete integrity and goodwill, are able to convince themselves that they choose and interpret the news objectively and on the basis of professional values. Internal censorship may arise inadvertently in response to public anger; John MacArthur, publisher of *Harper's* Magazine, notes that there used to be a public awareness that honest investigative journalism was innately valuable and that "the patriotic thing to do is to tell the American people the truth." Now however, says MacArthur, this impartiality has been re-cast as lack of patriotism; there is "tremendous hostility to the free press in this country."[94] Even more powerful than this external hostility, maintain Herman and Chomsky, are the internal and structural workings by which media manufactures consent, constraints which are "so powerful, and are built into the system in such a fundamental way, that alternative bases of news choices are hardly imaginable."[95]

Media ethicists have recognized that mainstream media were swept up in a patriotic fervor that impaired its sense of professionalism. In the United

States in particular, journalists and anchors confused support for their country with allegiance to the actions of their leaders. News networks tried to outdo each other in demonstrating loyalty. To be openly critical was dangerous: charges of being unpatriotic, even traitorous, were leveled against those questioning the actions of President Bush and his Cabinet. In a time when the government was over-riding the Constitution and expanding its powers in the name of national security, these were dangerous allegations. In this climate journalists, especially news anchors who became "icons of sentimental patriotism, resisted this role at their peril."[96] When PBS anchors on *The NewsHour with Jim Lehrer* refused to wear American flag pins on-air, stating that they believed it was important to maintain a distance from the government on which they reported, viewers denounced them as unpatriotic.[97] In contrast, Dan Rather said on David Letterman's show on September 17, 2001, "George Bush is the president, he makes the decisions, and, you know, as just one American, he wants me to line up, just tell me where." On the same show, a few weeks later, ABC's Cokie Roberts stated, "Look, I am, I will just confess to you, a total sucker for the guys who stand up with all the ribbons on and stuff and they say it's true and I'm ready to believe it."[98]

In the aftermath of 9/11, the media failed to ask the necessary hard questions, engaging instead in a competition to outdo each other in showing the flag, or the flag pin. "That's not what journalists should be doing," says Amy Goodman, "we should be independent," not just "the megaphone for officialdom."[99] Robert Jensen of the University of Texas School of Journalism raises further concerns about the relationship between patriotism and journalism. He argues that an ideology rooted in patriotism prevents many American journalists from clearly seeing their government's war agenda; it is precisely in times of war, he states, "when a democracy most desperately needs a critical, independent journalism working outside the ideological constraints of the culture," that commercial mainstream news media is most likely to "fail profoundly."[100]

The Fox network's success is one mark of this failure. Its formula of opinionated, conservative, patriotic news journalism has made it America's most watched cable news station. Other networks have followed suit, implementing programming changes that echo Fox-style news broadcasts, a pattern some call "the Fox Effect." Many networks, wary of critics who argued that journalistic traditions of objectivity and balance were simply masks for a liberal bias, adjusted the tone and content of their broadcasts to replicate those of Fox News. MSNBC, for example, added American flag graphics, a portrait of President Bush on the main set, and a studio wall devoted to "America's Bravest," the men and women serving in Iraq.[101] This, with MSNBC's cancellation of Donahue's program and its addition of conservative commentators, demonstrates the extent of the Fox Effect on other broadcasters. PBS also made changes to combat what is seen by some as an "anti-Bush" or "liberal" bias. In 2005, The Corporation for Public Broadcasting hired a White House staffer to add conservative voices to PBS in order to restore "objectivity and balance," despite survey results that suggested the public viewed PBS as objective and trustworthy.[102] MSNBC president Erik Sorenson justified such changes, saying "After Sept. 11 the country wants more optimism and benefit of the doubt. It's about being positive as opposed to being negative."[103] However, Andrew Heyward, president of CBS News, expressed caution over loss of objectivity in reporting: "There is a long-standing tradition in the mainstream press of middle-of-the-road journalism that is objective and fair. I would hate to see that fall victim to a panic about the Fox effect."[104]

Critical Journalism

By its nature, investigative journalism usually involves writing against the grain and confronting prevailing political orthodoxies. It lifts rocks, peers behind facades, refuses to accept official versions at face value, and is skeptical of vested interests. Inevitably, investigative reporters are treated with suspicion, sometimes hostility, by the subjects of their investigations. Despite this, there are journalists today who determinedly pursue stories and overcome obstacles placed in their way. Many are uncovering stories that profoundly affect our world. During the lead-up to the Iraq war and throughout the occupation, mainstream U.S. media failed to question the Bush administration's claims about its justifications for invasion and the conduct of the occupation. A few journalists, however, questioned the government line, uncovered important stories, and reported alternative narratives not shaped by government spin. Most of these operate outside the mainstream, as independent, web, or foreign-based; only a select few appear in major newspapers, journals, or on major television networks. One such news outlet was the Knight Ridder group (now The McClatchy Company), whose journalists and editors did not take government claims of Iraqi weapons of mass destruction (WMD) as absolute truth. At a time when mainstream papers faithfully repeated Bush administration claims about Saddam's nuclear ambitions and the danger posed by Iraq, Knight Ridder asked questions seldom raised elsewhere. After no stockpiles of WMD were found in Iraq after a year of occupation, other media outlets grew increasingly skeptical of the official story. The critical difference between the reporting done by Knight Ridder and the reporting done

by other newspapers, according to Knight Ridder Washington reporter War-
ren Strobel, was in their selection of sources: "I'm not saying we didn't have
any top-level sources, but we also made a conscious effort to talk to people
more in the bowels of government who have a less political approach to
things."[105]

Knight Ridder journalists faced intimidation from the Bush administration: the agency received angry phone calls from government officials, and
the White House attempted to keep its journalists from attending press brief-
ings. In an environment when critical coverage could be construed as unpatriotic, Knight Ridder stood out as a challenging voice. Its journalists were
the first to entertain the idea that the Bush administration manipulated intelligence to justify its designs to overthrow Saddam. Three years later, *The
London Times* covered the allegations when the Downing Street Memos were
made public, but the damning content of the memos came as no surprise to
the journalists at Knight Ridder.[106]

Another rare voice of dissent within an otherwise complacent mainstream
media comes from Seymour Hersh. Since uncovering the massacre at My Lai
and its cover-up, Hersh has been one of investigative journalism's key figures.
He has been consistently critical of the Bush administration's War on Terror;
in the spring of 2006, he published a story detailing the administration's
plans to topple the Iranian government, which included the option of using
nuclear weapons. His journalistic record, position within the mainstream,
and trustworthy reputation ensured that instead of being dismissed (as it was
by the Bush administration), Hersh's piece became front page news around
the world.[107] Hersh was the first American reporter to state that WMD
would not be found in Iraq, and was central in uncovering the Abu Ghraib
torture scandal and revealing the secret CIA "black sites" that housed ab-
ductees suspected of having links to terrorism.[108] Hersh has also weathered
intimidation: he was been accused of sympathizing with the enemy and in-
flaming anti-American sentiment around the world with his stories documenting atrocities at My Lai and Abu Ghraib. These accusations have not
stopped him from publishing stories that paint a sobering picture of the occupation of Iraq.

London-based journalist and documentary film-maker John Pilger has also
been a consistent critic of both the war on terror and the mainstream media's
acquiescence. Pilger has been vocal in illuminating and clarifying the extent
and nature of the Iraqi resistance. He insists that if the public wants news free
of obfuscation and misdirection, it needs to consider the contributions of citizen journalism: bloggers and internet sites, for example, were instrumental
in exposing U.S. use of the chemical agents white phosphorus and napalm

during the siege of Fallujah, something embedded journalists did not report. Pilger attributes this journalistic blind spot to mainstream journalists' lack of interviews with locals, victims of U.S. atrocities, or other, unembedded journalists. When citizen journalists forced the U.S. to admit its use of chemical agents, the mainstream media invariably cast the incident as a PR crisis, ignoring the larger point of the suffering experienced by the victims of chemical weapons. Pilger points to freelance journalists Jo Wilding and Dahr Jamail as examples of journalists who cover the human cost of such military operations by offering eyewitness reports and interviews with doctors, local officials, and families. Amy Goodman emphasizes the important political implications of this kind of journalism when she states, "If people in the U.S. had a true picture of war—dead babies, women with their legs blown off, dead and dying soldiers—they would say 'no'."[109] Pilger also lists important websites that are devoted to this kind of coverage, including zmag.org, truthout.com, informationclearinghouse.info, and counterpunch.org.[110]

Robert Fisk of the *Independent* is another prominent journalist who has worked outside the mainstream and offers a critical perspective of U.S. military involvement in the Middle East. Fisk has been a vocal critic of what he terms "hotel journalism," Western journalism that, because of Iraq's dangers, relies on Iraqi stringers and secondhand information for important news stories. Fisk views embedded journalism as detrimental to good journalism; he notes that "rarely, if ever, has a war been covered by reporters in so distant and restricted a way."[111] Fisk describes *New York Times* correspondents living in Baghdad behind massive stockades and protected by security guards. NBC reporters stay in a hotel with iron grills on their doors, forbidden by security advisers to go to the hotel pool or restaurant, "let alone the rest of Baghdad," for fear of attack. Many Western journalists simply do not leave their rooms while in Baghdad, a situation, says one long-time American correspondent, that the military couldn't be happier with, since "They know that if they bomb a house of innocent people, they can claim it was a 'terrorist' base and get away with it. They don't want us roaming around Iraq and so the 'terrorist' threat is great news for them. They can claim they've shot 600 or 1,000 insurgents and we have no way of checking because we can't go to the cemetery or visit the hospitals because we don't want to get kidnapped and have our throats cut."[112]

Amy Goodman has been a consistent supporter of independent media and a critic of the war on terror. She has critically addressed the administration's claims used to justify war with Iraq, the marginalizing of progressive voices in the mainstream media, and the program of "embedded" journalists.[113] She argues that "the Bush Administration not finding weapons of mass destruction laid bare more than the Bush Administration. It laid bare media that act as a conveyer belt for the lies of the Administration. You know governments are going to lie, but not the media. So I think people started to seek out other forms of information."[114] Another critical voice can be found in *Washington Post* correspondent Ellen Knickmeyer, who exposed the massacre in Haditha. Her coverage demonstrates what John Pilger advocates: a humanizing concern for the people of Iraq, conveyed through the use of interviews with local officials, doctors, coroners, and families of victims. Knickmeyer also documents statements from human rights organizations like Human Rights Watch.[115] Another key figure, author and Pulitzer Prize-winning journalist Dana Priest, has been prominent in the uncovering of so-called CIA "black sites." In the *Washington Post,* Priest has dedicated column space to the questions of morality and legality surrounding the use of secret prisons by the CIA to hold and interrogate terror suspects.[116]

With today's technology, citizens have greater access to a variety of news, analysis and commentary than ever before. The internet enables people to post their own stories and opinions online; its ability to allow wide dissemination of viewpoints and information is revolutionary in the same way that the invention of the printing press spread revolutionary social, political and scientific change across fifteenth-century Europe. The reach of the internet and the growth of news-related websites give people the means to gather and share perspectives online. With the rise of blogging, citizen journalism is on the increase. As a result, the number of alternative news and opinion sources have multiplied in the past decade, appealing to a younger demographic, who have grown up with all the internet offerings of communication, recreation, and entertainment, and who do not look automatically to television or print media for information. In an interview on PBS's *Media War*, Jeff Fager, executive producer of *60 Minutes*, discussed the CBS partnership with Yahoo! News. "We haven't seen the model for how broadcast journalism is going to end up on the Internet," he says. "But it has to go there. I mean, you don't see anybody between 20 and 30 getting their news from the evening news; you see them getting it online."[117]

Falling newspaper circulation figures and declining audience shares of mainstream radio and television all suggest the extent of contemporary media upheaval. Markos Moulitsas, author the blog *Daily Kos*, which reportedly receives 3 to 5 million visitors per week, explains that "People want to be part of the media: they don't want to sit there and listen anymore. They're too educated. They're taught to be go-getters and not to sit back and be passive consumers. And the traditional media is still predicated on the passive consumer model—you sit there and watch."[118] Being "part of the media" rather than subject to it lies in finding supplements and alternatives: Faisal al-Kasim, host of the al-Jazeera program *The Opposite Direction*, observed that "as a result of the perceived failure of western media to reflect the full picture, more people were turning to Arabic media."[119] Not only Arabs living abroad but increasing numbers of westerners turn to English-language Arab media to get a perspective unrepresented in the one-sided coverage of the West. Faisal did not claim there was no bias in the Arabic media but at least, he said, it offers an alternative voice and therefore allows the audience to make its own decision as to where the truth lies.

An interplay of overlapping, contiguous, and oppositional perspectives from a range of sources and contexts might represent our best hope of detecting a greater truth. But if traditional investigative journalism has been hampered by its assigned wartime role as stenographer to power, if media monopolies have ensured that limited interests will dominate, and if media is both unconsciously shaped by its frames and consciously shaping in its metaphors, how is this to happen? The consequences of not extricating ourselves from this dilemma, as suggested by the rise of both domestic and international backlash, are increasingly critical.

Notes

1. Philippa Strum. "The Journalist as Historian: Anthony Lewis, Civil Liberties, and the Supreme Court." *Journal of Supreme Court History*. Volume 29, Issue 2, July 2004: 191–206.

2. Norman Fairclough. *Language and Power*. London: Longman, 1989: 54.

3. bell hooks. [videorecording] bell hooks: *Cultural Criticism and Transformation*. Media Education Foundation, 1997.

4. Greg Philo. "Television News and Audience Understanding of War, Conflict and Disaster." In *Journalism Studies*, 3(2), May 2002: 173–86.

5. Ruth Wodak. "Discourse and Racism" in Deborah Schiffrin, Deborah Tannen and Heidi Hamilton (eds). *The Handbook of Discourse Analysis*. London: Blackwell, 2001: 372.

6. *Program on International Policy Attitudes (PIPA)*. "Study Finds Direct Link Between Misinformation and Public Misconception." October 2, 2003. See www.truthout .org/docs _03/100403F.shtml (July 11, 2007).

7. PIPA. "Study Finds Direct Link Between Misinformation and Public Misconception."

8. spin. "Bookseller of Baghdad."*Gbytes of Gbytes*. April 6, 2007. See gbytes.gsood .com/catagory/middle-east>. (July 11, 2007).

9. Howard Zinn. "Lessons of Iraq War start with U.S. history." *The Progressive Media Project*. March 8, 2006. See www.progressive.org/media_mpzinn030806 (July 11, 2007).

10. Michael Parenti. "Monopoly Media Manipulation." *Michael Parenti.org.* May 2001. See www.michaelparenti.org/MonopolyMedia.html (July 10, 2007).

11. Michael Parenti. "Monopoly Media Manipulation."

12. Michael Parenti. "Monopoly Media Manipulation."

13. Michael Parenti. "Monopoly Media Manipulation."

14. Karim. H. Karim. *Islamic Peril: Media and Global Violence.* Montreal: Black Rose Books, 2003.

15. Noam Chomsky. "Interviews." *Manufacturing Consent: Noam Chomsky and the Media.* [Videorecording]. Mark Achbar and Peter Wintonick. Necessary Illusions.1992.

16. Gary Kamiya. "Iraq: Why the Media Failed." *Salon.* April 10, 2007. See www.salon.com/opinion/Kamiya/2007/04/10/media_failure (July 11, 2007).

17. David Edwards. "The Media Is Tough on Terrorism but Not Tough on the Causes of Terrorism." *Media Lens.* September 2001. See www.medialens.org/articles/the_articles/articles _2001/de_tough_on_terrorism.html (July 11, 2007).

18. David Edwards. "The Media Is Tough on Terrorism."

19. David Edwards. "The Media Is Tough on Terrorism."

20. Kenneth Payne. "The Media as an Instrument of War." *Parameters.* Spring 2005.

21. Kenneth Payne. "The Media as an Instrument of War."

22. *Cited in AlertNet.* "Media Ignore Iraq's Humanitarian Issues." November 13, 2006. See www.globalpolicy.org/security/issues/iraq/media/2006/1113ignores.htm (July 17, 2007).

23. Julia Day. "US Media at 'all-time low.'" *The Guardian.* February 2, 2006.

24. Les Roberts, Riyadh Lafta, Richard Garfield, Jamal Khudhairi, and Gilbert Burnham. "Mortality before and after the 2003 invasion of Iraq: cluster sample survey." *Lancet.* October 29, 2004.

25. Judith Coburn. "Unnamed and Unnoticed: Iraqi Casualties." *TomDispatch.* July 18, 2005. See www.tomdispatch.com/index.mhtml?pid=6963 (July 15, 2007).

26. William Blum. "Civilian Casualties: Theirs and Ours." *Counter Punch.* December 17, 2001. See www.counterpunch.org/blumcasualties.html (July 15, 2007).

27. Robert Parry. "So Bush did steal the White House." *Asheville Global Report.* No. 150, Nov. 29–Dec. 5, 2001. See www.agrnews.org/issues/150/commentary.html (July 17, 2007).

28. Dave Markland. "Media blind to Afghan civilian deaths." *Seven Oaks Magazine.* December 29, 2006. See www.sevenoaksmag.com/features/civiliancasualties.html (July 15, 2007).

29. Editor and Publisher Staff. "Public Faults Media on Military Issues, Poll Finds." *Editor & Publisher.* August 8, 2005. See www.mediatank.org/resources/articles/2005/08/08/publicfaultsmedia.html (July 15, 2007).

30. Haider Rizvi. "Frustration Marks Another War Anniversary." *Global Policy.* March 19, 2007. See www.globalpolicy.org/ngos/role/iraq.htm (July 15. 2007).

31. BBC. "Millions join anti-war protests worldwide." *BBC News Online,* February 17, 2003.

32. Virginia Grantier. "Journalist Laments State of War Coverage." *Bismarck Tribune* (North Dakota). October 10, 2004.

33. Edward S. Herman and Noam Chomsky. *Manufacturing Consent: the Political Economy of the Mass Media*. New York: Pantheon, 1988.

34. Tami Silico interview with Joan Pliego. "The Reality had to get out." *Real Change News*.October 28, 2004. See www.realchangenews.org/2004/2004_10_28 /issue/current/coverstory.html (July 12, 2007).

35. Adam Taylor. "UD Professor Sue over DAFB photos." *The News Journal*. October 5, 2004. See www.delawareonline.com/newsjournal/local/2005/04/28pentagon release.html (June 1, 2007).

36. Doug Struck. "In Canada, An Uproar Over Army Casualties." *Washington Post Foreign Service*. April 26, 2006.

37. *Military Families Speak Out*. "The Flag-Draped Coffins." March 14th, 2004. See www.mfso.org/article.php?id=316 (July 15, 2007).

38. Aly Colon. "Embed Journalists Everywhere." *Poynter.org*. March 17, 2003. See www.poynter.org/column.asp?id=58&aid=25265 (July 15, 2007).

39. Henry Michaels. "Pentagon, media agree on Iraq war censorship." *World Socialist Web Site*. March 5, 2003. See www.wsws.org/articles/2003/mar2003/med-m05 .shtml (July 15, 2007).

40. Terence Smith. "Battlefield Bylines." *PBS NewsHour* Online. February 18, 2003. See www.pbs.org/newshour/bb/military/jan-june03/bylinesb_2-18.html (July 15, 2007).

41. Inquisitor U.S. editor. "Controlling the News with Embedded Journalists." *Inquisitor*. April 27, 2003. See www.inquisitoronline.com/news/0304embedded.html (July 15, 2007).

42. Sourcewatch. "Embedded." Sourcewatch. March 31, 2005. See www.source watch.org/index.php?title=Embedded (July 15, 2007).

43. Kenneth Payne. "The Media as an Instrument of War."

44. Kenneth Payne. "The Media as an Instrument of War."

45. Tom Regan. "U.S. military planting stories in Iraqi papers." *Christian Science Monitor.com*. December 1, 2005. See www.csmonitor.com/2005/1201/dailyUpdate.html (July 15, 2007).

46. Tom Regan. "U.S. military planting stories in Iraqi papers."

47. John Pilger. "The Real First Casualty of War." *Lewrockwell*. April 21, 2006. See www.lewrockwell.com/pilger/pilger40.html (July 15, 2007).

48. Dave Edwards. "Beating up the cheerleader." *Znet*. July 29, 2003. See www .zmag.org/Sustainers/Content/2003-07/29edwards.cfm (July 15, 2007).

49. Dave Edwards. "Beating up the cheerleader."

50. Dave Edwards. "Beating up the cheerleader."

51. Jebediah Reed. "The Iraq Gamble: At the pundits' table, the losing bet still takes the pot." *Radar Magazine*. January 2007. See www.radarmagazine.come/features /2007/01/betting_on (July 15, 2007).

52. Frank Rich. "Operation Iraqi Infoganda." *New York Times*. March 28, 2004.

53. Robert Love. "Before Jon Stewart."*Columbia Journalism Review*. March/April 2007. See www.cjr.org/feature/before_jon_stewart.php (July 15, 2007).

54. Norman Solomon. "The Military-Industrial-Media Complex: Why war is covered from the warriors' perspective." *FAIR/Extra!* July/August 2005. See www.fair.org /index .php?pag e=2627 (July 15, 2007).

55. Steve Rendall and Tara Broughel. "Amplifying Officials, Squelching Dissent FAIR study finds democracy poorly served by war coverage." *FAIR Extra.* May/June 2003. See www.fair.org/index.php?page=1145 (July 15, 2007).

56. Norman Solomon. "The Military-Industrial-Media Complex: Why war is covered from the warriors' perspective."

57. Guy Reel. "The Military-Mass Media Complex." *CommonDreams.org.* May 6, 2004. See www.commondreams.org/views04/0506-06.htm (July 15, 2007).

58. Norman Solomon. "Media and the Politics of Empathy." *CommonDreams.org.* April 18, 2003. See www.commondreams.org/views03/0418-08.htm (July 15, 2007).

59. FAIR. "Networks Accept Government Guidance." *FAIR.* October 12, 2001. <http://www.fair.org/press-releases/network-pressure.html> (July 15, 2007).

60. *Media Tank.* "Ties That Bind: An Assortment of Interlocking Interests." *Media Tank.* See www.mediatank.org/resources/peace/conflicts/ (July 15, 2007).

61. Ben H. Bagdikian. *The Media Monopoly*, Sixth Edition. New York: Beacon Press, 2000.

62. Robert Parry. "The Price of the Liberal Media Myth." *Consortiumnews.com.* January 1 2003. See consortiumnews.com/2002/123102a.html (July 15, 2007).

63. Roy Greenslade. "Their Masters'Voice." *The Guardian.* February 17, 2003.

64. *Center for American Progress.* "Who is Rupert Murdoch?" July 16, 2004. See www.americanprogress.org/issues/2004/07/b122948.html (July 15, 2007).

65. Margo Kingston. "Murdoch's War on Truth in War Reporting." *Sydney Morning Herald.* April 7, 2003. See www.smh.com.au/articles/2003/04/07/1049567619708 .html (July 15, 2007).

66. Margo Kingston. "Murdoch's War on Truth in War Reporting."

67. Richard Neville. "Rupert Murdoch's Victims." *Counter Punch.* September 1, 2006. See www.counterpunch.org/neville09012006.html (July 15, 2007).

68. *Media Matters for America.* "33 internal FOX editorial memos reviewed by MMFA reveal FOX News Channel's inner workings." July 14, 2004. See mediamatters .org/items/200407140002 (July 15, 2007).

69. Gary Kamiya. "Iraq: Why the Media Failed."

70. Edward S. Herman and Noam Chomsky. *Manufacturing Consent.*

71. Jon Prestage. "Mainstream Journalism: Shredding the First Amendment." *Truthout.* November 7, 2002. See www.truthout.org/doc_02/11.11.shred.1.amend.htm (July 15, 2007).

72. Darrell Satzman. "Advertising likely to wane against a backdrop of battle." *Los Angeles Business Journal.* Feb 3, 2003.

73. Deborah Johns and Michelle Souza. "Letter from CA Marine Moms & Military Families." posted on Marooned in Marin. See maroonedinmarin.blogspot.com /2006/06/kfbk-goes-liberal-fires-mark-williams.html (July 15, 2007).

74. *New York Times.* "MTV Refuses Antiwar Commercial." *New York Times.* March 13, 2003.

75. *New York Times.* "MTV Refuses Antiwar Commercial."

76. Barbara Leiterman. "The Ascendancy of Conrad Black." *FAIR Extra.* November/December 1996.

77. FAIR press release. "Who's on the News: study shows network news sources skew white male and elite." *FAIR.* January 1, 2001. See www.fair.org/index.php?page=1865 (July 15, 2001).

78. Steve Rendall and Tara Broughel. "Amplifying Officials, Squelching Dissent."

79. Robert W. McChesney. "Journalism, Democracy, and Class Struggle." *Monthly Review.* Volume 52, Number 6, 2000.

80. Steve Rendall and Tara Broughel. "Amplifying Officials, Squelching Dissent."

81. Trudy Lieberman. *Slanting the Story: the Forces That Shape the News.* New York: The New Press, 2000.

82. Trudy Lieberman. *Slanting the Story.*

83. Edward S. Herman and Noam Chomsky. *Manufacturing Consent.*

84. Steve Rendall and Tara Broughel. "Amplifying Officials, Squelching Dissent."

85. Steve Rendall and Tara Broughel. "Amplifying Officials, Squelching Dissent."

86. Julia Day. "US media at 'all-time low'." *The Guardian.* February 2, 2006.

87. Robert W. McChesney. "Journalism, Democracy, and Class Struggle."

88. Ben H. Bagdikian. *The Media Monopoly.*

89. Rick Ellis. "The Surrender Of MSNBC." *AllYourTV.com.* Wednesday, February 26, 2003. See www.commondreams.org/views03/0226-11.htm (July 15, 2007).

90. *Media Matters for America.* "Phil Donahue on his 2003 MSNBC firing." October 29, 2004. <http://mediamatters.org/items/200410290004> (July 15, 2007).

91. BBC NEWS. "Veteran CBS News Anchor Dan Rather speaks out." *BBC Newsnight* May 16, 2002. See www.bbc.co.uk/pressoffice/pressreleases/stories/2002/05_may/16/dan_rather .shtml (July 15, 2007).

92. PEW. "Self Censorship: How Often and Why. Journalists Avoiding the News." *PEW Research center for People and the Press.* April 30, 2000. See people-press.org/reports/dislay .php3?ReportID=39 (July 15, 2007).

93. Leilani Sweeney. "Americans'confidence in military news coverage takes steep drop." *Mccormick Tribune.* August 24, 2005. See www.mccormicktribune.org/news/2005/pr082405.aspx (July 15, 2007).

94. Robert Hackett. "Covering up the "War on Terrorism." *Canadian Association of Journalists.* See www.caj.ca/mediamag/fall2001/analysis.html (July 15, 2007).

95. Edward S. Herman and Noam Chomsky. *Manufacturing Consent.*

96. *Center for Social Media.* "Journalists became icons of sentimental patriotism." 2002. See www.centerforsocialmedia.org/challengestojournalism.html (July 27, 2007).

97. PEW. "Self Censorship: How Often and Why. Journalists Avoiding the News." *PEW Research center for People and the Press.* April 30, 2000. See people-press.org/reports/dislay .php3?ReportID=39 (July 15, 2007).

98. James Sandrolini. "Propaganda: The Art of War." *Chicago Media Watch.* Fall 2002. See www.chicagomediawatch.org/02_3_artofwar.shtml (July 15, 2007).

99. Amy Goodman. "Interview." *Hardball with Chris Matthews,* MSNBC. December 3, 2004. See www.democracynow.org/hardball-041203.shtml (July 15, 2007).

100. Robert Jensen. "Dan Rather's the Problem with Patriotism: Steps toward the redemption of American journalism and democracy." *Global Media Journal*, 2: 3 (Fall 2003).

101. Jim Rutenberg. "Cable's War Coverage Suggests a New 'Fox Effect' on Television." *New York Times*. April 16, 2003.

102. Stephen Labatan, Lorne Manly and Elizabeth Jensen. "Republican Chairman Exerts Pressure on PBS, Alleging Biases." *New York Times*. May 2, 2005.

103. Jim Rutenberg. "Cable's War Coverage Suggests a New 'Fox Effect' on Television."

104. Jim Rutenberg. "Cable's War Coverage Suggests a New 'Fox Effect' on Television."

105. Steve Ritea. "Accolades now come to Knight Ridder for its prescient reports expressing skepticism about claims that Iraq had weapons of mass destruction." *American Journalism Review*. August/September 2004.

106. Steve Ritea. "Accolades now come to Knight Ridder."

107. Julian Borger . "'I feel like I did in the Vietnam days—I hate to pay taxes just so they can go and bomb more people.'" *The Guardian*. April 14, 2006.

108. Bonnie Azab Powell. "Investigative journalist Seymour Hersh spills the secrets of the Iraq quagmire and the war on terror." *University of California Berkeley NewsCenter*. October 11, 2004. See www.berkeley.edu/news/media/releases/2004/10/11_hersh.shtml (July 15, 2007).

109. Julia Day. "US media at 'all-time low'."

110. John Pilger. "Recommends the World Wide Web." *New Statesman*. November 28, 2005. See www.newstatesman.com/200511280013 (July 15, 2007).

111. Robert Fisk. "The US Press in Iraq: Hotel Room Journalism." *Counter Punch*. January 17, 2005. See www.counterpunch.org/fisk01172005.html (July 15, 2007).

112. Robert Fisk. "The US Press in Iraq: Hotel Room Journalism."

113. Lizzy Ratner. "Amy Goodman's 'Empire'." *The Nation*. May 5, 2005. See www.thenation.com/doc/20050523/ratner (July 15, 2007).

114. Lizzy Ratner. "Amy Goodman's 'Empire'." *The Nation*. May 5, 2005. See www.thenation.com/doc/20050523/ratner (July 15, 2007).

115. Ellen Knickmeyer. " Memories of a Massacre:Iraqi Townspeople Describe Slaying of 24 Civilians by Marines in Nov. 19 Incident." *Washington Post*. May 27, 2006.

116. Dana Priest. "CIA Holds Terror Suspects in Secret Prisons."

117. PBS. "Media Wars." *PBS Frontline* series. See www.pbs.org/wgbh/pages/frontline/newswar/view (July 15, 2007).

118. *PBS*. "Media Wars."

119. Julia Day. "US media at 'all time low'."

CHAPTER EIGHT

Boiling the Blood and Narrowing the Mind: Fomenting Backlash

Since 9/11, every time there is an incident overseas attributed to Muslims or Arabs, we go on orange alert ourselves.

—Sohail Mohammed[1]

"It's a bad time to be named Ahmed," jokes comedian Ahmed Ahmed. This is especially true at airports and border crossings: the New York Times observes that "travelling makes many Muslim Americans feel like second-class citizens."[2] The experience is so widespread that it has come to be a staple of Muslim-American satire: Ahmed travels "wearing a T-shirt that says "Got Rights?'"[3] Stand-up comic Azhar Usman who, despite pressure, refuses to shave the long beard that denotes "someone trying to live a religious life," jokes in the comedy revue "Allah Made Me Funny" that it's ironic his "obviously Muslim appearance" associates him with terrorism: "If I were a crazy Muslim fundamentalist, this is not the disguise I would go with."[4]

There is, however, a sobering reality behind the wry comedy. Like Ahmed Ahmed, Taleb Salhab and his wife were taken away in handcuffs while traveling. The sound-track to their detention at the Port Huron border crossing, however, was not the murmur of curious fellow travelers, nor the laughter of a comedy-club audience, but the wailing of their two pre-school daughters, who watched from the car as their parents were dragged away in restraints, with no explanation from customs officials, for four hours of questioning. It was harrowing for the children, says Salhab, describing how "officers, their hands on their guns, swarmed around his vehicle, barking at him to get out as alarm bells clanged." He feared for his life, said Salhab, adding that now whenever his four-year-old daughter "sees uniformed officers, she asks if they are going to take him away."[5]

The response of comedians such as Ahmed and Usman to the denial of fundamental civil liberties is a generous one. It takes a bitter situation and turns it into humane laughter, simultaneously satirizing the fear-driven behavior shaping their daily experience and inviting a critical re-examination of those fears. Salhab's more poignant story suggests a different potential reaction: the inchoate terror of children made to witness their parents' humiliation, too young to detect irony, too fearful to be able to take control of the experience by re-casting it as comedic performance. Such situations will almost inevitably brew a potent mixture of helplessness, fear and rage; what will happen if we continually steep our youngest, most impressionable citizens in such a bitter brew? When we act out of a need to heighten our sense of security, we must be alert to the implications of our actions; through trying so rigorously to manage risk, are we ironically setting up the very conditions of outrage and impotence which create it? According to many foreign-policy analysts, the answer is yes. The Terrorism Index, a gauge of progress in the war on terror developed by the journal *Foreign Policy* and the Center for American Progress, finds that foreign-policy experts "see a world that is growing more dangerous, a national security strategy in disarray, and a war in Iraq that is alarmingly off-track."[6] The consequences of our social, political, and discursive choices are simply too significant to overlook.

Fatally interconnected, war and racism fuel each other.[7] Racism feeds war's atrocities, offering us a perverse permission to punish demonized others not so much for their actions as for their difference. War, in turn, supports racism's most dangerous assumptions about that difference, urging that our best hope for security lies in eradicating it in any of its guises: soldier or civilian, villain or victim, adult or child. Ironically, the more racism feeds fear's voice, telling us that our very nature, civilization, and identity are under attack because "they hate us,"[8] the more annihilating our wars become in response; thus we generate the very hatred we most resent. President Bush's cultivation of national fears by "portraying himself as the defender of 'Western civilization,'" says the Committee Against Anti-Asian Violence, is only the most recent expression of a "deep-rooted" pattern of "U.S. governments using racism to build support for colonial wars of conquest."[9] It is perhaps inevitable that the violence of 9/11 and the violence of the subsequent war on terror have, taken together, created a double-edged backlash. One blade strikes internally at Arab-Americans and Muslims in a retaliatory rage fostered by insistently racist government and media discourses, and generating its own terror among its victims. The other blade strikes internationally, as Western policies, hardened and intensified by fears of terrorist threats, generate resentment by those they knowingly or unknowingly victimize.

The first type of backlash can be most clearly detected in the rise of hate crimes against immigrants and North Americans of Middle Eastern origin. According to a Zogby Survey, 75 percent of American Muslims reported that they or someone they knew have been subject to harassment and discrimination since 9/11.[10] The European Monitoring Centre for Racism and Xenophobia documented many counts of verbal abuse blaming all Muslims for the attacks, as well as women having their hijab torn from their heads, male and female Muslims assaulted.[11] In Canada, mosques are vandalized, and Canada's Muslim and Arab communities experience insults, threats, attacks, and intolerance. Inaccurate reporting about them, Muslims believe, derives from and re-creates misinformation and stereotypes. Switch on the television, says a Pakistani-Dutch sociologist, Mustafa Hassain, "and you have the impression that Muslims are all fanatics, that Muslims don't understand Western liberal values."[12] Many Muslims agree that the Western media is preoccupied less with Islam than with its own false stereotypes. Sheikh Ahmed Kutty, Imam of the Islamic Foundation of Toronto, the largest Muslim center in Canada, says: The media "only seek evidence that confirms their preconceived notions of Islam and Muslims."[13]

One of the most insidious ways the media bigotry shows up is in linguistically denying Muslim-Canadian identity. Journalist Robert Fisk points out how the Canadian press has begun calling Canadian Muslims suspected of terrorist activities "Canadian-born" or "home-grown" rather than Canadians: "The vicious insinuation is that Muslim-Canadians are not really citizens."[14] A 2002 survey found that 60 percent of Canadian Muslims experienced discrimination following 9/11 and 82 percent knew of at least one fellow Muslim who had received this treatment. Paralleling this is the increased use of racial profiling, supported in the minds of the public, governments, and security by years of media stereotyping that continually linked Islam and the Middle East to terrorism. As early as 1991, an ABC News poll revealed 59 percent of Americans saw Arabs as "terrorists," while 58 percent saw them as "violent" and 56 percent as "religious fanatics."[15] A Gallup poll conducted two years later found that two-thirds of Americans believed there were "too many" Arab immigrants. The 9/11 attacks reinforced and furthered these views, solidifying the connection of Middle Eastern violence, terrorism, religious fanaticism. Civil rights lawyer Alia Malek describes watching "brown" Americans, anxious about reprisals following terrorist attacks, "rushing to affirm their allegiance and their American-ness," apologizing for the tragedy "as if we share the blame."[16] This anxiety is "not just collective hysteria," says Malek, referencing a recent Boston Globe survey showed "almost half of all Americans think Arabs in this country should carry special identification cards," and an Associated Press poll that one-third of Americans surveyed "support the creation of internment camps."[17] Islamophobia is so widespread in Europe that columnist Ziauddin Sardar wonders whether Muslims will be the victims of the next pogroms.[18] Rather than being publically denounced by politicians, political rhetoric often invited such views. Former U.S. senator Rick Santorum, for example, told an audience of university students that "radical Islam is as dangerous a threat to the U.S. as Nazi Germany to Britain in 1940," and warned of "Islamic fascists" who want to conquer the world.[19] The widespread public discourse of infiltration and infestation cements such fears. The media's emphasis on "sleepers," or terrorist plants who assume an unremarkable American life until "activated," is one aspect of the infiltration trope. Malek describes another aspect: days after 9/11, Washington, D.C. buses ran Washington Mutual ads with a picture of a Middle Eastern man and the caption, "Worry About Your New Neighbors, Not About Your Loan." These messages made clear, says Malek, that the "Arab enemies among us" might seen civilized, "but in the end their ultimate allegiance is our destruction."[20]

In 1997, England's Runnymede Trust, a policy research organization promoting multiculturalism, investigated Islamophobia in the UK. Islamophobia, it notes, assumes at root that Islam is innately alien, barbaric, resistant to change and aggressively anti-Western. Many prominent western leaders speak from an Islamophobic stance: influential televangelist Pat Robertson, for example, equates Muslims with termites "destroying institutions that have been built by Christians."[21] Echoing an exterminationist rhetoric familiar from military propaganda, but more startling in the mouth of a man of faith, Robertson warns, "the time has arrived for a godly fumigation."[22] Former Southern Baptist Convention president Reverend Jerry Vines blames America's problems on religious pluralism; speaking at a pastors' conference in 2002, he called Islam's founder "a demon-possessed pedophile"; only the Christian God, he claimed, is "not going to turn you into a terrorist that'll try to bomb people."[23] Vines' comments dismayed the Council of American-Islamic Relations (CAIR): "It's really unfortunate that a top leader in a mainstream Christian church would use such hate-filled and bigoted language in describing the faith of one-fifth of the world's population."[24]

Cultures of Fear

Racial profiling assumes certain racial minorities have proclivities to certain criminal acts. CAIR's 2005 report, "Unequal Protection: The Status of Muslim Civil Rights in the United States," notes that of the 1,552 incidents of anti-Muslim violence, discrimination, and harassment it documents in 2004, nearly 25 percent were unwarranted arrests and police searches, as compared to only 7 percent in the year previous.[25] In *Racial Profiling after September 11*, Kevin Johnson notes that: "Non-citizen Arabs and Muslims were subjected to special scrutiny at airports across the country and a new phrase, "Flying While Arab," entered the national vocabulary."[26] "Flying While Arab" is the War on Terror's version of "Driving While Black," which describes the tendency of police to pull over African-American drivers without evidence of criminal activity. An Arab-sounding name can now be enough to raise red flags at airport check-in counters. At New York's Kennedy airport, *The New York Times* reported, law enforcement officers searched passengers based on race: "Anyone with dark skin or who spoke with an accent was taken aside and searched," one passenger said, as was "any male with too much facial hair."[27]

The same assumptions have prompted physical and verbal abuse, often targeting individuals who only appear to be Arab or Muslim. Many victims of anti-terrorist anger have been people of Indian origin, especially devout male members of the Sikh community who wear a turban; nine days after 9/11, U.S. Representative John Cooksey told a radio audience that anyone "wearing a diaper on his head" should expect to be interrogated about the attacks. Cooksey later acknowledged that some of those wearing turbans are American citizens, and that not everyone wearing a turban is Arab or Muslim, "but bin Laden does," he insisted. "Bin Laden always wears a turban, and I think a lot of his followers—if they were not based here and trying to blend into our society—would be wearing them, too."[28]

The terrorist attacks in the U.S. in 2001 and the subway bombings in London in 2005 allowed authorities to suspend many democratic rights. The U.S. Patriot Act and Britain's Terrorism Bill have, by permitting legal principles to be breached in the name of combating terrorism, given "police unfettered powers to act as judge, jury and executioner" as Bill Van Auken reports in an article about the victims of "state 'anti-terror' killings."[29] Van Auken describes the death of Brazilian immigrant Jean Charles de Menezes, gunned down by plainclothes police on a London subway. Many inconsistencies arose between independent accounts and the police version of events; police initially reported that de Menezes was seen leaving the home of a suspected terrorist and wearing a bulky jacket on a warm day, leading them to suspect he was carrying a bomb. They claimed to have challenged him at the entrance to the subway station, whereupon he fled; he was shot to prevent him from detonating a bomb. Van Auken contradicts this version, insisting de Menezes lived in a different apartment than the terrorist suspects, was not wearing a heavy coat, and was never challenged by police. Instead, he was seated in the subway car when, without warning, he was seized and shot several times by police. After it became apparent that they had killed an innocent man, explanations were created to exonerate the officers and "uphold the infallibility of the security forces."[30] The killing was defended as inevitable collateral damage in the global war on terror. Such things are necessary, we are told, in order to keep us safe.

Governments have institutionalized discrimination through racial profiling and race-based travel restrictions. Many civilians have been severely injured or incarcerated based on suspicions, however flimsy, that they are terrorists. After the 9/11 attacks, Johnson writes that "hundreds of Arab and Muslim non-citizens were arrested, questioned, detained, and deported" in a "dragnet" that often netted South Asian Sikhs and Latin American Christians as well as innocent Arab Muslims.[31] The victims of mistaken identity have little recourse.

Amidst a climate of fear, hostility, and suspicion, the loss of fundamental civil liberties affects all American citizens. The rising intolerance for criticism of American international policy is analogous, says the American Civil Liberties Union (ACLU)'s Nadine Strossen, to the rise of McCarthyism in the 1950s: "The term 'terrorism' is taking on the same kind of characteristics as the term 'communism' did in the 1950s. It stops people in their tracks, and they're willing to give up their freedoms. . . . They are too willing to give up their rights and to scapegoat people, especially immigrants and people who criticize the war."[32] As in McCarthyism, political conformity is now replacing freedom of speech, threatening and silencing voices of dissent. Matthew Rothschild documents cases of government agencies harassing artists and activists, as when the Art Car Museum's show "Secret Wars" was inspected by officials from the FBI and Secret Service, who took notes on the artists, and "things that they thought were negative." They asked the museum's frightened tour guide "if [her] parents knew if [she] worked at a place like this."[33] Another young woman, Durham Tech freshman A. J. Brown, found two agents from the Secret Service at her door one evening, announcing "We're here because we have a report that you have un-American material in your apartment." They inspected her political posters, including a Pink Floyd poster bearing the phrase "Mother should I trust the government?" took information, and asked her if she had "any pro-Taliban stuff" in her apartment. They also asked if it were true that her mother was in the armed forces. "Obviously," said Brown, "I'm on some list somewhere."[34] Welcome, says Rothschild, to the era of the New McCarthyism.

Intensified security requirements cultivate a constant sense of danger. They create a culture of fear that requires that adults and children alike be constantly vigilant to the reality of a new terrorist threat, a threat immediate and palpable yet simultaneously vague and abstract. In contrast to the amorphous enemy, the new security measures are reassuringly concrete. The threat of terrorism becomes inseparable from a generalized sense of fear. In cultures of fear, people often end up accepting social contracts infringing on personal freedoms and democratic rights in exchange for an increased sense of security. Extraordinary measures in the name of national security have alienated many citizens domestically, while weakened individual rights and respect for international law has undermined North America's moral authority to speak out against human rights violations in other parts of the world.[35]

Fomenting a Racist War against the Developing World

Flouting international law and the Geneva conventions has earned the U.S. widespread animosity. Irene Khan, Secretary General of Amnesty International, states that "Through short sighted, fear-mongering and divisive policies, governments are undermining the rule of law and human rights, feeding racism and xenophobia, dividing communities, intensifying inequalities and sowing the seeds for more violence and conflict."[36]

The resulting global and domestic anger will take a long time to heal. The war on terror has ironically become a form of terror, generating its own backlash. As long as the mainstream media persist in painting all Muslims as terrorists and implicitly supporting the violence perpetrated upon them, those who see their faith and culture under siege by the West have ample evidence of a modern-day crusade against Islam. The Arab world is continually reinforced in its "feeling that there is a deep racism underlying the occupiers' attitudes to Arabs, Muslims and the Third World generally."[37] At the same time new technologies mean that "graphic digital evidence of these losses and humiliations is available to anyone with a computer," says Naomi Klein, evidence that creates a "lethal cocktail of racism and torture" that is "burning through the veins of angry young men."[38] To mask our role in creating this rage, politicians re-cast it as an expression of the clash of civilizations, claiming that "they hate us for our freedoms." A 2004 report from a federal advisory committee for the U.S. Secretary of Defense noted explicitly that "Muslims do not hate our freedom, but rather they hate our policies."[39] America's one-sided support of Israel and lack of concern for the rights of Palestinians are contentious for Muslims, as is its "long-standing, even increasing, support for what Muslims collectively see as tyrannies, most notably in Egypt, Saudi Arabia, Jordan, Pakistan and the Gulf states. Thus, when American public diplomacy talks about bringing democracy to Islamic societies, this is seen as no more than self-serving hypocrisy."[40]

While many in the West have been taught to regard Muslim anger and re-sentment towards the West as generalized and irrational, part of the inevitable dynamic of hostile difference between East and West, it is actually a specific re-sponse to specific Western actions and policies. According to Chalmers John-son, "to think that a colonial power can treat another people as subhuman, steal their land, contain them in open-air prisons, detain their elected leaders, and subject them to starvation and then express shock and dismay when the poor wretches say something nasty . . . is the height of imperial hubris."[41]

Acting out of this hubris, we create the conditions that give rise to "blow-back," a CIA term for the unintended consequences of the U.S. govern-ment's international activities. Johnson accuses the U.S. of engaging in "bla-tant displays of global hegemony" through "organizations they control"[42] such as the International Monetary Fund, the World Trade Organization and the World Bank, each targeted by anti-globalization and anti-poverty pro-testers because of lending policies detrimental to impoverished countries. The war on terror has caused many formerly-indifferent or even pro-Western Arabs to become sympathetic to the terrorists or even engage in terrorist acts themselves. The destruction of their homes and infrastructure, the loss of livelihood, and the lack of progress in rebuilding has angered Iraqis. The senseless deaths of hundreds of thousands of innocent Iraqis, all of whom leave behind grieving families and friends, has ensured that rage and loss will create new terrorists to replace those captured or killed. As a result, the threat of terrorism has indisputably grown despite the harsh military crack-down on suspected terrorists at home and abroad.

What underlies the war on terror, according to David du Bois, is "the con-viction among white Americans that people of color are inherently inferior to whites and are therefore capable of committing, indeed eager to commit, the most heinous of crimes against 'the hated and envied European/American.'"[43] Such racist attitudes do not go unnoticed in the rest of the world; as Klein ob-serves, "Racism is the terrorists' greatest recruitment tool." She reports that Hussein Osman, apprehended in connection to the 2005 failed bombing at-tempt in London, told police that he prepared for the mission by watching films on the war in Iraq, "especially those where women and children were be-ing killed and exterminated by British and American soldiers."[44] This suggests "a possible motive for acts of terror against the UK: rage at perceived extreme racism." And what else, asks Klein, can we call the belief "that American and European lives are worth more than the lives of Arabs and Muslims, so much more that their deaths in Iraq are not even counted?"[45]

A bitter irony lies at the heart of all this: indisputably, it seems, our na-tional insecurities about the state of national security has made us significantly less secure. This is not speculation: American intelligence officials agree that "the Iraq war has made the overall terrorism problem worse."[46] The *New York Times* reports that American intelligence agencies now concur that the invasion and occupation of Iraq have "helped spawn a new generation of Islamic radicalism," resulting in a significant increase in the "overall terrorist threat."[47] Eighty percent of foreign-policy experts participating in the Terrorism Index report assert that the war in Iraq has had a negative effect "on protecting the American people from global terrorist networks and in advancing U.S. national security goals."[48] Significantly, 30 percent of those analysts rank the project of "winning the hearts and minds" of the Muslim world as the most urgent U.S. policy objective for the next five years, as opposed to only 15 percent who consider creating a "stable, secure Iraq" the most essential endeavor. The sense of the pressing consequence of the war in Iraq is shared among many expert observers. "The National Intelligence Estimate attributes a more direct role to the Iraq war in fueling radicalism than that presented either in recent White House documents or in a report released Wednesday by the House Intelligence Committee," writes Mark Mazzetti, asserting that since the beginning of the war on terror, "Islamic radicalism, rather than being in retreat, has metastasized and spread across the globe," resulting in a "diffusion of jihad ideology."[49] Ironically, the same seeds of the attitudes about race that underlie our aggression in Iraq and are "exacerbating domestic conflicts" and "fomenting radical ideologies" can be found in the language of the *New York Times* article that is earnestly exposing its dangers. When Islamic radicalism is represented in the article as something that, like vermin, "spawns," or that, like cancer "metastasizes and spreads," we find ourselves almost before we're aware of it enmeshed in the same dehumanizing metaphors that shape our perspectives, bind our thinking, and limit our responses. As the Intelligence Estimate's grim survey of heightened terrorist threat makes clear, the consequences of allowing such metaphors to govern our thinking and our policies are not abstract, but terrifyingly concrete.

Notes

1. Masnet and News Agencies. "Beheadings in Iraq and Saudi Arabia Fuel Backlash Against American Muslims." *Muslim American Society*. June 25, 2004. See www .masnet.org/news.asp?id=1329 (July 22, 2007).

2. Neil MacFarguhar. "U.S. Muslims Say Terror Fears Hamper Their Right to Travel." *New York Times*. June 1, 2006.

3. Neil MacFarguhar. "U.S. Muslims Say Terror Fears Hamper Their Right to Travel."

4. Neil MacFarguhar. "U.S. Muslims Say Terror Fears Hamper Their Right to Travel."

5. Neil MacFarguhar. "U.S. Muslims Say Terror Fears Hamper Their Right to Travel."

6. Foreign Policy. "The Terrorism Index." *Foreign Policy*. September/October 2007.

7. *Racial Justice*. "Mission Statement."*Racial Justice*. See racialjustice911.org /homehk.htm (July 17, 2007).

8. George W. Bush. "Address to a Joint Session of Congress and the American People." *The White House.gov*. See www.whitehouse.gov/news/releases/2001/09/2001 0920-8.html (July 17, 2007).

9. *Racial Justice*. "Mission Statement."

10. Abdul Malik Mujahid. "Demonization of Muslims Caused the Iraq Abuse." *Sound Vision*. May 19, 2004. See www.soundvision.com/info/peace/demonization.asp (July 17, 2007).

11. C. Allen and J. S. Nielsen. "Summary report on Islamophobia in the EU after 11 September 2001." *European Monitoring Centre on Racism and Xenophobia*. Vienna, Austria, 2002.

12. Mustafa Hassain cited in Geoffrey Wheatcroft. "Cartoon Characters: Whose fault is it that the media presents Muslims as fanatics?" *Slate*. February 9, 2006.

13. Ahmed Kutty cited in Faisal Kutty. "Canada's Nearly 400,000 Muslims Concerned about Media Stereotypes." *Washington Report on Middle East Affairs*, October 1993: 54.

14. *New Socialist*. "Racism, the Right and the Toronto 'Terrorism.'" *New Socialist* See www.newsocialist.org/newsite/index.php?id=988 (July 23, 2007).

15. Steven W. Bender. "Sight, Sound, and Stereotype: The War on Terrorism and Its Consequences for Latinas/os." *Oregon Law Review*. Vol. 81, 2002.

16. Alia Malek "Beware Thy neighbour?" *John Hopkins Magazine*. November 2001. See www.jhu.edu/~jhumag/1101web/ruminate.html (July 23, 2007).

17. Alia Malek "Beware Thy neighbour?"

18. Ziauddin Sardar. "The next holocaust." *New Statesman*, December 5, 2005.

19. Irene Chen. "Forget the War on Terror." *Brown Alumni magazine*. May/June 2007. See brownalumnimagazine.com/under-the-elm/forget_the_war_on-terror.html (July 17, 2007).

20. Alia Malek. "Beware Thy neighbour?"

21. Pat Robertson. *New York Magazine*. August 18, 1986.

22. Pat Robertson. *New York Magazine*.

23. Allen G. Breed. "Muslims Angered by Comments at Gathering of Southern Baptists." *Associated Press*. June 9–10, 2002.

24. Allen G. Breed. "Muslims Angered by Comments at Gathering of Southern Baptists."

25. Cited in Jim Lobe. "Fear of Islam on the Rise—Muslim Group." *LewRockwell .com*. May 12, 2005. See www.lewrockwell.com/ips/lobe210.html (July 17, 2007).

26. Kevin R. Johnson. "Racial Profiling after September 11: the Department of Justice's 2003 Guidelines." *Loyola Law Review*, Spring 2004.

27. Damien Cave. "Round up the usual suspects: How far should ethnic profiling go in the quest to nab the World Trade Center terrorists?" *Salon*. Sept. 14, 2001. See archive.salon .com/news/feature/2001/09/14/profiling/ (July 17, 2001).

28. Joan Mckinney. "Cooksey: Expect racial profiling." *Advocate*. September 19, 2001.

29. Bill Van Auken. "Rigoberto Alpizar and Jean Charles de Menezes: Two victims of state "anti-terror" killings." *World Socialist Website*. December 12, 2005. See www .wsws.org/articles/2005/dec2005/kill-d12.shtml (July 17, 2007).

30. Bill Van Auken. "Rigoberto Alpizar and Jean Charles de Menezes."

31. Kevin R. Johnson. "Racial Profiling after September 11: the Department of Justice's 2003 Guidelines." *Loyola Law Review*, Spring 2004.

32. Matthew Rothschild. "The New McCarthyism." *Progressive*. January 2002. See www.progressive.org/0901/roth0102.html (July 23, 2007).

33. Matthew Rothschild. "The New McCarthyism."

34. Matthew Rothschild. "The New McCarthyism."

35. Irene Khan, "Security for Whom? A Human Rights Response." *Amnesty International*. 2003. See web.amnesty.org/report2003/message-eng (July 20, 2007).

36. *Amnesty International*. "Politics of Fear Creating a Dangerously Divided World." *Amnesty International* Press Release. May 23, 2007.

37. Norman Solomon. "This War and Racism." Z. June 2004.

38. Naomi Klein. "Terror's Greatest Recruitment Tool." *The Nation*. August 29, 2005.

39. Tom Regan. "They hate our policies, not our freedom: Pentagon report contains major criticisms of administration." *Christian Science Monitor*. November 29, 2004.

40. Marjorie Cohn. "Chickens Come Home to Roost." *Truthout*. December 7, 2004. See www.truthout.org/docs_04/120704A.shtml (July 22, 2007).

41. Chalmers Johnson. *Blowback: The Costs and Consequences of American Empire*. New York: Henry Holt, 2000.

42. Chalmers Johnson. *Blowback*.

43. David Graham du Bois. "A War Like NO Other? You Bet!" Black Electorate .com. November 27, 2001. See www.blackelectorate.com/articles.asp?ID=492 (July 23, 2007).

44. Naomi Klein. "Terror's Greatest Recruitment Tool."

45. Naomi Klein. "Terror's Greatest Recruitment Tool."

46. Mark Mazzetti. "Spy Agencies Say Iraq War Worsens Terrorism Threat." *New York Times*. September 24, 2006.

47. Mark Mazzetti. "Spy Agencies Say Iraq War Worsens Terrorism Threat."

48. Mark Mazzetti. "Spy Agencies Say Iraq War Worsens Terrorism Threat."

49. Mark Mazzetti. "Spy Agencies Say Iraq War Worsens Terrorism Threat."

CHAPTER NINE

Talking Our Way to Peace:
New Metaphors for Change

The nature of society is measured in part by the kind of metaphors it induces or allows . . . by our metaphors you shall know us.

—Trevor Barnes and James Duncan[1]

The Wolves We Feed

Terrorism, clearly, is never justifiable. Terrorism undermines the security and peace of a country; creates suspicion towards others of different ethnicity; devastates families; disrupts economies and causes governments to divert resources into the military rather than investing in education, health care or housing. Eradicating terrorism is an important goal, but terrorism is, at root, such a complex phenomenon that no simple or reductive approach can ever successfully accomplish this. Instead, we need to examine terrorism and its contexts, and the public and media rhetoric surrounding it. To end terrorism, it must first be understood. Attempts to understand it have existed since well before the events of 9/11. In August 1996, U.S. president Bill Clinton proclaimed to an audience at George Washington University that "Terrorism is the enemy of our generation."[2] Five years before the fall of the twin towers, acts of terrorism were seen as something largely limited to strife-torn areas like the Middle East or Northern Ireland. Clinton's comment foreshadowed both the rapid spread of global terrorism and the intensification of public discourse addressing it. While notorious earlier cases like the Unabomber, the 1993 attack on the World Trade Center, the Oklahoma City bombing, and the Columbine shootings caused public comment and distress, it was not until September 2001 that talk about terrorism began to permeate the media in a manner so discursively charged that it shaped both public opinion and the domestic and foreign policies of several countries, none more so the U.S. Because of the far-reaching ramifications of both terrorism and the dangerous discourses surrounding it, we need to develop a metaphoric frame that will allow us to fruitfully "unpack" terrorism, so that we may understand, through an enlarged and nuanced comprehension the weighty freight it carries. Stephen R. Shalom explicitly links such an understanding to the necessity for productively addressing terrorism. In *Confronting Terrorism and the War*, Shalom states, "Sometimes when we examine terrorist acts—whether small-scale, like Columbine, or large-scale, like September 11—we will find that the terror breeds on legitimate grievances. When this is the case, addressing those grievances will be the most sensible way to reduce the likelihood of a recurrence of the terrorism."[3]

It is not without precedent that we seek such understanding through investigation and discussion. As Shalom notes, when Eric Harris and Dylan Klebold methodically shot fellow Columbine High School students before taking their own lives, officials and observers tried to understand what led the two teens to commit this act of violence. We did not excuse the killings, Shalom explains, nor did we justify them. But we did hope that "by understanding what happened we could take steps to reduce the likelihood of recurrence—perhaps designing programs to reduce alienation among teenagers or to make students more tolerant of those who don't fit in or making it more difficult for kids to obtain guns."

The discourses through which we publicly discuss terrorism, however, are largely not helping us to understand it. Instead of looking at each case and taking steps to comprehend or address specific contexts, situations or grievances, we have instead attempted to eradicate terrorism through the blunt instruments of force and the suspension of civil liberties. Examining the way terrorism is discussed in the mainstream media and government statements shows that understanding terrorism and its roots and contexts is not foremost on the agenda. The persistent vocabulary that dominates the rhetoric of public discussion of terrorism creates a picture, sometimes subtle, sometimes overwhelmingly clear, of Arab terrorists as essentially alien, fundamentally different from us. The more dissimilar this image is from our image of ourselves, the easier it is to dehumanize the enemy-Other and, by association, others of their community. The consequences of that dehumanization, as this book documents, can be deadly not just for the dehumanized Other but for our own diminishing security, a security ill-served by the metaphoric frames that re-engender violence.

Calls for understanding of the contexts, conflicts, and productions of terrorism are often criticized by those embracing the war metaphor. They are denounced as, at best, weak, self-indulgent, and soft, at worst, as traitorous and
self-destructive. Another way of considering this call for understanding, however, might see it as by far the more difficult and more rigorous road of response,
one vastly more challenging and demanding than the relatively straightforward route of military response. At what is hard not to see as a crossroads in
our political landscape, the path we choose at this juncture will resonate in-
escapably into our future. It might be worth remembering the Native American teaching story featuring an elder who tells his grandchildren that every human has within them two wolves engaged in fierce battle; one represents fear,
anger, resentment, greed arrogance, lies, pride and ego, and the other peace,
joy, friendship, empathy, truth, and compassion. When asked by his grandchild
which wolf will win the battle, the elder replies, whichever one you feed.[4] If
this is so, then we would do well to choose our metaphoric language with care,
since metaphors can provide potent nourishment.

Changing our Metaphors and Language

Metaphor offers us a unique index to our ideas and assumptions, at once reflecting and shaping the spectrum of our values. The role of metaphor and
the discourses it sustains are so fundamental that, as E. L. Doctorow has argued, "The development of civilizations is essentially a progression of
metaphors."[5] Our cultural lexicon of dehumanizing metaphor is remarkably
enduring; not only has it colonized discussion of the war on terror, it has per-
meated our public conversations about other denigrated or marginalized
groups. The rat metaphor, in particular, creeps eagerly into many discourses
of judgment: an article in The 13th, a right-wing Catholic newspaper, claims
that "Homosexuals, like rats, are crawling out of their holes, only to be fed
lovingly by church people and politicians."[6] This language is echoed by an
American televangelist who said homosexuals are "like rats, skulking in their
closets, copulating in mad frenzies, unable to control their appetites, sniffing
around the doors of school classrooms for fresh prey."[7] Paul Cameron, chairman of the Family Research Institute, has advocated facial tattoos for AIDS
victims and the castration, deportation to a former leper colony, and even extermination of homosexuals.[8] Vermin metaphors are also regularly applied to
immigrant groups, especially when increases in immigration begin to be perceived as a threat to security. In Brown Tide Rising, Otto Santa Ana documents how media discourse on immigration typically uses "overtly racist and
dehumanizing" terms. Animal images provide the dominant metaphor for

immigrants, with secondary metaphors of the hunt supporting and reinforcing it. Illegal immigrants are described as "hunted down," "baited," "lured"
and "ferreted out." News reports frequently talk about the "hordes" "pouring"
across the border instead of employing more accurate, more neutral descriptions such as "people walking across." [9] Santa Ana argues that far from being
mere figures of speech, such metaphors produce and support negative public
perceptions of the Latino community; he reveals how metaphorical language
repeatedly publically portrays Latinos as invaders, outsiders, burdens, parasites, diseases, animals, and weeds.

These metaphors are not simply artful descriptors or enlivening figures of
speech. As Donald Schon has influentially argued, the work of metaphor
goes much further: metaphors represent a manner of perception, a special
way of seeing. The way in which we frame social problems has a significant
impact on the way we identify and structure solutions to them; for Schon,
"the framing of problems often depends upon the metaphors underlying the
stories which generate problem setting and set the direction of problem solv-
ing."[10] To exemplify this claim, he compares the treatment of two problematic housing developments; in one, slum areas were metaphorically defined
as a "blight" or "disease"; in the other, they were perceived as "natural communities." The medical metaphor implicit in the first situation justifies a
medical response, such as figurative radical surgery, to eliminate the disease;
the other metaphorical model, in contrast, calls for ways of acknowledging
and enhancing the life of those communities.

Metaphors offer a way of selecting, labeling, and understanding "facts," a
process that may filter or distort what is perceived. If we are unaware of the
ways in which our metaphors influence and shape our perception and understanding of social situations, Schon says, then this process of influence is
even more powerful. When metaphors remain tacit or implicit, they can condition the way in which a situation is understood as problematic. The consequences of buried, indirect, or hidden metaphors can therefore be dangerously counter-productive, constraining and sometimes negatively controlling
the way in which individuals and groups construct the world in which they
live and act. If the metaphor no longer remains tacit, however, because an effort is made to make it visible and conscious, then possibilities which were
suppressed when the dominant metaphor was only implied may emerge. The
assumptions which arise from the metaphor can then be evaluated deliberately, and the metaphor can be kept or discarded depending upon its appropriateness and usefulness. We can find an example of a deliberate discarding
of a stale, pejorative metaphoric frame in the recent decision of the British
government officially to renounce the use of the phrase "war on terror," the
metaphor previously so dominant as to eclipse all others in public and pri-

vate discourse. Sir Ken MacDonald, Director of Public Prosecutions, said the British government will "resist the language of warfare," refuting phrases that entrench and frame all discussion of public attack in martial terms. Such war-like language creates "fear-driven and inappropriate" responses that, Mac-Donald warns, might lure the British public into disregarding due process of law. When critique and examination of the martial metaphor becomes part of legitimated public debate, metaphoric space is opened up for new and more liberatory framings. [11]

Schon insists on the importance of adopting a conscious process of frame restructuring, involving the design of a new narrative or metaphor that sets the problem in a new way. Within the new metaphor, conflicting frames may be integrated by including features and relations drawn from earlier metaphors without sacrificing internal coherence, forcefulness, or clarity. Instead of preventing or limiting action, a conscious integration of metaphor may allow for new and enlarged possibilities of action.

Blechman and Docherty propose, therefore, that we choose more constructive metaphoric frameworks, such as education, medicine, or crime, to replace the dominant war metaphor. Each of these allows for productive possibilities that are precluded by the war metaphor. The crime metaphor, for example, has the benefit of allowing citizens to "assist law enforcement personnel by endorsing social sanctions, depriving criminals of their cover, and aiding officials when asked to do so."[12] If "the goal of a justice system is restoration, not punishment," add Blechman and Doherty, then the criminal metaphor, unlike the war metaphor, can offer "a platform for a restorative model of interaction with the terrorists."[13]

We need to actively seek out a workable, effective alternative to the war metaphor because our history is already "too full of the stories of war and too short on the stories of peace." Instead, we require a new narrative, with a better conclusion; perhaps in place of the narrative of the leader-as-general, who responds to attack with annihilating aggression, we might substitute the story, suggest Blechman and Doherty, "about the wise leader who listened to all the counselors and then chose the path of peace, reconciliation and justice."[14] New stories also create freedom by allowing us to adopt new roles within them, letting us move from passivity and conformity to creativity and possibility. When leaders regretfully tell us we must follow their injunctions because there are simply no other possibilities, Blechman and Doherty urge us to respond from these newly enlarged roles: "Wait, we can think of other options you haven't tried."[15]

Treating terrorist attacks as criminal acts within a legal rather than military frame also allows us to consider effective and contextualized responses; Stephen R. Shalom urges us to consider the crime analogy as a way to treat underlying causes rather than merely symptoms. "Some people brought up in grueling poverty become anti-social criminals" who "need to be brought to justice," Shalom argues; when analysts point out that poverty breeds crime, it "doesn't mean that criminals should be permitted to continue their crime sprees or that somehow they were justified in slitting the throat of this or that innocent victim,"[16] but it does mean that the continuing condition of poverty will continue to create new criminals without some serious intervention or redress. Richard Haass, a former director of policy planning in the U.S. State Department and president of the Council on Foreign Relations, also suggests that the most important first move in fighting terrorism is to dispense with "the metaphor of a war on terrorism"; terrorism cannot, he insists, "be defeated by arms alone. Other instruments of policy including intelligence, police work and diplomacy, are likely to play a larger part."[17] But much more important, he argues, is to "persuade young men and women not to become terrorists in the first place." Terrorism needs to be stripped not only of its legitimacy but, even more importantly, of its motivation. This translates, says Haass, into changes in foreign policy, with the aim of creating an environment in which terrorism is "neither acceptable nor necessary."[18] The conscious disposal of the metaphors that have not served us well, as more diverse voices are beginning to urge, is a crucial first step in moving towards that environment, a world in which terrorism is not defeated but made irrelevant.

Journalism and Peace

Some of these creative new options are beginning to emerge from sources outside of mainstream media and traditional government. Peace journalism, in particular, sets itself against the methods of mainstream news reporting, insisting that journalists have a choice in how they cover violent conflict. By rejecting the formats and formula of traditional journalism, journalists can shed light on issues of human rights and their violation, focus coverage on hate crimes and hate groups, and publicize important humanitarian efforts. A more emancipatory media framing can help formulate solutions to what seem like intractable conflicts rather than framing conflicts as inevitable because they emerge from fundamental and essential difference. A critical and self-aware media can also help reduce the dominance of rumor and propaganda.[19] In these ways, says Robert Karl Manoff, media can play a key role in preventing and moderating conflict. This means, of course, that media can also do the opposite. If it chooses to be complicit as, John Pilger argues, it often is in demonizing the enemy and enlisting public support for governments' war policies, then it gives up its vaunted and largely illusory objectivity in the service of war.[20] Why not instead, ask the new peace journalists, serve something else? Rune Ottosen rejects "war journalism" as "violence-oriented, propaganda-oriented, elite-oriented and victory-oriented"; this orientation not only reinforces official propaganda, Ottosen says, it also often plays a significant role in escalating conflicts.[21]

In order to resist this role, John Galtung has identified key journalistic problems common to traditional reporting. In covering conflict, mainstream news media risk intensifying that conflict through its metaphoric frames and representations. These media representations, Galtung observes, tend to decontextualize violence, focusing on its irrational elements and overlooking the reasons for conflict and polarization. They indulge in an often simplistic dualism, reducing parties in a conflict to only two, when there are frequently many more, and then splitting the two parties into the "good" and the "evil." They present violence as inevitable, failing to depict or even suggest possible alternatives, and focus on individual acts of violence while avoiding causes. By omitting and excluding the voices of the bereaved, for example, they fail to provide a way to understand contexts, acts of revenge and spirals of violence. Just as they fail to explore peace proposals and "offer images of peaceful outcomes," they "fail to explore the goals of outside interventionists," especially major powers, and further fail to "explore the causes of escalation and the impact of media coverage itself."[22] As a consequence of these failures, traditional news coverage tends to confuse peace with cease-fire and negotiations, and to omit representing actual reconciliation; if, Galtung argues, sufficient effort is not put into healing fractured societies, then conflicts generally re-emerge, often in an intensified form. Worse, if media fail to provide news about attempts to resolve conflicts, then an oppressive sense of fatalism is reinforced; if "people have no images or information about possible peaceful outcomes and the promise of healing" to balance the fatalism, further violence may be engendered.[23]

Given that media can play an important role in creating the conditions for peace and can act as a mediator and communication medium for non-violent conflict resolution, peace radio in particular stands out as having the capability of bridging even the most insurmountable of divides. One such radio station is 107.2 FM Radio All for Peace in Israel-Palestine, a collaborative effort between Palestinian and Jewish organizations. Their goal is to expose people in both Palestine and Israel to positive messages of "peace, cooperation, mutual understanding, coexistence and hope."[24]

Conclusion

Metaphors matter. They are figures of thought as much as figures of speech, and in their framing of events and identities they offer a way to understand our world and to act within it. With this power to generate and shape action, metaphor is a potent force; it is no wonder that Nietzsche described truth as a "mobile army of metaphors."[25] This potency is greatest when it attacks both overtly and covertly; at their most effective, metaphors are surreptitious. When we use our intelligence to scout them out, however, stripping them of their camouflage and bringing them into the light, we empower ourselves. If awareness is one of the most contested terrains on the battlefield, then every time we critically disinter a metaphor, we gain metaphorical ground. As T. J. Barnes insists, "in a very real sense, there is nothing trifling about a metaphor . . . we must eventually think critically about the metaphors we choose—where they come from, why they were proposed, in whose interest they represent, and the nature of their implications."[26] If we don't engage in these acts of critical consciousness, Barnes warns, we may find ourselves "the slave of some defunct maker of metaphors."[27]

One sobering example of a slavish attachment to destructive metaphor may be found in a recent 2007 cartoon by Michael Ramirez[28], which shows a map of the Middle East with, in its center, the country Iran replaced by a huge sewer grating. The associative linking of country with sewer is difficult to miss, but in case we do, Ramirez' image makes it clear by labeling the sewer "Iran" and adding, in much smaller, harder to make out typeface, the additional word "Extremism." Out of the sewer cover, in an image by now familiar, swarms a mass of loathsome cockroaches spreading inexorably into the surrounding countries of Iraq, Pakistan, Afghanistan, Turkey, and Saudi Arabia. "It is very sad," says Ali Sheikholeskami, executive director of the Islamic Cultural Center of Northern California, "that American media has come down to such a level and that there is no outcry of the American public against these types of cartoons or this type of dehumanization of an entire nation."[29] Perhaps even more sad is the tenaciousness of our attachment to these dehumanizing metaphors, and the way they both chronicle and are used to justify further conquest; in the fall of 2007 *Time* magazine reported that "The prospect of war with Iran is beginning to look real."[30] This is a prediction that might singularly fail to surprise us, if we are alert to the transpositions of these wearily familiar images representing the enemy-Other from Iraq to Iran, as we see so clearly in Ramirez's cartoon. If, as Seymour Hirsch quotes a former U.S. intelligence official as saying, "There is a desperate effort by Cheney et al. to bring military action to Iran as soon as possible,"[31] then one way to rally public support for wars as yet undeclared is to rally the public around such images of primal infestation and threat. The enemy as cockroach, used to justify war and genocide, is clearly not even close to being, in Barnes' terms, "defunct." It is for this reason that metaphor remains so critical. While philosophers like Richard Rorty who analyze metaphor have been criticized for not paying enough attention to how power and material economic conditions can influence the workings of metaphor and who controls and deploys metaphoric systems, Rorty's work is nevertheless suggestive in its assertion that to change metaphors is to change the conversation; at the very least, he says, coining a new metaphor can produce a new vivacity of speech, or turn the conversation to a new direction.[32]

Turning the conversation is often an admirable goal in itself; it allows for the entry of new ideas and new voices and can realign a dangerous trajectory. For a conversation to be turned, however, it must first exist as a dialogue: a speech, tirade, or monologue is much harder to interrupt, break into, or turn aside. Sometimes, then, we must undertake a more fundamental task in order simply to allow the conversation to begin. If, as Nelson suggests, we talk our way into war with rhetoric and propaganda and talk our way out of it with negotiations and treaties, we might consider the possibility of using talk to turn aside from war, to turn to new alternatives and talk our way to new solutions.[33] We might insist on new metaphors to take us to these decisive turns. We might ask of ourselves and our leaders, in what service is our army of metaphors deployed? And, more importantly, what would happen if we disbanded our metaphoric army, not only finally discharging those metaphors that are irreparably linked to difference and denigration, but, more radically, enlisting a new conceptual model altogether? The more fundamental and deep-rooted our present metaphors, the more powerful and far-reaching the change we initiate when we alter them. If we currently face, as Gibson Winter argues, a "crisis of root metaphors," then "a shift in metaphors may open new vistas of human possibilities."[34] Freeing ourselves from our "dead metaphors," Orla Schantz argues, will "free us to develop a talent for speaking differently," a talent that will allow us to discover that "it is rhetorical innovation" that is ultimately the "chief instrument of cultural and political change."[35] If our identities are tied up in the language we use, the metaphors we create, and the stories we tell, then when we choose to change that language, those metaphors, and those stories, we exert a powerful freedom to change not only the enemy, but ourselves. If, as Rorty urged, we ourselves are a narrative, a text of identity always being written, then in choosing to change the metaphors by which we dehumanize the enemy, we can commensurately and productively change our own story. "Our language," says Schantz, "exhibits sheer contingency, thus we are not forever bound to the vocabularies of our ancestors or their gods. We need not worship the corpses of their dead metaphors."[36] We can, if we choose, exert a textual autonomy that rejects the divisiveness of the dominant discourse, that rejects the binaries endlessly subdividing the "us" from the "them," the "I" from the "Other." And if, as peace scholars affirm, "the struggle for identity lies at the nexus of war and peace," with the prognosis for peace rising when identities are not at risk,[37] then changing the conversation becomes as radical an act as changing the world.

Notes

1. Trevor Barnes and James Duncan. *Writing Worlds: Discourse, Text and Metaphor in the Representation of Landscape*. London and New York: Routledge, 1992:12.

2. Bill Clinton speech. "Remarks on American security in a changing world at George Washington University." *American Presidency Project*. August 5, 1996. See www.presidency .ucsb.edu/ws/index.php?pid=53161 (July 26, 2007).

3. Stephen R. Shalom. "Confronting Terrorism and War." *New Politics*, vol. 8, no. 4, Winter 2002.

4. Mickey Z. "Which Wolf Will You Feed in 2006?" *Dissidentvoice.org*. December 31, 2005. See http://www.dissidentvoice.org/Dec05/MickeyZ1231.htm (March 28, 2008).

5. E. L. Doctorow. "False documents." *American Review*. Volume, 29. 1977: 231–32.

6. Cited in *hatecrime.org*. "Nazi Anti-Jewish Speech VS. Religious Right Anti-Gay Speech." See www.hatecrime.org/subpages/hitler/hitler.html (July 25, 2007).

7. Cited in Jack Nichols. *The Gay Agenda: Talking Back to the Fundamentalists*. Amherst, NY: Prometheus Books, 1996.

8. *sourcewatch*. "Paul Cameron." See www.sourcewatch.org/index.php?title=Paul_Cameron (July 25, 2007).

9. Otto Santa Ana. *Brown Tide Rising*. Austin, TX: University of Texas Press, 2002.

10. Donald Schon. "Generative metaphor: a perspective on problem setting in social policy." In Andrew Ortony (Ed). *Metaphor and Thought*. Cambridge: Cambridge University Press, 1979: 254–83.

11. Clare Dyer, "There is no 'war on terror'." *The Guardian*. January 24, 2007.

12. Frank Blechman and Jayne Seminare Docherty "Frameworks Other Than War." *Beyond September 11*. September 14, 2001. See www.emu.edu/ctp/bse-metaphor3.html (June 26, 2007).

13. Frank Blechman and Jayne Seminare Docherty. "Frameworks Other Than War."

14. Frank Blechman and Jayne Seminare Docherty. "Frameworks Other Than War."

15. Frank Blechman and Jayne Seminare Docherty. "Frameworks Other Than War."

16. Stephen R. Shalom. "Confronting Terrorism and War." *New Politics*. Vol. 8, no. 4, Winter 2002.

17. Richard N. Haass. "Fighting terror—We are still behind the curve." *Council on Foreign Relations*. August 11, 2006. See www.cfr.org/publication/11281/fighting_terror_we _are_still_behind_the_curve.html (July 28, 2007).

18. Richard N. Haass. "Fighting terror."

UNIVERSITY OF CHESTER, WARRINGTON CAMPUS

19. Robert Karl Manoff. "The Media's Role in Preventing and Moderating Conflict." *Virtual Diplomacy conference hosted by United States Institute of Peace* in Washington, D.C., April 1–2, 1997.

20. Rune Ottosen. "Emphasising Images in Peace Journalism," *Conflict and Communication online.* Vol. 6, No.1, 2007.

21. Rune Ottosen. "Emphasising Images in Peace Journalism."

22. John Galtung cited in Danny Schechter. "Covering Violence: How Should Media Handle Conflict?" *Media Channel.* July 18, 2001. See www.mediachannel.org/views/dissector/coveringviolence.shtml (July 28, 2007).

23. Danny Schechter. "Covering Violence."

24. *Bulletin of Regional Cooperation in the Middle East.* "All for Peace Radio." 2004. See www.sfcg.org/bulletin/2004/bulletin2e.doc (July 26, 2007).

25. Friedrich Nietzsche cited in Orla Schantz. "Richard Rorty: In Memorium." *The Enlightenment Underground.* June 11, 2007. See enlightenmentunderground.blogspot.com (July 22, 2007).

26. Trevor Barnes. "Metaphors and Conversations in Economic Geography: Richard Rorty and the Gravity Mold." Geografiska Annaler. Series B, Human geography, Volume 73, No. 2, 1991: 111–20.

27. Trevor Barnes "Metaphors and Conversations in Economic Geography."

28. Michael Ramirez. Untitled cartoon. *Columbus Dispatch.* September 4, 2007.

29. Cited in Omid Memarian. "US cartoon no joke to Iranians." *Asia Times.* September 20, 2007.

30. Scott MacLeod. "Iran War Drumbeat Grows Louder." *Time,* October 26, 2007.

31. Cited in Scott Peterson. "Are U.S. and Iran headed for war? *Christian Science Monitor.* October 3, 2007.

32. Trevor Barnes "Metaphors and Conversations in Economic Geography."

33. Daniel Nelson. "Word Peace." In *At War With Words.* Eds. Mirjana Dedaic and Daniel Nelson. Berlin: Mouton de Gruyter, 2003: 449.

34. Gibson Winter. *Liberating Creation: Foundations of Religious Social Ethics.* New York, Crossroad, 1981.

35. Orla Schantz. "Richard Rorty: In Memorium." *The Enlightenment Underground.* June 11, 2007. See enlightenmentunderground.blogspot.com (July 22, 2007).

36. Orla Schantz. "Richard Rorty: In Memorium."

37. Daniel Nelson. "Word Peace."

Bibliography

Abraham, Nabeel. "The Gulf Crisis and Anti-Arab Racism in America." In *Collateral Damage: The New World Order at Home and Abroad*. Cynthia Peters (ed). Boston: South End Press, 1991. *The Advertiser*. December 15, 2003.

Agence France Presse—English. April 1, 2006.

———. October 15, 2004.

Albert, Michael. "After The "Turkey Shoot." Z. See www.zmag.org/zmag/articles /albertold19.htm (June 26, 2007).

Ali, Tariq. "This is the real outrage." *The Guardian* February 13, 2006. See www .guardian.co.uk/cartoonprotests/story/0,,1708319,00.html (July 3, 2007).

Allen, C. and J. S. Nielsen. "Summary report on Islamophobia in the EU after 11 September 2001." *European Monitoring Centre on Racism and Xenophobia*. Vienna, Austria, 2002.

Allen, Christopher. "Islamophobia in the Media Since 911."*Forum against Islamophobia and Racism UK (FAIRUK)*. September 29, 2001. See www.fairuk.org/docs /Islamophobia-in-the-Media-since-911-ChristopherAllen.pdf (June 26, 2007).

Allen, Joe. "Vietnam: The War the U.S. Lost." *International Socialist Review*, January/February 2004. See www.thirdworldtraveler.com/Asia/Vietnam_War_US _Lost.html (June 26, 2007).

"America's Mad as Hell Humor Page." See www.almostaproverb.com

Ammitzbøll, Pernille and Lorenzo Vidino. "After the Danish Cartoon Controversy." *Middle East Quarterly*. Winter 2007. See www.meforum.org/article/1437#_ftn14>. (July 3, 2007).

Amnesty International. "Human dignity denied Torture and accountability in the 'war on terror.'" October 27, 2004. See web.amnesty.org/library/Index/ENGAMR51145 2004>. (June 29, 2007).

————. "Politics of Fear Creating a Dangerously Divided World." Press Release. May 23, 2007.

Anti-Defamation League. "Racist Groups Using Computer Gaming to Promote Violence Against Blacks, Latinos and Jews." February 12, 2002. See www.adl.org/video games/default.asp (July 3, 2007).

Apter, David (ed). *The Legitimation of Violence.* London: Macmillan. 1997.

Artz, Lee W., and Mark A Pollock. "Limiting the Options: Anti-Arab Images in U.S. Media Coverage of the Persian Gulf Crisis." in *The U.S. Media and the Middle East: Images and Perception.* Kamalipour, Yahya R (Ed). Westport, CT: Greenwood Press, 1995.

As'ad. "Danish Cartoons (not pastries)." *Angry Arab.* February 04, 2006. See angryarab .blogspot.com/2006/02/danish-cartoons-not-pastries.html>. (July 3, 2007).

Ashrawi, Hannan. "Anatomy of Racism." Z. October 18, 2000. See www.zmag.org /meastwatch/anatomy_of_racism.htm (June 26, 2007).

Aslan, Reza. "Depicting Mohammed: Why I'm offended by the Danish cartoons of the prophet." *Slate.* February 8, 2006. See www.slate.com/id/2135661/ (July 3, 2007).

Associated Press. "Evidence suggests Haditha killings deliberate: Pentagon source." August 2, 2006.

The Australian. August 6, 2003.

————. December 18, 2003.

————. May 2, 2003.

————. October 22, 2002.

Bacon, Kenneth H. "DoD News Briefing." U.S. Department of Defense. April 24, 1995. See www.defenselink.mil/transcripts/transcript.aspx?transcriptid=123>. (July 3, 2007).

Bagdikian, Ben H. *The Media Monopoly*, Sixth Edition. New York: Beacon Press, 2000.

Baldilocks. "Spain's the Target." March 11, 2004.See baldilocks.typepad.com /baldilocks/2004/03/spains_the_targ.html (June 26, 2007). See also http://bancroft .berkeley.edu/Exhibits/nativeamericans/10.html (June 26, 2007).

Barnes, Trevor, and James Duncan. *Writing Worlds: Discourse, Text and Metaphor in the Representation of Landscape.* London and New York: Routledge, 1992: 12.

Barnes, Trevor. "Metaphors and Conversations in Economic Geography: Richard Rorty and the Gravity Mold." Geografiska Annaler. Series B, Human geography, Volume 73, No. 2, 1991: 111–20.

Barsamian, David. "Dateline Baghdad: An Interview with Dahr Jamail." Z. December 2005. See zmagsite.zmag.org/Dec2005/barsamian1205.html (June 26, 2007).

Bath Chronicle. February 8, 2006.

Baudrillard, Jean. "War Porn." *International Journal of Baudrillard Studies.* Volume 2, Number 1, January 2005.

BBC. "Al-Jazeera English TV date set." BBC. November 1, 2006. See news.bbc.co .uk/2/hi/middle_east/6105952.stm (July 3, 2007).

————. "Cartoons row hits Danish exports." *BBC News.* September 9, 2006. See news .bbc.co.uk/2/hi/europe/5329642.stm (July 3, 2007).

———. "Millions join anti-war protests worldwide." *BBC News Online*, February 17, 2003.

———. *Monitoring International Reports*, January 4, 2004.

———. "Veteran CBS News Anchor Dan Rather speaks out." *BBC Newsnight*. May 16, 2002. See www.bbc.co.uk/pressoffice/pressreleases/stories/2002/05_may/16/dan_rather.shtml (July 15, 2007).

Belman, Jonathan. "A Cockroach cannot give birth to a butterfly and other messages of hate propaganda." *Peace, War and Human Nature*. May 2004. See www.gse.harvard.edu/~t656_web/peace/Articles_Spring_2004/Belman_Jonathan_hate_propaganda.htm (June 27, 2007).

Bender, Steven W. "Sight, Sound, and Stereotype: The War on Terrorism and Its Consequences for Latinas/os." *Oregon Law Review*. Vol. 81, 2002.

Bendib, Khalil. "Your Islamophobic Fist Must Stop At My Muslim Nose." *altmuslim.com*. February 17, 2006. See www.altmuslim.com/perm.php?id=1658_0_25_0_C42 (July 3, 2007).

Biedermann, Hans. *Dictionary of Symbolism*. New York City: Facts on File, 1992: viii.

Birmingham Post. March 13, 2003.

Black, Ian. "End growing anti-muslim prejudice, EU report urges." *The Guardian*. May 4, 2002.

Blechman, Frank, and Jayne Seminare Docherty "Frameworks Other Than War." *Beyond September 11*. September 14, 2001. See www.emu.edu/ctp/bse-metaphor3.html (June 26, 2007).

Blum, William. "Civilian Casualties: Theirs and Ours." *Counter Punch*. December 17, 2001. See www.counterpunch.org/blumcasualties.html (July 15, 2007).

Blumenthal, Sidney. "The right wing's summer of hate." *Salon*. August 15, 2003. See dir.salon.com/story/opinion/feature/2003/08/15/hate/index.html (July 3, 2007).

Boggs, Carl, and Tom Pollard. *The Hollywood War Machine*. Boulder, CO: Paradigm Publishers, 2006: 9.

Borger, Julian. "'I feel like I did in the Vietnam days—I hate to pay taxes just so they can go and bomb more people.'" *The Guardian*. April 14, 2006.

Boston Herald. December 15, 2003.

Bouvier, Virginia. "Imaging a Nation: U.S. political cartoons and the war of 1898." In *Whose War; the War of 1898 and the Battles to Define the Nation*. Virginia Marie Bouvier (ed). Westport, CT: Praeger, 2001.

Breed, Allen G. "Muslims Angered by Comments at Gathering of Southern Baptists." *Associated Press*. June 9–10, 2002.

Breen, Steve. "Untitled." *San Diego Union-Tribune*. September 13, 2001.

Bronski, Michael. "Brain drain: In defense of Susan Sontag, Noam Chomsky, and Gore Vidal." *The Phoenix.com*. September 19, 2002. See 72.166.46.24/boston/news_features/other_stories/multipage/documents/02441651.htm (June 26, 2007).

Buch-Andersen, Thomas. "Denmark targets extremist media." *BBC News*. August 17, 2005. See newsvote.bbc.co.uk/mpapps/pagetools/print/news.bbc.co.uk/1/hi/world/europe/4159220. stm (July 3, 2007).

Buckingham, Mike. "1991 massacre of thousands of fleeing Iraqi troops was part of U.S. 'total war.'" *Hartford Web Publishing*. February 8, 2003. See www.hartfordhwp .com/archives/27c/069.html (June 26, 2007).

Bulletin of Regional Cooperation in the Middle East. "All for Peace Radio." 2004. See www.sfcg.org/bulletin/2004/bulletin2e.doc (July 26, 2007).

Buncombe, Andrew, and Justin Huggler. "*Iraq: Abuse Crisis: Abu Ghraib: inmates raped, ridden like animals.*" *Independent* (London). May 22, 2004.

Burke, Kenneth. *Language as Symbolic Action: Essays on Life, Literature and Method.* Berkeley, CA: University of California Press, 1968.

Burnette, Ann E., and Wayne L. Kraemer. "Putting a Face on Evil: The Rhetorical Creation of an Enemy in the U.S. War on Terrorism." Presentation to the *National Communication Association Convention*, 2003.

Bush, George W. "Address to a Joint Session of Congress and the American People." *The White House.gov.* See www.whitehouse.gov/news/releases/2001/09/20010920-8 .html (July 17, 2007).

Cafepress: *Shop, sell or create what's on your mind.* See www.cafepress.com

Cageprisoners. "Profile: Mamdouh Habib." January 29, 2005. See www.cageprisoners .com/articles.php?id=5011

Cagle, Daryl. "Dead or Alive." *MSNBC.Com.* September 20, 2001.

———. "Saddam Skin Rug." *MSNBC.com.* December 29, 2006.

———. "Taliban Bugs Windshield." *MSNBC.com.* October 30, 2001. *The Calgary Sun.* July 17, 2005.

Cappella, Joseph, Joseph Turow, and Kathleen Hall. "Call-In Political Talk Radio: Background, Content, Audiences, Portrayal in Mainstream Media." *University of Pennsylvania Annenberg Public Policy Center*, July 22, 1996.

Cardow, Cameron. "Canada Buggy Flag." *Ottawa Citizen.* June 11, 2006.

Carillo, Jose A. "English Plain and Simple." *Manila Times.* May 27, 2003. See www .manilatimes.net/national/2003/may/27/top_stories/20030527top13.html (June 28, 2007).

Carlson, Margaret. "Public Eye." *Time.* January 23, 1995.

Carmon, Yigal. "Option Paper: Creating Awareness: Education, Media and Memory." *Stockholm International Forum.* January 26–28, 2004. See www.manskligarattigheter .gov.se/stockholmforum/2004/page1589.html (July 3, 2007).

Carr, David. "Deadly Intent: Ann Coulter, Word Warrior." *New York Times.* June 12, 2006.

Caswell, Lucy Shelton. "Drawing Swords: War in American Editorial Cartoons." *American Journalism.* 21(2), 2004: 13–45.

Cave, Damien. "Round up the usual suspects: How far should ethnic profiling go in the quest to nab the World Trade Center terrorists?" *Salon.* Sept. 14, 2001. See archive.salon.com/news/feature/2001/09/14/profiling/ (July 17, 2001).

Center for American Progress. "Who is Rupert Murdoch?" July 16, 2004. See www .americanprogress.org/issues/2004/07/b122948.html (July 15, 2007).

Center for Social Media. "Journalists became icons of sentimental patriotism." 2002. See www.centerforsocialmedia.org/challengestojournalism.html (July 27, 2007).

Cfinstr. "End Islam." *Jihad Chat*. February 6, 2007. See www.jihadchat.com/index .php?showtopic=521&pid=2174&mode=threaded&start=—30k—(June 28, 2007).

Chen, Irene. "Forget the War on Terror." *Brown Alumni magazine*. May/June 2007. See brownalumnimagazine.com/under-the-elm/forget_the_war_on-terror.html (July 17, 2007).

China Daily, December 15, 2003.

Chomsky, Noam. "Interviews." *Manufacturing Consent: Noam Chomsky and the Media*. [Videorecording]. Mark Achbar and Peter Wintonick. Necessary Illusions, 1992.

———. "Propaganda, American-Style." *Z*. September 17, 2001. See www.zpub.com /un/chomsky.html (June 26, 2007).

The Christchurch Press. December 16, 2003.

Clark, Ramsey. "War Crimes: A Report on United States War Crimes against Iraq." *War Crimes: A report on United States War Crimes against Iraq*. New York: Maisonneuve Press, 1992.

Clinton, Bill speech. "Remarks on American security in a changing world at George Washington University." *American Presidency Project*. August 5, 1996. See www .presidency.ucsb.edu/ws/index.php?pid=53161 (July 26, 2007).

CNN. "In Libya, 11 reportedly die in cartoon protests." February 18, 2006. See edition .cnn.com/2006/WORLD/africa/02/17/libya.cartoons/index.html

Coburn, Judith. "Unnamed and Unnoticed: Iraqi Casualties." *TomDispatch*. July 18, 2005. See www.tomdispatch.com/index.mhtml?pid=6963 (July 15, 2007).

Cohen, Jeff, and Steve Rendall. "Can a Man Who Has a Problem with People of Color Be a Color Commentator on 'Monday Night Football'?" *Los Angeles Times*. June 7, 2000.

Cohn, Marjorie. "Chickens Come Home to Roost." *Truthout*. December 7, 2004. See www.truthout.org/docs_04/120704A.shtml (July 22, 2007).

Colon, Aly. "Embed Journalists Everywhere." *Poynter.org*. March 17, 2003. See www .poynter.org/column.asp?id=58&aid=25265 (July 15, 2007).

Conan. "Untitled." *Scotsman*. June 4, 2007. See www.scotsman.com/?id=869642007 (June 28, 2007).

Conners, J. L. "Hussein as enemy: The Persian Gulf War in political cartoons." *Harvard International Journal of Press/Politics*. 3 (3), 96–114. 1998.

Conway, Mike, and Maria Grabe. "Content analysis of O'Reilly's rhetoric finds spin to be a 'factor.'" *Indiana University Press Release*. (May 2, 2007). See newsinfo.iu .edu/news/page/normal/5535.html (July 3, 2007).

Copeland, Libby. "Spider hole's web of meanings." *Washington Post*. December 18, 2003.

Corn, David. "George Won't Be Reading This: the President Prefers Spin to News." *Los Angeles Weekly*. October 23, 2003. See www.laweekly.com/news/news/george-wont-be-reading-this/2295/ (June 28, 2007).

Coulter, Ann. *How to Talk to a Liberal (If You Must)*. New York City: Crown Publishing Group, 2004.

Cox, John, and Allen Forkum. "Forked Tongue." *Cox and Forkum.com*. June 18, 2006. See www.coxandforkum.com/archives/000868.html (July 3, 2007).

———. "Metastasis." *Cox and Forkum.com*. July 02, 2007. See www.coxandforkum .com/archives/000868.html (July 3, 2007).

Cox News Service, December 30, 2003.

Crockett's Almanac. Philadelphia, New York, Boston and Baltimore: Fisher & Brothers, 1841, 1847, and 1852. The Theodore H. Koundakjian Collection of American Humour.

Daily Herald, Portland (Maine), September 16, 2001.

Daily Mirror (UK), March 2, 1991. Cited in John Pilger, *Hidden Agendas*. New York: The New Press. 1998.

Daily Post (Liverpool), April 15, 2003.

Daily News (New York), July 8, 2005.

———. July 20, 2005.

———. May 9, 2007.

Daily Star (UK), January 16, 2007.

———. July 16, 2005.

Daily Telegraph (London), April 19, 2004.

Daily Telegraph (Sydney, Australia), April 16, 2003.

———. July 14, 2005.

Danchev, Alex. "Like a Dog!"Humiliation and Shame in the War on Terror." *Alternatives: Global, Local, Political*. Volume 31, Issue3, July 2006: 259–83.

Davis, David Brion. "The Problem of Slavery." In *Slavery, Secession and Southern History*, Robert Louis Paquette and Louis A. Ferleger (eds). Charlottesville, VA: University Press of Virginia, 2000.

Day, Julia. "US Media at 'all-time low.'" *The Guardian*. February 2, 2006.

Debusmann, Bernd. "Radio Hoax Reveals U.S. Anti-Muslim Sentiment in U.S., fear and distrust of Muslims runs deep." *Reuters*. December 1, 2006.

Dedaic, Mirjana, and Daniel Nelson, eds. *At War with Words*. New York: Mouton de Gruter. 2003.

Delgado, Richard, and Jean Stefancic. *Understanding Words That Wound*. Boulder, CO: Westview Press, 2004:16.

Democracy Now. "Report: U.S. Treated Elderly Woman Like a Donkey." *Democracy Now*. May 6, 2004. See www.democracynow.org/article.pl?sid=04/05/06/149239

Deseret Morning News (Salt Lake City), May 29, 2004.

DeSousa, Michael, and Martin Medhurst. "Political cartoons and American Culture: Significant Symbols of campaign 1980," *Studies in Visual Communication*. 8:1 Winter 1982.

"Detention of Enemy Combatants Act."109th Congress 1st Session H. R. 1076. March 3, 2005.

de Rooj, Paul. "Glossary of the Iraqi Occupation." *Dissident Voice*. April 29, 2004. See www.dissidentvoice.org/April2004/DeRooij0429.htm (June 26, 2007).

Deutsche Presse-Agentur, May 13, 2007.

Docherty, Jayne. "Four Reasons to Use the War Metaphor with Caution." *Beyond September 11*. See www.emu.edu/ctp/bse-metaphor.html (June 26, 2007).

———. "Revisiting the War Metaphor." *Beyond September 11*. September 25, 2001. See www.emu.edu/ctp/bse-metaphor2.html (June 26, 2007).

Doctorow, E. L. "False documents." *American Review*. Volume, 29. 1977: 231–32.

Dodd, Vikram, and Tania Branigan. "US Abuse Could Be War Crime." *Guardian*. August 5, 2004.

Dower, John. *War without Mercy: Race and Power in the Pacific War*. New York: Pantheon Books, 1986.

Drinnon, Richard. *Facing West: The Metaphysics of Indian-Hating and Empire-Building*. Norman, OK: University of Oklahoma Press, 1997.

Du Bois, David Graham. "A War Like NO Other? You Bet!" BlackElectorate.com. November 27, 2001. See www.blackelectorate.com/articles.asp?ID=492 (July 23, 2007).

Dyer, Clare. "There is no 'war on terror'." *The Guardian*. January 24, 2007.

Edelman, Murray. *Politics as Symbolic Action: Mass Arousal and Quiescence*. Chicago: Markham,1971.

Editor & Publisher Staff. "Public Faults Media on Military Issues, Poll Finds." *Editor & Publisher*. August 8, 2005. See www.mediatank.org/resources/articles/2005/08/08/publicfaultsmedia.html (July 15, 2007).

Edwards, Dave. "Beating up the cheerleader." *Znet*. July 29, 2003. See www.zmag.org/Sustainers/Content/2003-07/29edwards.cfm (July 15, 2007).

———. "The Media Is Tough on Terrorism but Not Tough on the Causes of Terrorism." *Media Lens*. September 2001. See www.medialens.org/articles/the_articles/articles_2001/de_tough_on_terrorism.html (July 11, 2007).

El-Amine, Rayan. "The Making of the Arab Menace." *Left Turn Magazine*. May 1, 2005. See www.leftturn.org/?q=node/345. (June 26, 2007).

Ellis, Rick. "The Surrender of MSNBC." *AllYourTV.com*. Wednesday, February 26, 2003. See www.commondreams.org/views03/0226-11.htm (July 15, 2007).

Ellul, Jacques. *Propaganda: The Formation of Men's Attitudes*. New York: Vintage Books. 1973.

El Refaie, Elizabeth. "Understanding Visual Metaphor: the example of newspaper cartoons." *Visual Communication*. 2 (1), 2003: 75–95.

Emmerson, Rod. "Untitled." *The New Zealand Herald*. April 23, 2004.

Engelhardt, Tom. "War Porn." *Z*. June 14, 2006. See www.zmag.org/content/showarticle.cfm?ItemID =10429

Environmental Working Group. "Luntz Memo on the environment."*Environmental Working Group*. See www.ewg.org:16080/briefings/luntzmemo/ (June 26, 2007).

Epstein, Edward. "How many Iraqis died?"*San Francisco Chronicle*. May 3, 2003.

Erard, Michael. "Frame Wars." *Texas Observer*. Posted on *Alternet*. November 18, 2004. See www.alternet.org/election04/20537/ (June 26, 2007).

Fairclough, Norman. *Language and Power*. London: Longman, 1989.

Fairness and Accuracy in Reporting. "Networks Accept Government Guidance." *FAIR*. October 12, 2001See www.fair.org/press-releases/network-pressure.html (July 15, 2007).

———. "HBO Recycling Gulf War Hoax?"*FAIR*. December 4, 2002. See www.fair .org/activism/hbo-gulf-hoax.html (June 26, 2007).

———. "Iraq and the Media." *FAIR*. March 19, 2007. See www.fair.org/index.php? page=3062 (July 10, 2007).

———. "Media March to War." *FAIR*. September 17, 2001. See www.fair.org/index .php?page =1853 (June 26, 2007).

———. "Media Pundits Advocate Civilian Targets." *FAIR*. September 21, 2001. See www.fair.org/index.php?page=1675 (July 10, 2007).

———. "Savage Homophobia on MSNBC." *FAIR*. July 7, 2003. See www.fair.org/index .php?page =1621 (July 10, 2007).

———. "Who's on the News: study shows network news sources skew white male and elite." *FAIR*. January 1, 2001. See www.fair.org/index.php?page=1865 (July 15, 2001).

Falcon, Allen Lauzon. "Saddam Rat Caught." *Caglecartoons.com*. December 14, 2003.

Fard, Hara M. "Islam, America's Cancer." *Dhimmi Wits*. May 17, 2007. See upyourcult .blogspot.com/ (June1, 2007).

Financial Express, May 18, 2002.

Fish, Stanley. *Is There a Text in This Class? The Authority of Interpretive Communities*. Cambridge, MA: Harvard University Press, 1980.

Fisk, Robert. "The US Press in Iraq: Hotel Room Journalism." *Counter Punch*. January 17, 2005. See www.counterpunch.org/fisk01172005.html (July 15, 2007).

Florian. "Islam: The Cancer of the Earth." *florians-insensitivity-training*. February 7, 2007. See florians-insensitivity-training.blogspot.com/2007/02/islam-cancer-of-earth.html>. (June 28, 2007).

Florida Times-Union (Jacksonville, FL), December 18, 2003.

Ford, Peter. "Europe cringes at Bush 'crusade' against terrorists."*The Christian Science Monitor*. September 19, 2001. See www.csmonitor.com/2001/0919/ p12s2-woeu.html (June 26, 2007).

Foreign Policy. "The Terrorism Index." *Foreign Policy*. September/October 2007.

Forresloon. "London Terrorist Bombings." *This is North Scotland Bulletin*. July 10, 2005. See www.nepforums.co.uk/thisisnorthscotland/showflat.php?Cat=&Number=17594 &page= view=&sb=5&o=&fpart=all&vc=1 (June 28, 2007).

Foulkrod, Patricia. *The Ground Truth: After the Killing Ends*. [Videorecording]. 2006.

Frank, Jerome D. and Andrei Y. Melville. "The Image of the Enemy and the Process of Change." In Anatolii Andreevich Gromyko and Martin E Hellman (Eds). *Breakthrough: Emerging New Thinking*, Beyond War Foundation, online edition, 1988.

Frank Mack 23rd Bomb. "Enemies Both." *U.S. government poster*.1944. USGPO 44PA 720. Still Pictures Branch, U.S. National Archives and Records Administration.

Gamson, William and D. Stuart. "Media Discourse as a Symbolic Contest: the Bomb in Political Cartoons." *Sociological Forum*. Vol. 7, No. 1 1992: 55–86.

germaninamerica. "bomb islam." *Jihadwatch*. December 9, 2006. See www.jihadwatch .org/archives/014346.php (June 28, 2007).

Goff, Stan. " Hold On to Your Humanity: An Open Letter to GIs in Iraq." *Military Families Speak Out*. See www.mfso.org/article.php?id=225 (June 26, 2007).

Goldman, Lea. "The Celebrity 100." *Forbes*. July 3, 2006.

Goodman, Amy. "Interview." *Hardball with Chris Matthews, MSNBC*. December 3, 2004. See www.democracynow.org/hardball-041203.shtml (July 15, 2007).

Gourevitch, Philip. *We wish to inform you that tomorrow we will be killed with our families: Stories from Rwanda*. New York City: Picador, 1998.

Gilbert, Gustave M. *Nuremberg Diary*. New York: Farrar, Straus and Co. 1947.

Grand Rapid Press (Michigan), June 9, 2005.

———. March 15, 2003.

———. October 31, 2005.

Grantier, Virginia. "Journalist Laments State of War Coverage." *Bismarck Tribune* (North Dakota). October 10, 2004.

Greenslade, Roy. "Their Masters' Voice." *The Guardian*. February 17, 2003.

Gregory, Ted. "Right and wrong; Rush Limbaugh critics want to set the facts straight, but it's not easy." *Chicago Tribune*. August 18, 1995.

Grunberger, Richard. *Twelve-Year Reich: A Social History of Nazi Germany*. New York: Holt, Rinehart & Winston, 1971.

Haass, Richard N. "Fighting terror—We are still behind the curve." *Council on Foreign Relations*. August 11, 2006. See www.cfr.org/publication/11281/fighting _terror_we _are_still_behind_the_curve.html (July 28, 2007).

Hackett, Robert. "Covering up the "War on Terrorism." *Canadian Association of Journalists*. See www.caj.ca/mediamag/fall2001/analysis.html (July 15, 2007).

Hamilton Spectator (Ontario, Canada), July 16, 2004.

Hart, William, and Fran Hassencahl. "Dehumanizing the enemy in editorial cartoons." In B. S. Greeberge (ed). *Communication and Terrorism: Public and Media Responses to 9/11*. Cresskill, NJ: Hampton Press, 2002: 137–51.

Hatecrime.org. "Nazi Anti-Jewish Speech VS. Religious Right Anti-Gay Speech." See www.hatecrime.org/subpages/hitler/hitler.html (July 25, 2007).

Havrilesky, Heather. "The selling of 9/11." *Salon*. September 7, 2002. See dir.salon.com/story/mwt/feature/2002/09/07/purchase_power/index.html?pn=2 (July 1, 2007).

Hawkes, T. *Metaphor*. London: Methuen. 1972: 1.

The Herald (Scotland) April 25, 2003.

———. May 7, 2004.

———. September 4, 2004.

Herman, Edward. "Power and the Semantics of Terrorism,"*Covert Action Information Bulletin*, Vol. 26, 1986: 9–16.

Herman, Edward S., and Noam Chomsky. Manufacturing Consent: the Political Economy of the Mass Media. New York: Pantheon, 1988.

Higham, Scott, and Joe Stephens. "New Details of Prison Abuse Emerge: Abu Ghraib Detainees' Statements Describe Sexual Humiliation And Savage Beatings." *Washington Post*. May 21, 2004.

Hodges, Darrin. "Muslim vermin seething." *Voice of the Shire*. May 28, 2007. See voiceoftheshire.blogspot.com/ (June 28, 2007).

Hoffman, Gene Knudsen. "Taking it from the personal to the global via Compassionate Listening." *Peace Heroes*. January 2002. See www.peaceheroes.com/PeaceHeroes/jeanknudsenhoffman.htm (June 26, 2007).

Holland, Joshua. "The Structural Imbalance of Political Talk Radio." *alternet.org*. June 29, 2007. See alternet.org/mediaculture/55269/?comments=view&cID=686257&pID=686181 (July 3, 2007).

Hornshoj-Moller, Stig. "On The Eternal Jew." *Holocaust-History*, 1999. See www.holocaust-history.org/der-ewige-jude/ (June 26, 2007).

———. "Still images from the Eternal Jew." *Holocaust-History*, 1999. See www.holocaust-history.org/der-ewige-jude/stills.shtml (June 26, 2007).

Houston Chronicle, December 16, 2003.

Huffaker, Sandy. "Al Jazeera." *Cagle Cartoons*. March 27, 2003.

Human Rights Watch. Leave None to Tell the Story: Genocide in Rwanda. April 1, 2004. See www.hrw.org/reports/1999/rwanda/ (June 26, 2007).

Huntley, E. W. H. "United Kingdom: Desert Rats." *allstates-flag*. December 6, 2002. See www.allstates-flag.com/fotw/flags/gb%5Edesrt.html (July 22, 2007).

Huntington, Samuel P. "The Clash of Civilizations?" *Foreign Affairs*, Summer 1993, Volume 72.3: 22–49.

Inquisitor U.S. editor. "Controlling the News with Embedded Journalists." *Inquisitor*. April 27, 2003. See www.inquisitoronline.com/news/0304embedded.html (July 15, 2007).

The Independent (London), January 24, 2004.

Irish News, June 07, 2005.

Irish Times, October 4, 2005.

Jackson, Janine, and Jim Naureckas. *The Fair Reader: An Extra! Review of Press and Politics in the '90s*. Boulder, CO: Westview Press, 1996.

Jamail, Dahr. "Trophy Hunting in Iraq." *AntiWar*. December 5, 2004. See www.antiwar.com/jamail/?articleid=4112

Jensen, Robert. "Dan Rather's the Problem with Patriotism: Steps toward the redemption of American journalism and democracy." *Global Media Journal*, 2: 3 (Fall 2003).

Jester. "Untitled." My Pet Jawa. October 30, 2005. See mypetjawa.mu.nu/archives/129768.php (June 28, 2007).

JihadWatch. See www.jihadwatch.org/archives/016467.php

Johns, Deborah, and Michelle Souza. "Letter from CA Marine Moms & Military Families." Posted on Marooned in Marin. See maroonedinmarin.blogspot.com/2006/06/kfbk-goes-liberal-fires-mark-williams.html (July 15, 2007).

Johnson, Chalmers. *Blowback. The Costs and Consequences of American Empire*. New York: Henry Holt, 2000.

Johnson, Kevin R. "Racial Profiling after September 11: the Department of Justice's 2003 Guidelines." *Loyola Law Review*, Spring 2004.

Jowett, Garth S., and Victoria O'Donnell, *Propaganda and Persuasion*. Thousand Oaks, CA: Sage Publications, 3rd edition, 1999.

Kagwi-Ndungu, Charity. "The challenges in prosecuting print media for incitement to genocide." *International Development Research Centre*. See www.idrc.ca/fr/ev-108292-201-1-DO_TOPIC.html (July 10, 2007). Document(s) 34 de 37.

Kallen, Evelyn. "Hate on the Net: A Question of Rights/A Question of Power." *Electronic Journal of Sociology*. 1998. See www.sociology.org/content/vol003.002/kallen.html (July 4, 2007).

Kamiya, Gary. " Iraq: Why the Media Failed." *Salon*. April 10, 2007. See www.salon.com/opinion/Kamiya/2007/04/10/media_failure (July 11, 2007).

The Kansas City Star, June 23, 2004.

Karim, Karim. H. *Islamic Peril: Media and Global Violence*. Montreal: Black Rose Books, 2003.

Kava, Brad. "Experts predict move to civility on talk radio after Imus firing." *San Jose Mercury News*. April 13, 2007.

Keen, Sam interviewed in Bill Jersey and Jeffrey Friedman. *Faces of the Enemy* [Video recording]. California NewsReel. 1987.

———. *Faces of the Enemy: Reflections of the Hostile Imagination*. New York: Harper Collins; Reprint edition (September 1991).

Kellner, Douglas. *The Persian Gulf TV War*. 1992. San Francisco: Westview Press.

Khan, Irene, "Security for Whom? A Human Rights Response." *Amnesty International*. 2003. See web.amnesty.org/report2003/message-eng (July 20, 2007).

Killology Research Group. "Psychological Effects of Combat." *Killology Research Group*. 1999. See www.killology.com/art_psych_resistance.htm (June 26, 2007).

Kingston, Margo. "Murdoch's War on Truth in War Reporting." *Sydney Morning Herald*. April 7, 2003. See www.smh.com.au/articles/2003/04/07/1049567619708.html (July 15, 2007).

Klein, Naomi. "Terror's Greatest Recruitment Tool." *The Nation*. August 29, 2005.

Knickmeyer, Ellen. " Memories of a Massacre:Iraqi Townspeople Describe Slaying of 24 Civilians by Marines in Nov. 19 Incident." *Washington Post*. May 27, 2006.

Knish, Sultan. "Whatever You Do, Don't Fight Back." *Sultanknish*. February 28, 2007. See sultanknish.blogspot.com/index.html (June 28, 2007).

Konkle, Maureen. *Writing Indian Nations: Native Intellectuals and the Politics of Historiography, 1827–1863*. Chapel Hill, NC: University of North Carolina Press, 2003.

Kopple, Barbara. *Shut Up and Sing*. 2006 [Videorecording].

Kranish, Michael, and Bryan Bender. "Bush Backs Cheney on Assertion linking Hussein, Al qaeda." *Boston Globe.* June 16, 2004.

Kumar, Shanti. "Religious Tolerance versus Tolerance of Religion: A Critique of the Cartoon Controversy in Jyllands-Posten." *FlowTV.* March 10, 2006. See flowtv.org /?p=150 (July 3, 2007).

Kutty, Faisal. "Canada's Nearly 400,000 Muslims Concerned about Media Stereotypes." *Washington Report on Middle East Affairs,* October 1993: 54.

Labatan, Stephen, Lorne Manly, and Elizabeth Jensen. "Republican Chairman Exerts Pressure on PBS, Alleging Biases." *New York Times.* May 2, 2005.

Labbé, Theola. "Suicides in Iraq, Questions at Home Pentagon Tight-Lipped as Self-Inflicted Deaths Mount in Military." *Washington Post.* February 19, 2004.

Lakoff, George, and Evan Frisch "Five Years After 9/11: Drop the War Metaphor." *Commondreams.* September 11, 2006. See www.commondreams.org/views06/0911 20.htm (June 26, 2007).

Lakoff, George, and Mark Johnson. *Metaphors We Live By.* Chicago: University Of Chicago Press, 2nd edition, 1980: 4

Lakoff, George. " Metaphor and War, Again." *AlterNet.* March 18, 2003. See www .alternet.org/story/15414/ (July 3, 2007).

———. "Metaphors of War." *In These Times.* October 29, 2001. See www.inthesetimes .com/issue/25/24/lakoff2524.html (June 28, 2007).

Lancaster New Era (Lancaster, PA), April 2, 2003.

Laswell, Fred. "Louseous Japanicas: Bugs every marine should know." *Leatherneck.* March 28, 1945: 35–27.

Lawrence, Bruce. Review of *The New Crusades: Constructing the Muslim Enemy.* Emran Qureshi and Michael A. Sells (Eds). New York: Columbia University Press, 2003. Posted on Columbia University Press website. See www.columbia.edu /cu/cup/catalog/data/023112/0231126662.HTM (June 26, 2007).

Leiterman, Barbara. "The Ascendancy of Conrad Black." *FAIR Extra.* November /December 1996.

Lelchuk, Ilene. "'Convert or die' game divides Christians:Some ask Wal-Mart to drop Left Behind." San Francisco Chronicle. December 12, 2006. See sfgate.com /cgi-bin/article.cgi?file=/c/a/2006/12/12/MNG8TMU1KQ1.DTL&type=printable (July 3, 2007).

Lester, Mike. "Sam's Pest Control." *The Rome News-Tribune* (Georgia). April 4, 2003.

———. "Spawn." The Rome News-Tribune (Georgia). September 25, 2006.

Lewis, Bernard. "The Roots of Muslim Rage." *The Atlantic Monthly.* September 1990 Volume 266, No. 3: 47–60.

The Liberty Papers. May 18. 2007. See www.thelibertypapers.org/2007/05/18 /explaining-the-reaction-to-ron-paul/ (June 28, 2007).

Lieberman, Trudy. *Slanting the Story: the Forces That Shape the News.* New York: The New Press, 2000.

Lillpop, John. "Michael Savage Honored With Prestigious Freedom of Speech Award!" *Canada Free Press.* March 28, 2007. See www.canadafreepress.com/2007 /lillpop032807.htm (July 3, 2007).

Lithwick, Dahlia. "The Prisoners' Dilemma." *Slate*. April 20, 2004. See www.slate
.com/id/2099223/

Linder, Douglas. "The My Lai Courts-Martial" posted on website of *University of Missouri Kansas Law School*.1999. See www.law.umkc.edu/faculty/projects/ftrials/mylai
/mylai.htm (June 26, 2007).

The Literature of Justification. Lehigh University Digital Library. See digital.lib.lehigh
.edu/trial/justification/about/soundbites/ (June 26, 2007).

Lobe, Jim. "Fear of Islam on the Rise—Muslim Group." *LewRockwell.com*. May 12,
2005. See www.lewrockwell.com/ips/lobe210.html (July 17, 2007).

London Daily Telegraph, June 15, 2002.

London Sunday Times, March 23, 2003.

Love, Robert. "Before Jon Stewart."*Columbia Journalism Review*. March/April 2007.
See www.cjr.org/feature/before_jon_stewart.php (July 15, 2007).

Lummis, C. Douglas. "The Terrorist as a New Human Type: You Are Charged with
Being Evil. Defend Yourself!" Z. January 19, 2004. See www.zmag.org/content
/showarticle.cfm?ItemID=4853 (June 28, 2007).

MacFarguhar, Neil. "U.S. Muslims Say Terror Fears Hamper Their Right to Travel."
New York Times. June 1, 2006.

MacLeod, Scott. "Iran War Drumbeat Grows Louder." Time, October 26, 2007.

Malek, Alia. "Beware Thy neighbour?" *John Hopkins Magazine*. November 2001. See
www.jhu.edu/~jhumag/1101web/ruminate.html (July 23, 2007).

Manoff, Robert Karl. "The Media's Role in Preventing and Moderating Conflict."
Virtual Diplomacy conference hosted by United States Institute of Peace in Washington, D.C., April 1–2, 1997.

Marine Corps News Service. "War Trophies." *About.com*. August 20, 2003. See usmilitary
.about.com/cs/wars/a/wartrophies.htm

Markland, Dave. "Media blind to Afghan civilian deaths." *Seven Oaks Magazine*. December 29, 2006. See www.sevenoaksmag.com/features/civiliancasualties.html
(July 15, 2007).

Marlette, Doug. "Journalism's Wild Man." *American Journalism Review*. January/February
1992. See www.ajr.org/Article.asp?id=1444 (July 3, 2007).

Masnet and News Agencies. "Beheadings in Iraq and Saudi Arabia Fuel Backlash
against American Muslims."*Muslim American Society*. June 25, 2004. See www.masnet
.org/news.asp?id=1329 (July 22, 2007).

Matson, R. J. "Iraq Hornets." *St. Louis Post Dispatch*. March 24, 2006.

Mazzetti, Mark. "Spy Agencies Say Iraq War Worsens Terrorism Threat." *New York
Times*. September 24, 2006.

McChesney, Robert W. "Journalism, Democracy, and Class Struggle." *Monthly Review*.Volume 52, Number 6, 2000.

McDermott, Jim. "Rhetoric of the War Crusade." Speech to the U.S. House of Representatives. May 11, 2004. See www.house.gov/mcdermott/sp040511a.shtml (June
26, 2007).

McGuinness, Patrick. "Common Sense." *Freedoms Truth*. March 27, 2007. See freedoms
truth.blogspot.com/index.html (June 28, 2007).

Mckinney, Joan. "Cooksey: Expect racial profiling." *Advocate*. September 19, 2001.
  Media Ignore Iraq's Humanitarian Issues. November 13, 2006. See www.globalpolicy
  .org/security/issues/iraq/media/2006/1113ignores.htm (July 17, 2007).
Media Matters for America. "33 internal FOX editorial memos reviewed by MMFA reveal FOX News Channel's inner workings." *Media Matters for America*. July 14,
  2004. See mediamatters.org/items/200407140002 (July 15, 2007).
——. "Boortz: Islam is a "deadly virus" and "we're going to wait far too long to develop a vaccine to find a way to fight this." *Media Matters for America*. Wed, October 18, 2006. See mediamatters.org/items/200610180005 (June 26, 2007).
——. "Coulter's reward for her "downright hateful" comments: another appearance
  on CNN!" *Media Matters for America*. March 5, 2007. See mediamatters.org
  /items/200703050003 (July 4, 2007).
——. "Citing reader support, several papers will keep publishing Coulter." *Media
  Matters for America*. March 12, 2007. See mediamatters.org/items/200703120010
  (July 4, 2007).
——. "Help Stop Conservative Hate Speech on Public Airwaves." *Media Matters for
  America*. August 24, 2005. See mediamatters.org/items/200508240007 (July 4, 2007).
——. "Islam is "a car-burning cult" *Media Matters for America*. February 10, 2006.
  See mediamatters.org/items/200602100003 (July 3, 2007).
——. "O'Reilly: The Bush administration is in a war not only with the terrorists,
  but also with the far left in this country." *Media Matters for America*. Aug 23, 2006.
  See mediamatters.org/items/200608240001 (June 26, 2007).
——. "Phil Donahue on his 2003 MSNBC firing." *Media Matters for America*. Oc-
  tober 29, 2004. See mediamatters.org/items/200410290004 (July 15, 2007).
——. "Savage advocated "kill[ing] 100 million" Muslims." *Media Matters for Amer-
  ica*. April 19, 2006. See mediamatters.org/items/200604190001 (June 26, 2007).
——. "Savage: Arabs are "non-humans" and "racist, fascist bigots." *Media Matters
  for America*. May 14, 2004. See mediamatters.org/items/200405140003 (July 3,
  2007).
——. "Savage called Iraqi witnesses of alleged Haditha massacre 'vermin' and
  'scum,' proclaimed detained Marines are American 'POWs'." *Media Matters for
  America*. June 9, 2006. See mediamatters.org/items/200606090010 (July 3, 2007).
——. "Savage: Israel must ensure 'nothing is left living in Southern Lebanon' and
  must 'free itself of the men . . . act[ing] like Holocaust Jews hiding in the sewer'."
  Media Matters for America. July 31, 2006. See mediamatters.org/items/20060731
  0004 (July 3, 2007).
——. "Savage Nation: It's not just Rush; Talk radio host Michael Savage: 'I com-
  mend' prisoner abuse; 'we need more'." *Media Matters for America*. May 13, 2004.
  See mediamatters.org/items/200405130004 (July 3, 2007).
——. Savage: "Use a bunker-buster bomb on the U.N. *Media Matters for America*.
  July 24, 2006. See mediamatters.org/items/200607240007 (July3, 2007).
——. "O'Reilly: Iraqi people are 'primitive,' 'prehistoric group'." June 18, 2004
  4:44 P.M. EST See mediamatters.org/items/200406180005
Media Research Center. "Rush Limbaugh to accept media excellence award at MRC
  20th anniversary gala."*Media Research Center*. March 20, 2007. See www
  .mediaresearch.org/press/2007/press20070320.asp (July 30, 2007).

Media Tank. "Ties That Bind: An Assortment of Interlocking Interests." Media Tank. See www.mediatank.org/resources/peace/conflicts/ (July 15, 2007).

Memarian, Omid. "US cartoon no joke to Iranians." Asia Times. September 20, 2007.

Michaels, Henry. "Pentagon, media agree on Iraq war censorship." World Socialist Web Site. March 5, 2003. See www.wsws.org/articles/2003/mar2003/med-m05.shtml (July 15, 2007).

Mickey Z. "Which Wolf Will You Feed in 2006?" Dissidentvoice.org December 31, 2005. See www.dissidentvoice.org/Dec05/MickeyZ1231.htm (March 28, 2008).

Michalak, Laurence. "Arab in American Cinema." Social Studies Review. Fall 2002, 42(1), 11–17.

Mieder, Wolfgang. "Proverbs in Nazi Germany: The Promulgation of Anti-Semitism and Stereotypes through Folklore." The Journal of American Folklore. Volume 95, Issue 378, 1982: 435–64.

Miel, Deng Coy. "Terrorism as a Snake-hydra." The Straits Times (Singapore). November 27, 2005.

Military Families Speak Out. "The Flag-Draped Coffins." March 14, 2004. See www .mfso.org/article.php?id=316 (July 15, 2007).

Mills, Mary. "Propaganda and Children during the Hitler Years." The Nizkor Project. See www.nizkor.org/hweb/people/m/mills-mary/mills-00.html (June 26, 2007).

Morris, Nigel. "War on Terror: Guantanamo: I Was Tied up like a Beast and Beaten.'" The Independent (London), August 4, 2004.

Mujahid, Abdul Malik. "Demonization of Muslims Caused the Iraq Abuse." Sound Vision. May 19, 2004. See www.soundvision.com/info/peace/demonization.asp (July 17, 2007).

Mumby, D. K., and C. Spitzack. "Ideology and Television News: a Metaphoric Analysis of Political Stories." Central States Speech Journal. Vol. 34, 1983: 162–71.

Musolff, Andreas. "What role do metaphors play in racial prejudice? The function of anti Semitic imagery in Hitler's Mein Kampf." Patterns of Prejudice. Volume 41, Issue 1. February 2007: 21–43.

Nakamura, Norman. "The Nature of GI racism during the Vietnam War." Gidra, June/July 1970. Posted on Model Minority. See modelminority.com/modules.php?name=News&file =article&sid=74 (June 26, 2007).

The Nation (Kenya), September 15, 2006.

National Post, July 23, 2003.

Navarro, Anthony V. "A Critical Comparison Between Japanese and American Propaganda during World War II." Posted on website of Michigan State University. See www.msu.edu/~navarro6/srop.html (June 26, 2007).

Nelson, Daniel. "Word Peace." in At War With Words. Eds. Mirjana Dedaic and Daniel Nelson. Berlin: Mouton de Gruyter, 2003: 449.

Neville, Richard. "Rupert Murdoch's Victims." Counter Punch September 1, 2006. See www.counterpunch.org/neville09012006.html (July 15, 2007).

Newman, Andy. "US Army feels the strain." Socialist Unity Network. September 2004. See www.socialistunitynetwork.co.uk/news/strain.htm (June 26, 2007). See also news.bbc.co.uk/2/hi/programmes/newsnight/3045574.stm

New Socialist. "Racism, the Right and the Toronto "Terrorism." New Socialist. See www.newsocialist.org/newsite/index.php?id=988 (July 23, 2007).

New York Daily News, July 8, 2005.

New York Post, April 23, 2004.

———. December 2, 2001.

———. February 14, 2003.

———. February 18, 2003.

———. January 24, 2003.

———. May 23, 2006.

———. July 3, 2004.

———. May 25, 2002.

———. June 26, 2007.

New York Times, July 16, 2004.

———. "MTV Refuses Antiwar Commercial." *New York Times*. March 13, 2003.

———. October 11, 2002.

The New Zealand Herald, September 12, 2002.

News of the World (England), August 13, 2006.

Nichols, Jack. *The Gay Agenda: Talking Back to the Fundamentalists*. Prometheus Books, 1996.

Nimmo, Kurt. "Torture Party: Limbaugh and the Babes of Abu Ghraib." *Counter-Punch*. May 8–9, 2004. See www.counterpunch.org/nimmo05082004.html

Olsen, Ken. "Does Talk Radio Incite Hate?" *Tolerance*.org. April 25, 2003. See www.tolerance.org/news/article_tol.jsp?id=752 (July 3, 2007).

ONASA News Agency, November 22, 2003.

Opotow, Susan."Aggression and Violence." In *The Handbook of Conflict Resolution: Theory and Practice*. Morton Deutsch and Peter T. Coleman, eds. San Francisco, CA: Jossey-Bass Publishers, 2000.

The Oregonian (Portland, Oregon), December 29, 1998.

O'Reilly, Bill. "Newspaper Column List." *BillOReilly.com*. January 8, 2007. See www .billoreilly.com/pg/jsp/general/newspapercolumn.jsp (July 3, 2007).

Ottosen, Rune. "Emphasising Images in Peace Journalism," *Conflict and Communication online*. Vol. 6, No.1, 2007.

Pakistan Press, October 24, 2004.

Parenti, Michael. "Monopoly Media Manipulation." *Michael Parenti.org*. May 2001. See www.michaelparenti.org/MonopolyMedia.html (July 10, 2007).

Parker, Jeff. "9/11 Terror Eagle." *Florida Today*. September 7, 2002.

———. "Foxy Saddam." *Florida Today*. September 24, 2002.

———. "London Bombings." *Florida Today*. July 7, 2005.

Parry, Robert. "So Bush did steal the White House." *Asheville Global Report*. No. 150, November 29–December 5, 2001. See www.agrnews.org/issues/150/commentary.html (July 17, 2007).

———. "The Price of the Liberal Media Myth." *Consortiumnews.com*. January 1 2003. See consortiumnews.com/2002/123102a.html (July 15, 2007).

Pat. "Untitled."*patshideout*. March 14, 2002. See www.patshideout.com/theattic.htm (July 3, 2007).

Patterson, Charles, *Eternal Treblinka: Our treatment of animals and the holocaust.* New York: Lantern Books, 2002.

Payne, Kenneth. "The Media as an Instrument of War." *Parameters.* Spring 2005.

PBS. "Media Wars." PBS Frontline series. See www.pbs.org/wgbh/pages/frontline /newswar/view (July 15, 2007).

Peek, Lori. "Constructing the Enemy During Times of Crisis: America After 9/11." *Divide: Journal of Writing and Ideas.* 1(2), 2004: 26–30.

Peterson, Scott. "Are U.S. and Iran header for war? Christian Science Monitor. October 3, 2007.

PEW. "Self Censorship: How Often and Why. Journalists Avoiding the News." *PEW Research Center for People and the Press.* April 30, 2000. See peoplepress.org/reports /dislay.php3?ReportID=39 (July 15, 2007).

Pfauth, Ernst-Jan. "When Hate Speech Turns Deadly, Who Can Stop It?" *Inter-Press Service News Agency (IPS).* April 13, 2007. See ipsnews.net/news.asp?idnews= 37345 (July 4, 2007).

Philo, Greg. "Television News and Audience Understanding of War, Conflict and Disaster." In *Journalism Studies,* 3(2), May 2002:173–86.

Pilger, John. "Recommends the World Wide Web." *New Statesman.* November 28, 2005. See www.newstatesman.com/200511280013 (July 15, 2007).

———. "The Real First Casualty of War." *Lewrockwell.* April 21, 2006. See www .lewrockwell.com/pilger/pilger40.html (July 15, 2007).

Pipes, Daniel. "Sudden Jihad Syndrome." *FrontPageMagazine.com* March 14, 2006. See www.frontpagemagazinc.com/Articles/Read.aspx?GUID={730A921C-1FED -4DCD-9949 -D28A3390317D} (August 1, 2007).

The Post and Courier (Charleston, SC), October 9, 2003.

Powell, Bonnie Azab. "Investigative journalist Seymour Hersh spills the secrets of the Iraq quagmire and the war on terror." *University of California Berkeley NewsCenter.* October 11, 2004. See www.berkeley.edu/news/media/releases/2004/10/11_hersh .shtml (July 15, 2007).

Powers, John. "300: Racist War Propaganda with Septic Timing." *Art Threat Political Art Magazine.* March 2007. See www.artthreat.net/2007/03/95 (July 1, 2007).

Press Association (Central Command, Qatar), April 2, 2003.

Prestage, Jon. "Mainstream Journalism: Shredding the First Amendment." *Truthout.* November 7, 2002. See www.truthout.org/doc_02/11.11.shred.1.amend.htm (July 15, 2007).

Priest, Dana. "CIA Holds Terror Suspects in Secret Prisons." *Washington Post.* November 2, 2005.

Program on International Policy Attitudes. " Study Finds Direct Link between Misinformation and Public Misconception." *Program on International Policy Attitudes.* October 2, 2003. See www.truthout.org/docs_03/100403F.shtml (July 11, 2007).

Project for Excellence in Journalism. "Annual Report on American Journalism, 2007." *The State of the News Media.* Spring 2007. See www.stateofthenewsmedia.org/2007 (June 26, 2007).

Providence Journal-Bulletin (Rhode Island), April 16, 2003.

Purefoy, Christian Allen. "Five days of violence by Nigerian Christians and Muslims kill 150." *The Independent.* February 24, 2006. See news.independent.co.uk/world /Africa/article347374.ece (July 3, 2007).

Qureshi, Emran, and Michael A. Sells (Eds). *The New Crusades: Constructing the Muslim Enemy.* New York: Columbia University Press, 2003.

Racial Justice. "Mission Statement." See racialjustice911.org/homehk.htm (July 17, 2007).

Rahman al-Rashed, Abdel. "Innocent religion is now a message of hate." *Telegraph* (UK). September 5, 2004.

Raman, B. "Use a Cockroach to Catch a Cockroach." *South Asia Analysis Group.* September 19, 2001. See www.saag.org/papers4/paper316.html (June 28, 2007).

Ramirez, Michael. "Gotcha." *Los Angeles Times.* December 15, 2003.

Rampton, Sheldon, and John Stauber. "Trading On Fear." *The Guardian,* posted on *Commondreams.* Saturday, July 12, 2003. See www.commondreams.org/views03 /0712-01.htm (June 26, 2007).

———. "How to Sell a War." *In These Times.* April 8, 2003. See www.inthesetimes .com/comments.php?id=299_0_1_0_M (June 26, 2007).

Random House. "Author profile: Bill O'Reilly." *Random House.* See www.randomhouse .com/author/results.pperl?authorid=22596 (July 3,2007).

Rastaman. "Muslims Show Their Love of Children." February 27, 2007. *Islamanzi.* See islamanazi.com (June 28, 2007).

Ratner, Lizzy. "Amy Goodman's 'Empire'." *The Nation.* May 5, 2005. See www.thenation .com/doc/20050523/ratner (July 15, 2007).

Razack, Sherene. "When is Prisoner Abuse Racial Violence." Z. May 24, 2004. See www.zmag.org/content/showarticle.cfm?ItemID=5594

Reed, Jebediah. "The Iraq Gamble: At the pundits' table, the losing bet still takes the pot." *Radar Magazine.* January 2007. See www.radarmagazine.come/features/2007 /01/betting_on (July 15, 2007).

Reel, Guy. "The Military-Mass Media Complex." *CommonDreams.org.* May 6, 2004. See www.commondreams.org/views04/0506-06.htm (July 15, 2007).

Regan, Tom. "They hate our policies, not our freedom: Pentagon report contains major criticisms of administration." *Christian Science Monitor.* November 29, 2004.

———. "U.S. military planting stories in Iraqi papers." *Christian Science Monitor.com.* December 1, 2005. See www.csmonitor.com/2005/1201/dailyUpdate.html (July 15, 2007).

Rendall, Steve, and Tara Broughel. "Amplifying Officials, Squelching Dissent: FAIR study finds democracy poorly served by war coverage." *FAIR Extra.* May/June 2003. See www.fair.org/index.php?page=1145 (July 15, 2007).

Reuters. "U.S. soldiers' suicide rate in Iraq doubled in '05." Dec. 19, 2006.

Rich, Frank. "Operation Iraqi Infoganda." *New York Times.* March 28, 2004.

Ricks, Thomas E., and Ann Scott Tyson. "Troops at Odds with Ethics Standards." *The Washington Post.* May 5, 2007. Posted on *Truthout.* See www.truthout.org/docs _2006/050507Z.shtml (June 26, 2007).

The Right Things, Get Your Conservative Gear Here! See www.therightthings.com

Ritea, Steve. "Accolades now come to Knight Ridder for its prescient reports expressing skepticism about claims that Iraq had weapons of mass destruction." *American Journalism Review*. August/September 2004.

Ritter, Jim. "Muslims see a growing media bias." *Chicago Sun Times*. September 4, 2006.

Rizvi, Haider. "Frustration Marks Another War Anniversary." *Global Policy*. March 19, 2007. <http://www.globalpolicy.org/ngos/role/iraq.htm>. (July 15. 2007).

Robb, David. *Operation Hollywood: How the Pentagon Shapes and Censors the Movies*. New York: Prometheus Books. 2004.

Roberts, Les, Riyadh Lafta, Richard Garfield, Jamal Khudhairi, and Gilbert Burnham. "Mortality before and after the 2003 invasion of Iraq: cluster sample survey." *Lancet*. October 29, 2004.

Robertson, Pat. *New York Magazine*. August 18, 1986.

Ronin. "Blair, Pakistan PM to open conference on Islam." *Doctor Bulldog*. May 29, 2007. <http://doctorbulldog.wordpress.com>. (June 28, 2007).

Rose, Flemming. "Muhammeds ansigt." *Jyllands-Posten*, September 30, 2005.

———. "Why I Published Those Cartoons." *Washington Post*. February 19, 2006. <http://www.washingtonpost.com/wpdyn/content/article/2006/02/17/AR2006021702499.html>.(July 3, 2007).

Ross, John. "Everyone Knows This is Theater: Burying Iraq, Burying Bush (Part One)." *Counterpunch*. July 19, 2004. <http://www.counterpunch.org/ross07202004.html>.

Rothschild, Matthew. ""Deck of Weasels" Lists 54 "Anti-American, Pro-Saddam" Leaders and Celebs." *The Progressive*. May 14, 2003. <http://www.progressive.org/mag_mcweasel>. (July 1, 2007).

———. "The New McCarthyism." *Progressive*. January 2002. <http://www.progressive.org/0901/roth0102.html>. (July 23, 20027).

Rowland, Beryl. *Animals with Human Faces*. Knoxville, TN: University of Tennessee Press, 1973.

Roy, Celia. "The bug-eyed monkeys of Tojo: Using Animal Metaphors to Widen Racial Schisms." <journals.iranscience.net:800/mcel.pacificu.edu/mcel.pacificu.edu/jwasia/reviews/seebeesCR.html>. (August 27, 2003).

Rudolph, Barbara. "Racism in the Ranks." *Time Magazine*. January 30, 1995.

Russell, Edmund. *War and Nature*. London: Cambridge University Press, 2002.

Rutenberg, Jim. "Cable's War Coverage Suggests a New 'Fox Effect' on Television." *New York Times*. Wednesday, April 16, 2003.

Said, Edward. *Covering Islam: How the media and the experts determine how we see the rest of the world*. Revised Edition, New York: Vintage Books. 1997: xxii.

———. *On Orientalism*. 1998. [Videorecording]. Media Education Foundation.

———. *Orientalism*. New York: Vintage Books. 1979: 6.

———. "The Clash of Ignorance." *The Nation*. October 4, 2001. See www.thenation.com/doc/20011022/said (June 26, 2007).

Sandrolini, James. "Propaganda: The Art of War." *Chicago Media Watch*. Fall 2002. See www.chicagomediawatch.org/02_3_artofwar.shtml (June 26, 2007).

Santa Ana, Otto. *Brown Tide Rising*. Austin, TX: University of Texas Press, 2002.

Sardar, Ziauddin. "The next holocaust." *New Statesman*. December 5, 2005.

Satzman, Darrell. "Advertising likely to wane against a backdrop of battle." *Los Angeles Business Journal*. Feburary 3, 2003.

Scahill, Jeremy. "Did Bush Really Want to Bomb Al Jazeera?" *The Nation*. November 23, 2005. See www.thenation.com/doc/20051212/scahill (July 3, 2007).

Schantz, Orla. "Richard Rorty: In Memorium." *The Enlightenment Underground*. June 11, 2007. See enlightenmentunderground.blogspot.com (July 22, 2007).

Schechter, Danny. "Covering Violence: How Should Media Handle Conflict?" *Media Channel*. July 18, 2001. See www.mediachannel.org/views/dissector /coveringviolence.shtml (July 28, 2007).

Schmitt, Eric, and Carolyn Marshall. "Before and After Abu Ghraib, a U.S. Unit Abused Detainees." *New York Times*. March 19, 2006.

Schon, Donald. "Generative metaphor: a perspective on problem setting in social policy." In Andrew Ortony (Ed), *Metaphor and Thought*. Cambridge: Cambridge University Press, 1979: 254–83.

Schuh, Trish. "Racism and Religious Desecration as U.S. Policy: Islamophobia, a Retrospective." *Double Standards*. May 6, 2006. See www.doublestandards.org/schuh1 .html (June 26, 2007).

Schwartz, Marie Jenkins. *Birthing a Slave: Motherhood and Medicine in the Antebellum South*. Cambridge, MA: Harvard University Press, 2006.

Shaheen, Jack. Interviewed in *Reel Bad Arabs* [Videorecording]. 2006. Media Education Foundation.

———. *Reel Bad Arabs: How Hollywood Vilifies a People*. Interlink Publishing Group, 2001.

Shalom, Stephen R. "Confronting Terrorism and War." *New Politics*. Vol. 8, no. 4, Winter 2002.

Shapiro, Ben. "Civilian Casualties OK By Me." *TownHall*. July 25, 2002. See www.town hall.com/columnists/BenShapiro/2002/07/25/enemy_civilian_casualties_ok_by_me (June 26, 2007).

Shaw, Chris. "Don't look now: US soldiers' 'trophy videos' of Iraq make uncomfortable viewing for the American government next to TV networks' coverage." *Guardian*. August 4, 2006.

Shewchuk, Blair. " Terrorists and Freedom Fighters."CBC *News Online*. October 18, 2001. See www.cbc.ca/news/indepth/words/terrorists.html (June 26, 2007).

Shorb, Terril L., and Yvette A. Schnoeker-Shorb (eds). *Least Loved Beasts of the Really Wild West*. Prescott, AZ: Native West Press, 2003.

Siddiqui, Haroon. "Four telltale Themes: Anti-Muslim bigotry 'spreading like wildfire'." *Scholar Of The House*. November 24, 2002. See www.scholarofthehouse.org /fourtorstar1.html (June 26, 2007).

Silico, Tami. Interview with Joan Pliego. "The Reality had to get out." *Real Change News*. October 28, 2004. See www.realchangenews.org/2004/2004_10_28/issue /current/coverstory.html (July 12, 2007).

Skegness News, July 11, 2006.

Sleepycat. "Britain 'is now biggest security threat to US'." *JihadWatch*. August 26, 2006. See www.jihadwatch.org/archives/012914.php (June 28, 2007).

Smiley, Jane. "All-American Hate Speech." *The Huffington Post*. June 7, 2006. See www.huffingtonpost.com/jane-smiley/allamerican-hate-speech_b_22463.html (July 4, 2007).

Smith, Matt. "Soldiers put Iraq 'war trophies' on eBay." *CNN*. March 18, 2004. See www.cnn.com/2004/US/03/18/iraq.war.booty/

Smith, Sam. "The semiotics of a terrorist bombing." Insight on the News, June 5, 1995. See findarticles.com/p/articles/mi_m1571/is_n22_v11/ai_16936757 (July 3, 2007).

Smith, Terence. "Battlefield Bylines." *PBS NewsHour* Online. February 18, 2003. See www.pbs.org/newshour/bb/military/jan-june03/bylinesb_2-18.html (July 15, 2007).

Snow, Nancy. *Information War: American Propaganda, Free Speech and Opinion Control since 9-11*. New York: Seven Stories Press. 2003.

Socialist Worker. "The American way of war crimes." *Socialist Worker Online*. June 9, 2006. See www.socialistworker.org/2006-1/592/592_06_AmericanWay.shtml (June 26, 2007).

Solomon, Norman. "Picture-perfect killers: Military weapons are often technological marvels but always instruments of death." *San Francisco Chronicle*. June 19, 2005.

———. "Media and the Politics of Empathy." *CommonDreams.org*. April 18, 2003. See www.commondreams.org/views03/0418-08.htm (July 15, 2007).

———. "Media spin revolves around the word terrorist." Z. October 4, 2001. See www.zmag.org/solorerr.htm (June 26, 2007).

———. "The Military-Industrial-Media Complex: Why war is covered from the warriors' perspective." *FAIR/Extra!* July/August 2005. See www.fair.org/index.php?page=2627 (July 15, 2007).

———. "This War and Racism." Z. June 2004.

———. "War Needs Good Public Relations." *FAIR*. October 25, 2001. See www.fair.org/media-beat/011025.html (June 26, 2007).

Sontag, Susan. "Real Battles and Empty Metaphors."*New York Times*. September 10, 2002.

Soueif, Ahdaf. "A profound racism infects the US and British establishments." *The Guardian* (UK). May 5, 2004. Posted on www.arabworldbooks.com/arab/ahdaf3.htm (June 26, 2007).

Sourcewatch. "Embedded." *Sourcewatch*. March 31, 2005. See www.sourcewatch.org/index.php?title=Embedded (July 15, 2007).

Sourcewatch. "Paul Cameron." *Sourcewatch*. See www.sourcewatch.org/index.php?title=Paul_Cameron (July 25, 2007).

Spin. "Bookseller of Baghdad." *Gbytes of Gbytes*. April 6, 2007. See gbytes.gsood.com/category/middle-east (July 11, 2007).

Stanton, Gregory H. "The 8 Stages of Genocide." *Genocide Watch*. 1996. See www.genocidewatch.org/8stages1996.htm (June 26, 2007).

Stannard, David. *American Holocaust: The Conquest of the New World*. Oxford: Oxford University Press. 1993.

Stares, Paul, and Mona Yacoubian. "Terrorism as Virus." *The Washington Post*, August 23, 2005.

The Star-Ledger (Newark, New Jersey), March 27, 2003.

Stauber, John, and Sheldon Rampton. *Toxic Sludge is Good For You*. Monroe, ME: Common Courage Press, 1995.

St. Louis Post-Dispatch (Missouri), November 8, 2005.

———. November 13, 2004.

St. Petersburg Times (Florida), December 15, 2003.

Streeter, Mark. "Untitled." *The Savannah Morning News*. May 14, 2004.

Struck, Doug. "In Canada, An Uproar Over Army Casualties." *Washington Post Foreign Service*. April 26, 2006.

Strum, Philippa. "The Journalist as Historian: Anthony Lewis, Civil Liberties, and the Supreme Court." *Journal of Supreme Court History*. Volume 29, Issue 2, July 2004: 191–206.

Suarez-Diaz, Chanan. "Citizens' Hearing Panel Declares Iraq War Illegal." *wartribunal.org*. February 2, 2007. See www.wartribunal.org/

Subsunk. "Untitled." *An Idiot's Blog*. May 9, 2007. See kbarrett.cotse.net/idiot/index .php?title=feds_wonder_if_jihadis_nuke_us_who_do_we&more=1&c=1&tb=1& pb=1>.(June 28, 2007).

Sudbury Star. May 12, 2004.

Sulugiuc, Gelu. "Danish paper cleared in Muslim libel lawsuit: Muhammad cartoons." *National Post*. Oct 27, 2006: 12.

Sweeney, Leilani. "Americans'confidence in military news coverage takes steep drop." Mccormick Tribune. August 24, 2005. See www.mccormicktribune.org /news/2005/pr082405.aspx (July 15, 2007).

The Sun (UK), December 30, 2006.

———. September 23, 2005.

———. July 30, 2005.

Sunday Express (UK), April 13, 2003.

———. February 6, 2005.

Sunday Mercury, April 6, 2003.

Supercaffinated. "Untitled." *Storage Review*. July 7, 2005. See forums.storagereview .net/index.php?showtopic=20229 (June 28, 2007).

Talkers Magazine. "The 25 Greatest Radio Talk Show Hosts of All Time." *Talkers Magazine*. September 2002.

———. "Top Talk Personalities," *Talkers Magazine*. Spring 2006. See www.talkers .com/main/index.php?option=com_content&task=view&id=17&Itemid=34 (June 26, 2007).

Tampa Tribune (Florida), August 28, 2002.

Taylor, Adam. "UD Professor Sue over DAFB photos." *The News Journal*. October 5, 2004. See www.delawareonline.com/newsjournal/local/2005/04/28pentagonrelease .html (June 1, 2007).

Tétreault, Mary Ann. 'The Sexual Politics of Abu Ghraib: Hegemony, Spectacle, and the Global War on Terror." *NWSA Journal* 18.3, 2006: 33–50. See muse.jhu .edu/journals/nwsa _journal/v018/18.3tetreault.html

The Times (London), January 31, 2006.

———. July 24, 2004.

———. November 11, 2006.

Tirman, John. "Study: More Than 600,000 Dead in Iraq."*AlterNet*. October 11, 2006. See www.alternet.org/waroniraq/42867/ (June 26, 2007).

Toronto Star, June 22, 2003.

———. May 8, 2005.

———. November 26, 2006.

———. April 18, 2003.

———. April 4, 2003.

Trial Watch. "Julius Streicher." See www.trialch.org/en/trialwatch/profile/db/facts/julius _streicher_22.html; and, motlc.wiesenthal.com/site/pp.asp?c=gvKVLcMVIuG&b =395155>. (July 4, 2007).

Turkish Daily News, November 21, 2003.

Tyson, Ann Scott. "The other battle: coming home." *The Christian Science Monitor*. July 9, 2003. See www.csmonitor.com/2003/0709/p01s03-usmi.html (June 26, 2007).

University of Mississippi Libraries. "Scientists Say Negro Still in Ape Stage." *Inventory of the Klu Klux Klan collection*. See www.olemiss.edu/depts/general_library/files /archives/collections/guides/latesthtml/MUM00254.html (June 26, 2007).

UPI, January 20, 2005.

U.S. News and World Report, April 14, 2003.

Valenti, Jack. "Speech before the Los Angeles World Affairs Council." October 1, 1998. Posted on *Los Angeles World Affairs Council* web site, see www.lawac.org /speech/pre%20sept%2004%20speeches/valenti.html (July 3, 2007).

Van Auken, Bill. "Rigoberto Alpizar and Jean Charles de Menezes: Two victims of state "anti terror" killings." *World Socialist Website*. December 12, 2005. See www .wsws.org/articles/2005/dec2005/kill-d12.shtml (July 17, 2007).

Vargas, Jose Antonio. "Way Radical, Dude: Video Games with an Islamist Twist." *Washington Post*. October 9, 2006.

Varvel, Gary. "We Got Him." *The Indianapolis Star News*. May 2004.

Verkaik, Robert. "Joy and Despair: a Tale of Two Fathers." *The Independent* (London), March 10, 2004.

Verlaine, Paul. "Art Poétique." *Aesthetic Realism*. See www.aestheticrealism.net /poetry/art-poetique.htm (June 26, 2007).

Vickers, Brian. *In Defense of Rhetoric*. New York City: Clarendon Paperbacks. 1989: 299.

Warriors for Truth. See www.warriorsfortruth.com/mohammed%20cartoons.html (July 3, 2007).

Washington, Latrell. "Untitled." *Realm of the Sphinx*. June 2, 2007. See realmofthesphinx .blogspot.com/ (June 28, 2007).

Washington Monthly. "The Wisdom of Ann Coulter." The Wisdom of Ann Coulter. October 2001. See www.washingtonmonthly.com/features/2001/0111.coulterwisdom .html (July 10, 2007).

Washington Post, November 13, 2004.

Wax, Emily. "Journalists Sentenced In Rwanda Genocide. Prosecutor Said 'Hate Media' Urged Killings." *Washington Post Foreign Service*. December 4, 2003.

Weekend Australian, April 5, 2003.

——. September 9, 2006.

Wehner, Peter. "John Edwards's irresponsible and revealing address." *Townhall*. May 24, 2007. See www.townhall.com/columnists/PeterWehner/2007/05/24/john_edwardss _irresponsible_and_revealing_address (June 26, 2007).

Western Daily Press, November 17, 2004.

Weil, Dan. "Limbaugh's New Radio Contract Worth $285 Million." *The Palm Beach Post*. July 20, 2001.

Wheatcroft, Geoffrey. "Cartoon Characters: Whose fault is it that the media presents Muslims as fanatics?" *Slate*. February 9, 2006.

Wheeler, Thomas. "O'Reilly's Final Solution." Z. June 22, 2004. See www.zmag.org /content/showarticle.cfm?ItemID=5753 (July 10, 2007).

White, Joseph L. *Black Man Emerging: Facing the Past and Seizing a Future in America*. New York: Routledge. 1999.

Whittick, Arnold. *Symbols, Signs and Their Meaning*. Newton, MA: Charles T. Branford Co. 1971.

Wickham, DeWayne. "Iraq war 'souvenir' stories reawaken guilt." *USA Today*. April 28, 2004. See www.usatoday.com/news/opinion/columnist/wickham/2003-04-28-wickham_x.htm

Wing, Bob. "The Color of Abu Ghraib." *War Times*. May 17, 2004. See www.why-war .com/ news/read.php?id=4270

Winner, Ellen. *The Point of Words*. Cambridge, MA: Harvard University Press. 1988.

Winter, Gibson. *Liberating Creation: Foundations of Religious Social Ethics*. New York, Crossroad, 1981.

The Wisdom Fund. "The 'Who' In American Media." *The Wisdom Fund*. August 9, 1995. See www.twf.org/News/Y1997/Who.html (July 3, 2007).

Wodak, Ruth. "Discourse and Racism" in Deborah Schiffrin, Deborah Tannen and Heidi Hamilton (eds). The Handbook of Discourse Analysis. London: Blackwell, 2001: 372.

Wolverton, Monte. "Insurg-ants." *Cagle Cartoons*. February 20, 2005.

York, Bryon. "A New Attack on Rush." *The National Review on line*. May 28 2004. See www.nationalreview.com/york/york200405280844.asp (July 3, 2007).

The York Dispatch (York, PA), March 11, 2003.

Yorkshire Evening Post, November 8, 2004.

Your Dictionary. "Top Ten Word Lists of 2003." December 26, 2003. See www .yourdictionary.com/about/topten2003.html (June 28, 2007).

Zangana, Haifa. "All Iraq is Abu Ghraib." *Guardian*. July 5, 2006.

Zinn, Howard. "Lessons of Iraq War start with U.S. history." *The Progressive Media Project*. March 8, 2006. See www.progressive.org/media_mpzinn030806 (July 11, 2007).

Zornick, George. "The Porn of War." *The Nation*. September 22, 2005. See www.the nation.com/docprint.mhtml?i=20051010&s=the_porn_of_war

Index

About the Authors

Erin Steuter is associate professor of Sociology at Mount Allison University in Sackville, New Brunswick, Canada. Her MA and PhD theses examined ideological representations of the news. Recipient of multiple awards for her teaching and research, Erin Steuter is contacted regularly for interviews in connection with her research and published works, which have appeared in *Political Communication and Persuasion, Canadian Journal of Communication, Journal of American and Comparative Cultures*, and other noted academic journals. Because of her deep interest in promoting media literacy, Dr. Steuter conducts community workshops and visits schools to encourage greater understanding of the important issues of today.

Deborah Wills teaches in the English Department at Mount Allison University. She has published and presented papers in the areas of cultural studies, disability and illness in poetry, literary genre, eschatology, science fiction and cyberpunk, magic realism, creative nonfiction and, most recently, horror and neogothic literature and film. She is a recipient of the Herb and Leota Tucker Award for Excellence in Teaching.